GOD IN HISTORY

GOD IN HISTORY

Shapes of Freedom

Peter C. Hodgson

Abingdon Press/Nashville

GOD IN HISTORY: Shapes of Freedom

COVER DESIGN BY JOHN R. ROBINSON

This book is printed on acid-free paper.

Library of Congress Cataloging-in-Publication Data

Hodgson, Peter Crafts, 1934-
  God in history : shapes of freedom / Peter C. Hodgson.
    p.   cm.
  Includes index.
  ISBN 0-687-14969-X (alk. paper)
  1. History (Theology)   I. Title.
BR115.H5H64   1989   88-28621
231.7'6—dc19

MANUFACTURED IN THE UNITED STATES OF AMERICA

Contents

Preface

This book is an attempt to reconstruct a theology of history in light of the challenges of postmodernism—surely an audacious undertaking in view of the severity of these challenges, both cognitive and ethical, which have led to a widespread collapse of the classic framework of Christian faith known as "salvation history." The question of whether and in what sense we are able to speak anymore of God's redemptive presence in history poses one of the most difficult and inescapable theological dilemmas of our time. I do not claim to have found any definitive answers to the question but at best only to have pointed the discussion in what may prove to be a fruitful direction.

My efforts are focused on a particular line of argument, which, stated very briefly, is that God and history are in some sense correlative realities, and that their relationship focuses at the point of praxis—not an indiscriminate, amorphous praxis, but praxis that is liberating, emancipatory, transfigurative. Freedom involves an activity of shaping, configuring, synthesizing, presencing; it is an activity in which we experience ultimacy and are empowered by it, but always in an unfinished, open, plural process, which includes reversals and defeats as well as advances. God is present in history in the many shapes of freedom, among which there is for Christians a paradigmatic gestalt, the shape of love in freedom associated with Jesus' proclamation and crucifixion. The aim or goal of history, never achieved but only approximated in a plurality of ways, is to build up these shapes into a nexus of communicative freedom. The very extremities of our time call for the beginning of a history of the praxis of freedom if humanity is to survive.

Only themes and resources that bear directly on this argument (which is summarized more fully in the last section of the introductory chapter) are included in the present work. I make no pretense at an exhaustive treatment of theology of history, or of the doctrine of providence as it was traditionally called, partly because I have not wanted to lose the argument in a mass of details, and partly because of the complexity and difficulty of the issues, which resist any holistic treatment. It should be clear that what is offered here is not a "postmodernist" theology in the sense of accepting the "atheological" premises that many find to be required by the cultural and cognitive crises of our time; rather, what is offered is a "revisionist" theological response to the challenge of postmodernism (a challenge that I attempt to summarize and evaluate in the second section of the introductory chapter).

This book was written as I was completing nearly a decade of effort leading to a new edition and translation of Hegel's lectures on the philosophy of religion. Thus it will not be surprising that Hegel plays an important role in these pages. My use of Hegel can be viewed in part as an attempt to show both the possibilities and limits of Hegel's contribution to theological reconstruction in a postmodern framework. Readers familiar with Hegel will recognize that the expressions "God in history" and "shapes of freedom" have a Hegelian provenance. My work on Hegel and engagement with the question of theology of history have led to a new appreciation of Ernst Troeltsch, who in my view struggled more creatively than almost any other modern theologian with these issues. I have drawn as well on current philosophies and theologies of praxis, process, hermeneutics, and communication, and on recent structuralist and narrativist approaches to philosophy of history.

Financial support for the year of academic leave during which I completed research and began writing was provided by the Association of Theological Schools, the Vanderbilt University Research Council, and the Vanderbilt Divinity School. Some of my ideas were tested in lectures and conversations in Iceland, England, Northern Ireland, and Germany; and I am grateful to the friends who welcomed me in these countries, especially Sigurdur Thórdarson, Michael Stewart, Robert Bernasconi, Robert Morgan, Bernard Cullen, John Clayton, Walter Jaeschke, and Georg Dellbrügge. Students in my fall semester 1987 seminar on theology of history were subjected to a draft version of this manuscript, which they in turn subjected to vigorous discussion and critique, contributing to its improvement in many ways. Among this group I am especially indebted to Charlotte Joy Martin for her close reading and keen insight. David H. Fisher, Paul Lakeland, and Mark Kline Taylor each read the manuscript and offered detailed critical suggestions, which have led to several important modifications in the argument. I appreciate their interest in my work and the time they devoted to its improvement. Finally, I am grateful to Davis Perkins, senior editor of academic books at Abingdon Press, for his interest in and support of this project, and to Steven Cox and Holley Roberts for their careful copyediting and proofreading.

CHAPTER I

Introduction:
The End of Salvation History

1. The Classic Model

For centuries Christians and Jews have held on to a central, compelling, and crucial story as the very foundation of their faith in God and confidence in salvation. It is a story with which we are all familiar: the story of God's creation of the world, the fall of humanity into sin, the infectious spread of evil, and God's providential guidance of the affairs of history toward the end of salvation, an end already accomplished (for Christians) in the earthly appearance of the Messiah but to be consummated by the victorious return of Christ and the final destruction of evil powers at the close of world history. It is a story with a plot that unfolds along a line through a special sequence of events from beginning to middle to end; and it is by means of orientation to this plot that our individual lives are given coherence. In fact, our inner life histories are in many respects microcosms of this outer history, and without coherence on the macrocosmic scale we are threatened by chaos within. "To be a self is to have a god; to have a god is to have history, that is, events connected in a meaningful pattern; to have one god is to have one history."[1]

The God most Christians have had is a God who is believed to exercise world governance on the political model of the rule of a monarch over a realm. According to this royal metaphor, God exerts causality in world affairs by means of specific and decisive interventions, including not only global historical events but also specific theophanies, miracles, acts of inspiration, and punishments and rewards of individuals. An important corollary to this classic version of salvation history is the belief that God is able to accomplish what God wills to accomplish in earthly affairs, either

11

indirectly through the contingencies of nature and human purposes or, when necessary, by exercising a direct causality—the logic of divine sovereignty or triumph, as it has been called.[2]

This set of convictions, deeply rooted in the Jewish and Christian heritage, was not simply abandoned when religious belief was seriously questioned for the first time in the Enlightenment; instead it was secularized and reappeared in the form of a "myth" or "theory of progress" based solely on human accomplishment and the ability to control our own destiny. The discovery of evolution lent a scientific basis to this myth. Subsequently a rival version emerged in the form of the Marxist-Leninist theory of class struggle and the eventual abolition of all classes with the triumph of the proletariat. Yet all these versions of salvation history—the classic Judeo-Christian, the liberal-bourgeois, and the Marxist-Leninist—have been severely challenged in our time. It is this challenge, this veritable shaking of the foundations of Western historical confidence, that more than anything else constitutes the crisis of "postmodernism."[3]

Before turning to this crisis, it will be helpful to trace the "history" of salvation history and its accompanying logic of divine sovereignty. When and where did this mythos originate and how did it secure such a strong hold upon our collective psyches? We shall focus our attention on the contributions of a few major thinkers rather than attempt to provide an exhaustive account. Then, following our analysis of the challenge of postmodernism, the concluding section of this chapter will summarize the constructive argument of the book as a whole, which is an attempt to rethink the question of the relationship of God and history without relying on the classic model, but also without surrendering the core conviction of Christian faith that God is redemptively present in history.

Scriptural Foundations

The salvation history mythos is ultimately traceable, of course, to the Hebrew and Christian scriptures. The oldest of the

Hebraic credos, such as the one found in Deuteronomy 26:5-19, made no attempt to mark off decisive moments in the story of the people's relationship to God, since the picture presented was simple and compact enough to be intelligible. But, as Gerhard von Rad has pointed out, when various complexes of tradition containing quite diverse materials were joined together to form the Hexateuch, "it became essential to organize this history in some way, to divide it into periods." Following the primordial "history" (which included the creation of the world, the fall of humanity, the spread of sin, and the destruction of a corrupt human race by the great flood), the principle of organization was determined by the several covenants made by Yahweh with successive leaders of the people: Noah, Abraham, and Moses. The first of these ensured the preservation of human life; the second promised that the descendants of Abraham would become a great people; and the third established a special relationship of this people with God. Finally, the promise of the land of Canaan, initially made to Abraham, was fulfilled when Joshua led the people into the land of milk and honey. Thus the entire mass of Hexateuchal traditions was organized into a sequential story of salvation with decisive moments of transition marked by specific events: creation, fall, punishment, wanderings, bondage in Egypt, exodus, Sinai, and possession of the land. This theology of history was extended and refined by the Deuteronomist's account of the period of the judges and the monarchy. For the latter, the Deuteronomist operated with a very simple critical canon, namely, whether the kings of Israel and Judah recognized the temple in Jerusalem as the sole legitimate place for worshiping Yahweh, or whether they sacrificed to the Baals on the "high places."[4]

The theological assumptions underlying the salvation history of the Hexateuch and the Deuteronomist were radically altered by the political crisis that confronted Israel with the fall of Jerusalem in 587 B.C.E. This event and the ensuing exile destroyed the matrix in which Israel's understanding of its relationship to God—based upon the land, the temple, and a divinely sanctioned monarchy—had previously taken shape.

The prophets viewed the collapse of political power not as proving the impotence of God, but as the result of God's judgment on the chosen people. At the same time God was at work against the enemies of Israel, and eventually the people would be restored to the land and to prosperity with the coming of the promised messianic king. This belief was adopted and modified by the early Jewish-Christian communities, who proclaimed as their gospel that certain present events, associated with the life, death, and resurrection from the dead of the one they believed to be the Messiah, marked the beginning of a final intervention in human affairs by the same God who had acted in Israel's past. Thus a revised salvation history was fashioned by the author of Luke-Acts.

Roman Historia, *Tertullian, and the Imperial Theology*

There was, however, little concrete interest in *history* as the matrix of salvation on the part of first-century and early second-century Christians since they believed that the end of the present age was very nearly at hand. The construction of a fully elaborated salvation history was primarily the accomplishment of Latin Christianity during the period following the recognition of the church as the official religion of the Roman Empire by Constantine in the fourth century.[5] This "imperial theology" was, however, foreshadowed by the views of divine providence expressed in classical Roman *historia,* especially as adapted to a Christian framework by Tertullian at the end of the second century. The provenance of the category "history" was not the Hebrew Bible, despite the importance for it of historical traditions and the historical "acts" of God, but Greek and Roman historiography.

In light of the expansion and consolidation of Roman hegemony in the Mediterranean world, Latin philosophers, poets, and historians articulated a version of Roman destiny in which religion played a specific role. The gods imported from Greece, Asia Minor, and Africa were transformed into powers or utilities[6] on whose goodwill the political and commercial success of Rome, and the prosperity of her citizens, were directly dependent.

Sacrifices were offered to the gods and they were honored by elaborate festivals in order to obtain their providential guidance and protection—the so-called principle of *do ut des*, "I give so that you will give in return."[7] Cicero's *De republica* and Virgil's *Aeneid* were classical expressions of this theology. Later historians such as Livy and Tacitus, though affirming Rome's manifest destiny, warned against the dangers they perceived in the relaxation of discipline, morals, and piety and the spread of corruption.[8]

Of greater interest, however, is the way that Tertullian appropriated this Roman eschatology for his own purposes. Faced with the charge that Christians are atheists responsible for much misfortune because they do not worship the gods of the *imperium*, Tertullian in his *Apology* turned the tables on his critics: it is not the pagan deities but the true God of Israel and of Jesus Christ who determines the destinies of empires. If Rome has prospered, it cannot be because of imported foreign deities, who (he notes caustically) must have betrayed their own peoples if they are responsible for Rome's rise to power. Nor do the calamities presently besetting the Empire reflect the disfavor of these gods with the spread of Christianity. Rather, they are punishments inflicted by the Christian God, who has maintained the Empire in existence for God's own purposes, although its eventual destruction is foretold by Scripture.[9] R. G. Patterson observes that although Tertullian's remarks "certainly assume the common Roman notion that worship of the true God will issue in human security and prosperity, . . . their poignancy derives from the very fact that he believes that Rome's doom has already been pronounced. . . . His message stands in the tradition of Cicero and Virgil with the one, for him doubtless terrifying, difference that it announces not Rome's continuing grandeur but her inevitable doom."[10] It is not unfair to conclude that what Tertullian unwittingly brought about was the christianization of an essentially pagan view of salvation history—a view which, with its logic of divine governance, intervention, reward and punishment, and eventual triumph, was to have a far-reaching and fateful impact on subsequent Christian thought. It provided a frame of reference for reading the Hebrew scriptures, portions of which (especially those attributable to the Deuteronomist) lent themselves to such an interpretation.

This view was adapted to new circumstances when Christianity replaced paganism as the religion of the Empire. Now, obviously, Rome's doom could no longer be pronounced. It fell to Eusebius of Caesarea to fashion an imperial theology appropriate to the Constantinian age. He envisioned a divine *politeia*, a still-future but approaching stage of earthly perfection in the form of a Christian commonwealth, which would be larger than the church and more or less equivalent to the dominion of the Christian emperor, who is God's earthly regent. Subsequent theologians—Lactantius, Ambrose of Milan, and Prudentius— made it very clear that the Latin pagan interpretation of Rome's rise to greatness had been baptized by the church. The shared assumption was that peace and prosperity would be given to a people who turned for help to the God who was the true sovereign of history.[11] The assumption, however, was soon to be falsified by the course of events. The result of the change in imperial policy toward Christianity proved not to be a renewal of peace and prosperity but a worsening situation, leading to the year 410 when Gothic Arian Christian tribes invaded Rome and sacked it (an event that foreshadowed the fall of the Empire in 476). It was this crisis that confronted Augustine, evoking a much more profound theological reflection on the meaning of history than anything accomplished hitherto, in the form of the twenty-two books of his *City of God,* written between 413 and 426.

Augustine's City of God

In the first ten books, Augustine addressed the claim of pagan writers that human happiness in general, and the greatness of Rome in particular, are attributable to the pagan deities. Happiness, he contended in Book 5, is not a goddess (the goddess Fortuna) but the gift of God, the one true God whose providential rule is the cause of the greatness of empires. God has indeed granted the Romans an empire and has caused it to prosper without regard to their pagan worship; but God has done the same for the Assyrians and Persians. God gives power to emperors both good and bad, who serve the divine purposes without knowing it by pursuing their own passions: such is the "cunning" of divine providence.[12] Augustine also made the important point in this book that providence works in and through, not against, the free activity of human beings. God, he said, is the cause of all causes but not of all choices; what God foreknows is precisely our choices *as* choices. Human will prevails, but the power that "permits" this is God's: God *permits* us to sin and *pursues* us with mercy. Thus what Augustine offered (at least at the microcosmic level) is not an utterly totalitarian but a limited logic of sovereignty; divine causality is exercised not mechanically or coercively, but rather more like the kind of influence found in human relationships—although, to be sure, God does accomplish what God wills to accomplish.[13]

Patterson points out that in the first ten books Augustine was implicitly accepting the imperial theological principle, although he drew different conclusions from it. Two tendencies seem to be at work in his thought at this point: one toward accepting the providential nature of events along the lines of his predecessors, the other toward his own distinctive analysis of the divided self, which serves as the basis of his distinction between two human societies.[14] The second tendency prevails in the last twelve books, where Augustine undertook to write about the "origins, developments and appointed ends" of "the City of God and the city of the world," "as though they were two cities, although as far as human history goes, the former lives like an alien in the latter."[15]

Here the Roman providential scheme has been displaced, but at the same time Augustine seemed to reject any possibility of real historical transformation or change. The two cities are established from the beginning of creation; both spring from Adam, from "common clay," which God can and does mold as God wills, shaping from it a society of saints sufficient to replace the fallen angels, but leaving the great majority of persons to their deserved perdition. "In the torrential stream of human history, two currents meet and mix: the current of evil which

flows from Adam and that of good which comes from God."[16]
But nothing really ever changes in this relationship. They "meet
and mix" rather like oil and water. Even Israel, like every other
nation, belongs to the earthly city, for which there is no hope of
redemption. God will not restore the earthly Jerusalem but
rather preserve from destruction, during its earthly pilgrimage,
the heavenly Jerusalem, which is a metaphor of the City of God.
Although this metaphor is political, Augustine in the final
analysis thought not so much in political and historical categories
as aesthetic ones. God exercises worldly rule not really as a king
or politician, an agent of historical change, but rather as an artist,
an artificer who fashions the world in accord with that art which
is God's own eternal, unchanging, timeless wisdom. God's
artistry is such that the greatness of the divine masterpieces is not
lessened by the minor works. Everything has a place in the total
design; beauty is a matter of symmetry, proportion, order,
hierarchy. Salvation means the restoration of order, an "eternal
stillness of rest" from earthly toil, the "sabbath peace" in which
God is all in all.[17]

In conclusion, the specific kind of "salvation history" and
"logic of sovereignty" that we tend to think of as characteristic of
classical Christianity should be attributed not so much to
Augustine as to his Latin predecessors (Tertullian, Eusebius,
Lactantius) and successors (Orosius, Salvian, Gregory the
Great). But the price Augustine paid for his critique of imperial
theology was a lessening of interest in actual history. He had no
need for special divine providence since all earthly empires are
condemned in advance. The primary "work" of God in history is
to protect the heavenly city from destruction and to guide it to its
destined consummation. No earthly kingdom stands at the end
of history. "History's institutions and so the course of history
itself are left in the limbo of untransformed and unredeemed
ambiguity."[18] In the strict sense there is no *history* of salvation but
only an *eternal decree* and *telos* of salvation. To be sure, the decree
unfolds through certain distinguishable phases—Augustine
identified seven ages of world history corresponding to the
seven "days" of creation—but these do not constitute a historical

process. The only history one can speak of is a history of corruption, sin, and evil. Here a great deal "happens," and Augustine recorded it in exhausting detail, but it has little significance since the outcome of history is determined solely by God's electing will. Augustine *looked back* upon this weary spectacle from what he took to be the approaching end of the sixth stage, and he anticipated the coming tranquility and peace of the heavenly kingdom: his journey was over, his battle won.

Thus, despite his recognition of human freedom and rejection of the simple calculus of reward and punishment, from this global and eschatological perspective Augustine approximated a total divine determinism that devalues human history. He firmly believed that for the elect there is an escape from this history in the final blessed vision, whereas for modernity there is no such escape: we are all condemned to work out our salvation, if there is to be any at all, within history.

Thomas Aquinas on Providence

Thomas Aquinas addressed the specific question of divine providence in Question 5 of his treatise *De veritate*.[19] This scarcely represents a fully developed salvation history; indeed, history was not an operative category for Thomas, but he did think of the world as a living process of emanation from and return to God, an *exitus et reditus*. Thus there is an *economy* of salvation, which is set forth in the Thomistic *summas*. Thomas's brief discussion of providence is helpful not only because he articulated very clearly the sort of teleology or final causality that has become so problematic for postmodernism, but also because he modified in important respects Augustinian determinism.

Providence, said Thomas, is a kind of "prudence," which disposes in an orderly way means to an end by a kind of reasoning process, a practical reason. Divine providence is, therefore, *practical* divine knowledge, exercised in the mode of final causality—but persuasively, "reasonably," not coercively or mechanically. There must indeed be a final causality that pervades the natural and human worlds, since without it only the existence of effects is secured (through material and efficient causes), not their goodness; and, without such a causality, the apparent harmony and usefulness found in natural things would have to be regarded as the result of chance, which is absurd. Moreover, God's provident action is necessarily continuous because of the radical contingency of created things. We may understand God's governance or rule on the analogy of human rule, for example, that of a man over his family or of a ruler over his kingdom; in both cases, seeking the common good takes priority over the good of the individual. This is a hierarchical rule since beings are ranked according to their proximity to God, depending on the degree of their spirituality or materiality, and God exercises causality through higher forms on lower ones.[20]

Corruptible (i.e., finite) things are capable of corruption or failure since this is precisely what is meant by their corruptibility or impermanence. God permits such failures in order to be able to have things distinguishable from godself. Evil is the result of failure; God does not cause it but permits it. God does not do evil for the sake of the good; rather God directs evil to a good end, which is an act of goodness.[21]

Human beings are not only provided for by God's providence but are provident or prudent themselves. They exercise a choice in their own actions, and because of this they are culpable or accountable. Thomas was suggesting that God shares providentiality with human beings as well as other spiritual creatures. Divine providence has no need of canceling human freedom, and the two providences, divine and human, are capable of working together, cooperatively. Our will is a moved mover; what moves it must be an immaterial and intelligent power, namely, God.[22]

Thomas was considerably more forthcoming on this point than either Augustine or Calvin; and, as I have said, the analogy of prudence suggests a kind of causality that is exercised in a practical, persuasive way rather than in a mechanical, coercive one. In this respect Thomas anticipated distinctly modern concerns. Yet at the same time he was attracted to Augustine's aesthetic vision of the universe, which places great emphasis on hierarchical structure and views the whole as "excellently arranged." The question raised by postmodernism is whether the world can really be so regarded. Might it, instead, be an endless labyrinth or a bottomless abyss?

Calvin on God's Governance of History

Calvin's theology was anchored in what he himself confessed to be the "awful decree" of divine election, whereby God predestines some to salvation and others to destruction. He found that he *must* confess it because it is clearly revealed in scripture, and scripture is the sole basis for genuine knowledge of God. Also evident from scripture, he believed, is the fact that God's foreknowledge and predestination are independent of one another. If they were not, we could say that God condemns only those who are foreseen to be inclined toward wickedness and impiety. But this would be to make salvation a reward for good works, whereas God is utterly free to bestow grace on whomsoever God chooses, irrespective of human merit. All deserve to be condemned, but God by gratuitous mercy selects a remnant to be saved.[23] Given this foundational conviction, it might appear that the doctrine of election would eliminate salvation history for Calvin since in the strict sense salvation is not being "worked out" in history.

Election does not, however, preclude divine providence; rather, it is clearly taught by scripture that God, not chance, rules history. "All events are governed by God's secret plan," inanimate things as well as animate. God's omnipotence is "not the empty, idle, and almost unconscious sort that the Sophists imagine, but a watchful, effective, active sort, engaged in ceaseless activity." God rules not merely in a general way but through a very particular "special providence." Things may seem fortuitous to us because their order, reason, end, and necessity are for the most part concealed in the purpose of God. But in fact God's providence presides over and directs what we call "fortune" or "misfortune" to God's end. Chance is not lord, as the Stoics believed; rather God is the Lord of chance also.[24]

In a world ruled by God's "ceaseless activity," is any room left for human activity? Following the tradition established by Augustine and Thomas, Calvin argued that human free will is not obliterated by the decrees of God. This was a difficult question for him, and an inconsistency seemed to creep into his thought. On the one hand, we should not confuse the providence of God with the will of God: not everything that happens under God's *providence* is in accord with God's *will*. A thief, for example, is not "serving" God's will by plundering someone whom it has pleased the Lord to chastise with poverty. God does not command us to do evil things but rather knows how to use evil instruments to good ends.[25] But on the other hand, Calvin insisted, against Augustine and others, that it is a subterfuge to say that God permits evil but does not will it; scripture makes it plain, he believed, that God does not merely "permit" but "wills" that Satan should do his evil work.[26] Perhaps Calvin was trading here on two senses of the term "will," the one referring to God's purpose (which is not evil but salvific), the other to God's rule (which is utterly sovereign). In any event, it seems clear on Calvin's view, as Langdon Gilkey suggests, that in human affairs there is never simply a sole causality attributable to human will alone, but rather two levels of causality: "God's prior ordination from eternity and man's 'voluntary' (not compelled but willed) willing of the deed."[27]

Paradoxically, perhaps, knowledge of God's sovereign governance of history is not enervating but empowering; we are relieved, thereby, of "extreme anxiety," "pressing fear," and "every care." While the world totters, we remain secure: "We are not our own, but the Lord's."[28] This affirmation is the basis of Calvinist dynamism. Although the only true salvation is eschatological and transhistorical,[29] and though the outcome of salvation is not determined by the course of history, the work of providence is nonetheless concerned with the regeneration of history and the character of political institutions and social existence: the world is to be made to reflect God's glory.

How is this apparent tension in Calvin's thought to be accounted for? Gilkey suggests that one of the consequences of basing the knowledge of God solely on the scriptural word is that God is then understood in directly personal categories rather than in the classic categories of order and nature as employed by Augustine and Thomas. God becomes "the ordaining sovereign agent whose dynamic will orders events towards his own goal." Thus a "dynamic, process sense of history" begins to emerge, but at the same time human independence and responsibility are reduced by comparison with the views of Augustine and especially Thomas. Calvin's theology, moreover, is concerned primarily with the practical life of faith rather than with speculative or theoretical knowledge.[30] Belief in God as an "ordaining sovereign agent" who takes, as it were, a personal interest in the course of history, combined with an all-too-ready tendency to find proof of election in the active life of faith,[31] had an exhilarating but dangerous effect: it could lead to an ethic of creative transformation; but, applied uncritically, it could also lead to totalitarian religious and political ideologies. These tensions are deeply imbedded in Calvinism.

Modern Consciousness

The rise of natural science in the seventeenth and eighteenth centuries and of historical consciousness in the nineteenth had a profound impact on traditional views of salvation history and divine sovereignty. Natural science directly challenged teleological explanations of the cosmos, while historical consciousness introduced the critical concepts of change, process, becoming, relativity, as well as challenging references to any sort of transhistorical, supernatural, timeless-spaceless reality, whether conceived as a ground, cause, entity, realm, or telos. The full impact of these challenges to religious belief did not, however, take immediate effect.

Philosophical thought in the early modern period for the most part offered a defensive reaction. The rationalism of Descartes and especially Leibniz attempted to rehabilitate the classic doctrines of creation and providence in ways congenial to the spirit of modern science; Spinoza replaced the doctrines by an original and deeply religious pantheistic vision of the unity of God and nature; while deism preserved a place for a creator who set up a nearly perfect machine, functioning according to precise laws.[32] It was only with the skepticism of Hume and the critical philosophy of Kant that the spell was broken, but these philosophers offered little basis for rethinking what it might mean to speak of God's presence and action in history. That task was taken up in a powerful fashion by Hegel and the post-Hegelians, and subsequently by several strands of twentieth-century philosophical theology. It is to some of these contributions, with a focus on Hegel, that we shall turn in the next two chapters.

As far as theologians were concerned, the issue of historical consciousness and process was for the most part avoided by retreats into pietism, dogmatism, and confessionalism. The great exception, of course, was Friedrich Schleiermacher, but Schleiermacher remains profoundly unsatisfying precisely on the question of a post-Enlightenment theology of history. It is true that he demythologized the traditional supernatural versions of creation, providence, and salvation history; he understood "ethics" to be the "science of the principles of history"; and he had an important sense of the development and progression of consciousness through historical communities.[33]

But at the most fundamental level Schleiermacher's theology did not function with historical categories.[34] They were excluded by his philosophical determinism, on the one hand, and by his concentrated focus on religious feeling as a modification of self-consciousness, on the other. These combined to produce a view of the God-world relationship from which history is effectively excluded. God's primary attribute is "absolute causality," which is timeless, spaceless, omnipotent, omniscient, and unaffected by external relations to the world or human beings. The distinctively religious feeling is the feeling of "utter dependence," from which all reciprocity and variation are excluded. The latter are experienced by persons in relation to the world but not to God. The whole of dogmatics is ultimately derivable from "descriptions of human states of consciousness." These are not historical states but rather, on the one hand, a generic consciousness of the relationship of God and world, and, on the other, a determinate consciousness of the antithesis of sin and grace. Theology is oriented, ultimately, not to the knowledge of God or truth claims of any sort about objective reality, but to the practical life and piety of the church.[35] Thus, in the Protestant liberal heritage that flowed from Schleiermacher, dogmatic theology and historical theology were increasingly separated until, in the Ritschlian school, the former took on the character of a practical, confessional dogmatics, and the latter that of a scientific, purely descriptive discipline.[36] In other words, in order to save dogmatic theology from the challenge of modern historical consciousness, it was dehistoricized (or perhaps more accurately, it was never historicized).

Barth's Two Histories

Karl Barth restored the narrative structure of theology that was lost in Protestant liberalism, and history emerged as an important category for him (more so than for most theologians, ancient or modern); but at the same time his intention was clearly to reaffirm many of the elements of the classic paradigm, and he was resolutely antimodern in his determination to not allow post-Enlightenment methodological criteria, or the content of any of the modern academic disciplines, to influence the substance of theology. Thus his treatment of the doctrine of providence in volume 3 of the *Church Dogmatics* provides a convenient terminus for the history of the classic model of salvation history.[37]

Barth began by noting that medieval scholasticism treated *de providentia Dei* as part of the doctrine of God, whereas post-Reformation Protestant dogmatics located it under the doctrine of creation, thus distinguishing it as God's "outer work" from the doctrine of election or predestination, which is constitutive of the "inner work." Barth adopted the latter

arrangement because of his conviction that the actual relationship between creator and creature must not be imported into the
being of God. God "would be no less God even if the work of
creation had never been, if there were no creatures, and if the
whole doctrine of providence were therefore irrelevant. Hence
there can be no place for this doctrine in that of the being of
God."[38] Whatever else Barth wanted to say about the inner life of
God, it is clear that world-relatedness has no place in it; God and
world history are in no sense co-constitutive themes; the
Hegelian banner "without the world God is not God"[39] would
have to be viewed as blasphemy or pantheism.

Barth established a second, and for him equally crucial,
distinction between two histories: the history of creation (or of
the world) (*Schöpfungsgeschichte*), and the history of the covenant
(*Bundesgeschichte*) or of salvation (*Heilsgeschichte*). The first is the
domain of providence or God's work of "preserving," "accompanying," and "ruling" the world; the second, of reconciliation
or God's saving action in Jesus Christ. Barth conceived of the
relation between these two histories as that of two streams, one
broad and encompassing, the other narrow and particular.
Covenant history is "an astonishingly thin line" within creation
history, the latter being made up of "a confusion of apparently
much more powerful and conspicuous lines which seem to be
independent and mutually contradictory."[40] Sometimes Barth
indicated that the doctrine of providence is concerned not just
with one of these two histories (the "outer" stream) but with the
relationship between the two, the means by which God
"coordinates" them.

The fundamental affirmation of the doctrine of providence is
that God alone rules, a rule that is exercised through what is
ordinary, lawful, necessary, and continuous, as well as through
the extraordinary, novel, free, and discontinuous. The reason
for this affirmation is that, whereas the rule of all other (finite)
rulers leads ultimately only to oppression and confusion, God
alone is the one who rules in and on behalf of freedom. The
ground of this affirmation is faith alone, not worldly knowledge
or critical observation, for God's providential presence is

concealed in world occurrence and cannot be perceived or read off from it. God is providentially present only "nevertheless" (*dennoch*), despite the appearances. The "seeing" of God's presence is based solely on the paradigm of the special providence revealed in biblical history, which is the history of the covenant of God with Israel and the church.[41] Thus, while the history of providence or creation history is coextensive with secular history, it is strictly independent of scientific historiographical investigation. It has its own basis, which is that of God's revelation in the special history of Jesus Christ.

On this basis, the specifically Christian concept of divine rule may be formulated. God rules creaturely occurrence by *ordering* it and thereby *controlling* and *directing* it. In agreement with the mainstream Catholic tradition against Calvin, Barth affirmed that creatures use their freedom under divine permission rather than compulsion. God controls by giving permission to creaturely freedom, setting limits to it, and directing it to a common goal. This is accomplished by God's "ordering," "harmonizing," and "coordinating" of the antitheses, conflicts, and contradictions that are constitutive of world history.[42]

Barth was close here to certain insights that might be appropriated by a revisionist theology of history, except that he held on tenaciously to the privileged theological character of the insights and was all too ready to embrace the royal metaphor of God's kingly rule.[43] There may indeed be only "traces" of God's world governance in history, but why is it that these traces, these "signs and witnesses," can be decoded only by reference to Jesus Christ, as Barth insisted?[44] If the divine rule has any meaning at all with regard to harmonizing and coordinating the conflicts and contradictions of history, then it must bring about the shaping of partial syntheses, which if they really occur should be discernible to the trained and critical eye and should have an effect on the actual course of history. (Their attribution to the rule of God is of course a judgment of faith, but a judgment for which reasons may be given.) Barth insisted that God's "unified plan has nothing whatever to do with a levelling down and flattening out of individuals and individual groupings."[45] The plan does not take the form of a linear trajectory but of coordinating precisely the particular projects of human beings. Surely observations such as this are not deducible solely from a privileged disclosure based on Jesus Christ. If theological assertions about history are not publicly discussable—if they are not in some sense verifiable or falsifiable by reference to the actual configurations of history, the discernment and interpretation of which is a matter not of scriptural authority but of hermeneutical insight—then they must be regarded as meaningless or arbitrary.

Finally, why must the divine ordering, coordinating, harmonizing, and so forth, be construed as "controlling," "directing," "ruling," rather than as shaping, configuring, luring, persuading?[46] There seems to be no intrinsic necessity for it in Barth's theology other than his (Calvinist?) predilection for metaphors of sovereignty, royalty, and patriarchal authority—metaphors that stand in stark tension with, and indeed undermine, his commitment to religious socialism, his recognition of the approaching end of a cultural epoch, and his prophetic warning against totalitarian politics.

2. The Challenge of Postmodernism

The complications created by modern consciousness for traditional affirmations about the relationship of God and history have been intensified to the point of crisis by the cultural shift of our time known as "postmodernism." I am using this term, not in the specific sense in which it is often employed, namely, to describe certain recent shifts in literary, artistic, and architectural styles, but rather as a way of indicating a broad historical passage, comparable to the transition from the late medieval to the "modern" age, which occurred in the West with the emergence of scientific and historical-critical consciousness during the seventeenth and eighteenth centuries, culminating in the culture of the Enlightenment. Now, in the late twentieth century, there are abundant signs that the paradigm of modernity has run its course, even though it may in certain respects remain (in Habermas's words) "an incomplete project."[47] These signs are discernible in the cognitive, political, socioeconomic, religious, and historical crises of our time.[48] The recognition of and response to this complex situation is what I mean by "postmodernism."[49] Quite different kinds of response can be designated by the term; I am concerned in the following pages with what one critic has called the "postmodernism of resistance" rather than with the "postmodernism of reaction":

> The postmodernism of reaction is far better known: though not monolithic, it is singular in its repudiation of modernism. This repudiation, voiced most shrilly perhaps by neoconservatives but echoed everywhere, is strategic: . . . "adversary" culture is denounced even as the economic and political status quo is affirmed. . . . A postmodernism of resistance, then, arises as a counter-practice not only to the official culture of modernism but also to the "false normativity" of a reactionary postmodernism. In opposition (but not *only* in opposition), a resistant postmodernism is concerned with a critical deconstruction of tradition, . . . with a critique of origins, not a return to them.[50]

In theology, the postmodernism of reaction has taken the form of a call for a "postliberal" return to orthodox (or neo-orthodox) doctrine and confessional traditions, while the postmodernism of resistance can issue in either a deconstruction of all religious claims or a "revisionist" attempt, such as that represented by the present book, to retrieve and rethink the deconstructed tradition.

The Age of Anxiety, Pluralism, and Relativism

The *cognitive* crisis of postmodernity appears in the form of limits to technical rationality, which seems no longer capable of controlling, guiding, and ethically evaluating the immense power unleashed by technological advances; it also appears in the form of questioning all forms of philosophical rationality on the part of a deconstructionist critique of Western "logocentrism." The *political* crisis results from the dramatic decline in the

power and influence of Enlightenment culture, as seen from the
fact that only one of the current Big Four powers (the United
States, the Soviet Union, the People's Republic of China, and
Japan) remains Western in inheritance and values. The
socioeconomic crisis is reflected in the inability of both capitalist
and socialist systems to cope equitably and effectively with the
demands of the postindustrial age. The *religious* crisis stems
from the decline of Christianity in the West and the recognition
that the validity claims and truth claims of other great world
religions must be accorded equal respect.

My primary concern in this book is with the crisis of *history*
brought on by the collapse not only of traditional theological
views but also of their post-Enlightenment substitutes, namely,
liberal-bourgeois ideas of progress and Marxist-Leninist
theories of dialectical advance toward a classless society. Gilkey
points out that these secular salvation histories have mostly died
out in the cultures where they initially achieved dominance and
are alive today only among dissidents in the Communist world,
in Central and South America, and in Africa. In North America
and Western Europe as well as the Soviet Union, very little of an
ideal, transformative vision is left, and the most for which we
seem able collectively to hope is historical survival, "holding the
line," "defending our kind of world" against imagined aggres-
sors, whether communist or capitalist.[51]

It is not difficult to find the causes of this crisis of confidence.
Above all else, the deep experience of evil in the twentieth
century has permanently shaken confidence in historical
progress: two world wars, fascism, Stalinism, the Holocaust,
Vietnam and Cambodia, Central America, the madness of the
arms race, the possibility of irreversible ecological damage—
culminating with the threat of ultimate and irreversible evil in
the form of nuclear war. Corresponding to the outward terror is
a widespread loss of inner meaning brought on by the pursuit of
illusory values and the absence of any stable center or purpose to
life. To speak of our age as the "age of anxiety" is almost banal.
Indeed, in order to interpret the "shocks of non-being" that are
continually being experienced in our lives from without and

from within, Gilkey argues that powerful religious categories are required: "categories of ultimate violence, of the disintegration of meaning, of loss of soul, and of apocalyptic ending."[52]

Beyond this, ours is an age of thoroughgoing pluralism and relativism, an age for which there is no center but only a multiplicity of evanescent centers and value-free projects. This has been brought about partly by the pervasive cultural impact of natural science, especially the modern biological sciences, which have questioned whether change of any sort is teleologically oriented toward a progressively "better" goal. Instead of a purposive teleology in nature, some scientists find only "chance and necessity,"[53] and increasingly we suspect that the same may be true of history. An even more potent factor, however, is the appearance of a new kind of relativism that is characteristic of the postmodern age. This is not merely the religious and cultural relativism of which we have grown increasingly aware since the Enlightenment, but rather the relativization of the relativizing instrument itself, namely, Western critical consciousness, or "logocentrism." The very categories by which we have analyzed, distinguished, and constructed are said to be merely functions of this or that language game—and in the endless play of language everything seems to be dissolved: selves, thoughts, works, worlds, gods, history.

The New Historicism

One way of characterizing postmodernism is in terms of its radicalization of historical consciousness. William Dean advances this proposal in an article entitled "The Challenge of the New Historicism."[54] This is to be distinguished, he argues, from another, older historicism, whose roots lie in German critical and speculative philosophy and which views the world as fundamentally in process, a process determined by the interaction of freedom and destiny but grounded in an ultimate reality that does not itself change, or at least endures through change. By contrast, the new historicists insist "that there is not a deeper truth behind or beneath the events of social history"; rather, they have argued "that actual truths are entirely historical creatures, conceived within history, directed at history, and grown in a historical chain."[55] The denial of universal truths or extrahistorical realities by the new historicism amounts, then, "to a denial of the standard forms of foundationalism, of realism, and of the transcendentalized subject." In their place it accepts "unlimited pluralism," "radical empiricism," and "a pragmatism that arbitrates." Reality is entirely a product of "interpretive imagination": it is "composed of interpretations heaped upon interpretations"; it is a matter of "words all the way down."[56]

Dean has in mind primarily a group of American "neopragmatist" philosophers which includes Richard Rorty, Nelson Goodman, Hilary Putnam, Richard Bernstein, and Frank Lentricchia, and who are building on the tradition of American empiricism traceable to William James and John Dewey. His descriptive category, "new historicism," could be applied equally well, although in somewhat different terms, to the French deconstructionists or poststructuralists, and to the German critical social theorists, both of whom stand (in different ways) in the left-wing Hegelian, Marxist-Nietzschean-Freudian tradition. In later chapters I shall draw upon some of this literature in an attempt to describe both "the de-construction of history" (ch. 3.3) and "the turn to praxis" (ch. 4.1), which are important elements in any attempt to reconstruct a theology of history. Here I want to give a brief indication of just what "historicism" means in the works of two representative thinkers. It leads ultimately, I think, to a loss of interest in history.

In the introduction to his influential book, *Philosophy and the Mirror of Nature,* Richard Rorty suggests that "traditional philosophy" may be seen

> as an attempt to escape from history—an attempt to find nonhistorical conditions of any possible historical development. From this perspective, the common message of Wittgenstein, Dewey, and Heidegger is a historicist one. Each of the three reminds us that investigations of knowledge or morality or language or society may be simply apologetics, attempts to eternalize a certain contemporary language-game, social prac-

tice, or self-image. The moral of this book is also historicist, and
the three parts into which it is divided are intended to put the
notions of "mind," of "knowledge," and of "philosophy,"
respectively, in historical perspective.[57]

What Rorty offers, however, is certainly not a rigorous historical
analysis of these philosophical concepts in their own historical
contexts. He himself observes that "it is pictures rather than
propositions . . . which determine most of our philosophical
convictions,"[58] and his book provides a series of skillfully drawn,
beguiling pictures rather than philosophical or historical argument. He is led finally to the view that "the philosopher cannot
claim to know something about knowing which nobody else knows
so well," and that the sole remaining vocation of the philosopher is
"to keep the conversation of mankind going." This is an important
insight. Our very survival depends on keeping the conversation of
humanity going; the alternative to conversation is suspicion,
conflict, violence, and destruction. Above all in a nuclear age we
must not only keep the conversation going but use it to bring about
productive changes in the way we live. But Rorty tends to trivialize
the insight: perhaps something new and revitalizing will happen
through this conversation, he says, perhaps not; perhaps
philosophy will become "purely edifying," simply reading and
discussing books rather than solving problems. If so, then
practicing philosophy will be rather like fiddling while Rome
burns. Rorty acknowledges that the real threats to "free and
leisured conversation" and "abnormal discourse" do not come
from natural science and naturalistic philosophy. Rather, "they
come from the scarcity of food and the secret police." But that is
not the affair of the philosopher, who needs only "leisure and
libraries."[59] This damaging admission indicates, in my view, how
unhistorical and even impractical Rorty's neohistoricist, neopragmatist philosophy really is. At least Hegel, who may (with a certain
irony) have said something similar,[60] had a deeply historical sense
and a foreboding about his own time, and he recognized that the
philosophical interpretation of the shapes of freedom must

generate a history of the praxis of freedom if humanity is not only to survive but thrive.

Michel Foucault's seminal work, *The Archaeology of Knowledge*,[61] opens with what appears to be a discussion of shifts in historical knowledge toward the recognition of the role played in historical process by such phenomena as ruptures, discontinuities, displacements, breaks, thresholds, discrete series and strata, and so forth.[62] It soon becomes evident, however, that something much more radical is going on, and that the notion of historical process as such is under attack. Foucault's purpose is to define a "poststructuralist" method of analysis that will question all "teleologies and totalizations," purge all "anthropologism," decenter the self, and deconstruct the historical work, the *oeuvre*.[63] The deconstruction of "history" itself cannot be far behind, and indeed the word itself disappears, replaced by such terms as "archeology" and "archive." The archeology of knowledge

> does not establish the fact of our identity by the play of distinctions. It establishes that *we are difference,* that our reason is the difference of discourses, our history the difference of times, our selves the difference of masks. That difference, far from being the forgotten and recovered origin, is *this dispersion that we are and make.*[64]

The word *history* should here be placed within quotation marks since there is no recognizable sense in which the sheer "difference of times" constitutes *historia,* any more than a self "is" simply the "difference of masks." Sheer difference, sheer dispersion "is" not anything at all, it is "no thing," nothing, the *nihil;* and, taken at its most extreme, Foucault's case is that it is an illusion to think that there are such things as selves and history (to say nothing of works, worlds, and gods).

Foucault's more recent essay, "Nietzsche, Genealogy, History,"[65] makes this even clearer and spells out the ethical implications of his bleak vision of *humanitas*. A Nietzschean "genealogy" thematizes only "the endlessly repeated play of dominations" and "the staging of meticulously repeated scenes of violence." "Humanity does not gradually progress from combat to combat until it arrives at universal reciprocity, where the rule of law finally replaces warfare; humanity installs each of its violences in a system of rules and thus proceeds from domination to domination."[66] Nietzsche conceived of genealogy as "actual history" (*wirkliche Historie*), by contrast with what he took to be the traditional, make-believe history of most historians and philosophers. History becomes *wirklich* to the degree that "it introduces discontinuity into our very being." In a striking revision of Augustine, Foucault (following Nietzsche) writes: "The world of actual history knows only one kingdom, without providence or final cause, where there is only 'the iron hand of necessity shaking the dice-box of chance.' "[67] This is *The City of God* rewritten without the City of God in it. Foucault's kingdom of chance does, however, resemble Augustine's earthly city in the sense that while much happens, nothing ever really changes: both versions are strangely static with their endlessly repeated scenes of domination. Nietzsche's *wirkliche Historie,* just because it thematizes only discontinuity, only domination, proves to be strangely *unwirklich,* unreal. Sheer difference is indistinguishable from utter sameness, endless domination from eternal beatitude; what happens is always only the eternal return of the same.

Thus, ironically, the new historicism, when taken to extremes, ends in the destruction of history, at least as an intelligible category of interpretation. To avoid such a result, I believe that valuable resources can be appropriated both from the old historicism and from several strands in recent philosophy of history, notably those embodying analytic, structuralist, and narrativist approaches. Without in some way reconstructing the category of history, I know no way of speaking of God "in historicist terms," which Dean requires of us but gives no help in accomplishing. For one thing, it is clear that the old historicism and the philosophical theology associated with it did not naively postulate a transhistorical, extramundane, timeless essence as the "foundation" upon which to erect historical process, as Dean and others have suggested.[68] God is rather the primordial exemplification of history, time, process. The question we shall have to address is whether that can be understood in a way that is not reductive of either the reality of God or the experiences that have given rise to postmodernism.

Postmodernist Theology

Not much help toward this end is provided, in my view, by the theologians who thus far have imbibed the postmodernist *Geist* most fully. Just as the new historicism seems to end in the destruction of history, so too postmodernist theology seems to end in the destruction of theology. At the moment there are four principal contributors: Thomas Altizer, Carl Raschke, Mark C. Taylor, and Charles Winquist, all of whom draw in varying ways upon Derrida, Foucault, recent literary criticism, the late Heidegger, Freud, and Nietzsche. Taylor's *Erring* is probably the definitive representative of "postmodern a/theology," and I shall confine my remarks to his brilliant tour de force.[69]

The first part of the work, "Deconstructing Theology," progressively "unravels" the "Western theological network," attempting to show how the concepts "God," "self," "history," and "book" stand or fall together. The death of God leads to the disappearance of the self, the end of history, and the closure of the book. The second part, "Deconstructive A/theology," restores, after a fashion, what has been taken away. The death of the transcendent, sovereign God yields to "writing" as the "divine milieu"; a teleological history of salvation is replaced by "mazing grace"; and the closed book opens out into an unfinished, errant, endless "scripture."

My primary concern is with Taylor's critique of and alternatives to the classic conceptions of God and history. As far as God is concerned, traditional "ontotheology" is said to be based on the definition of being as "presence." Since God is being itself, God is absolute, total, eternal presence, and is present as such. But the dominant experience of postmodernism is that of the absence of such presence, and Taylor reminds us again and again that "absolute plenitude and total presence are nowhere to be found."[70] The God of ontotheology, therefore, has died and has been replaced, Taylor argues, in what is undoubtedly his most startling proposal, by *writing,* "scrip-ture," which is the "divine milieu." Why writing? Derrida provides a clue by pointing out that the first writing was "hieroglyphic" or "sacred inscription." Derridean deconstruction, at least, invests writing with a kind of sacrality, since it understands writing to be a self-referential interplay of signs, an endless milieu of significations that refers to nothing other than itself, the condition of possibility for consciousness and the object of consciousness, an unending play of differences in which the "ever-never-changing-same" eternally recurs in a *coincidentia oppositorum,* an "abiding passage."[71]

At this point I will make only the following observation about this intriguing proposal. The theological tradition never entertained the illusion that divine presence was totally, immediately available. It knew that God could be experienced and spoken of only indirectly, through signs and symbols, that God could only be "appresented"[72] in what is historically and experientially available, that God would be "all in all" only at the eschaton. Paradigmatic events, disclosures, and texts made it possible to live in the absence of presence, between the times. Ironically, those who cannot bear to live in the absence of presence are precisely those who speak most derisively of the metaphysics of presence. In them one senses a powerful eros for presence, and so the absent God is replaced by the signs and symbols themselves, the endless milieu of significations that is language. God becomes utterly immanent, totally incarnate in worldly inscription, in writing itself, which is "the creative/destructive medium of everything that is and all that is not." It is odd that the postmodernist sense of "incurable loss" and all-pervasive *différance* should here issue in the total "having" of divinity and an undialectical immediacy.

A similar displacement attends the fate of history. The "thread" that once drew history together into a coherent totality, a story with a beginning, middle, and end, the thread that traced the way out of the labyrinth, unravels under deconstructionist criticism and proves to be a figment of the imagination. Here

Taylor draws upon recent studies in literary criticism and philosophy of history that show the close connection between historical narrative and fictional narrative: both are imaginative constructs that articulate and interpret human experience in one way or another. Taylor concludes from this, however, that such constructs are inevitably illusory and deceptive. "The story of history is supposed to tame the grotesque monster that presides over/under/within the labyrinth. Historical narrative reflects the effort to ease the trauma of dislocation by weaving scattered events into a seamless web."[73] When the game is exposed, when the plot is lost, history becomes an "endgame," endless waiting and aimless wandering in the labyrinth from which there is no escape.[74] Yet within the maze we experience something like "mazing grace" when we discover that what we are waiting for will never arrive, and that "in the absence of a final telos . . . it is possible to affirm purposeless process." Then "the aimlessness of serpentine wandering liberates the drifter from obsessive preoccupation with the past and future," and we are able to receive the "grace that arrives only when God and self are dead and history is over." This grace appears in the form of purposeless play, which makes up the "carnival, comedy, and carnality" of life.[75]

Here again, I shall offer only a brief observation.[76] Taylor overstates what is being sought by the construction of historical accounts in the first place (a seamless web, an unambiguous teleology, etc.), and he understates the important differences between historical and fictional narrative that must be recognized along with their significant similarities. To say that history is a construct is not at all to say that it is a mere illusion, having no reference to reality whatsoever (this is a matter to which I shall return in chapter 3.3). Moreover, just as with God so also with history, Taylor gives back what he sought to take away, namely, saving presence. But it is given back in an utterly undialectical fashion. History may indeed be a maze or labyrinth rather than a straight and narrow path. But the purpose within the maze, I submit, is not to wander aimlessly seeking carn(iv)al pleasures and immediate satisfactions; rather, it is to build up structures of wholeness and integrity, to make this world a habitable place in which human beings can dwell. To find oneself empowered to do this, against overwhelming odds and in recognition that all such structures are fragmentary and ambiguous, is to experience grace, perhaps even amazing grace, within the maze.

3. Rethinking the Relationship of God and History

Unproductive Responses

Two unproductive responses to the postmodernist challenge in its various aspects are discernible in our time. In some respects these responses reinforce and feed upon each other, which is indicative of a tendency today to oscillate between dangerous extremes. The first response is essentially an attempt to avoid the threats and insecurities of historical passage by turning the clock back—indeed, by turning it back to pre-Enlightenment times, to traditional bases of authority and conventional forms of religious belief. The resurgence of evangelical Protestantism and of conservative attitudes in the Roman Catholic Church is symptomatic both of the magnitude of the experienced threat and of the deep desire to recover stable ethical and religious foundations in a topsy-turvy age. I do not intend to make light of evangelical religion as an authentic piety and vital conservative force; but, as Gilkey points out, its potential for idolatry and ideology must also be clearly acknowledged: its tendency to "overbelief" in face of the threats and insecurities of our time, its false securing based on illusory absolutes such as scriptural infallibility, fundamentalist doctrines, and flag-waving patriotism. Gilkey thinks the situation is especially dangerous when there appears on the national scene an "intricate interweaving of . . . two false but potent absolutes: a heteronomous and exclusivist Christianity and a rampant nationalistic and capitalistic ideology"—merging to produce the demand for a "Christian America," a demand that is capable of taking on not only theocratic but even fascist overtones.[77]

The second and diametrically opposed response arises from what Mark Taylor characterizes as the postmodernist sense of "irrevocable loss and incurable fault,"[78] which has the possibility of issuing in a radical relativism for which nothing is known, believed, or acted upon. Again, I do not intend to make light of the serious and baffling intellectual questions raised by postmodernist criticism, or to doubt for a moment the relativity of all thought and action; but the temptation here is to retreat into intellectual games and hedonistic play, which may very well be a mask for despair, cynicism, nihilism.[79] Ironically, such play assumes a stable order and has no staying power against demonic absolutes and political oppression.[80] In my view, Taylor's *Erring* is an example of this tendency. I have already alluded to his embrace of "carnival, comedy, and carnality" in lieu of historical purpose. His immanentized god of writing is designed, it appears to me, for those who do not need a real God—a God who saves from sin and death and the oppressive powers—because they already have all that life can offer; this is a god for those who have the leisure and economic resources to engage in an endless play of words, to spend themselves unreservedly in the carnival of life, to engage in solipsistic play primarily to avoid boredom and attain a certain aesthetic and erotic pleasure. The postmodernist mode of existence as depicted by Taylor is decidedly aesthetic rather than ethical or religious. Or in different terms, what we find here ultimately is a Nietzschean romantic embrace of the law of chance and necessity that manifests itself as eternal recurrence of the same. This acceptance of "fate" leaves utterly unchallenged the structures of domination and oppression from which the great majority of earth's population suffers. The economies of domination with which Taylor, too, is concerned are too restrictedly cognitive and insufficiently political.

Beyond Absolutism and Relativism, and the Turn to Praxis

The suffering experienced by Taylor is not physical, economic, or political but rather intellectual—the sense of the irrevocable loss of meaning and of the engulfing relativism characteristic of our time. This is an authentic suffering, which most of us have experienced to a considerable degree. The cure, however, is not to be found in the nihilistic play of the elite; nor is it to be sought in one or another of the illusory absolutes of popular culture. Rather, it appears to me, the way beyond absolutism and relativism may be found, if it is to be found at all, through engagement in some form of transformative, emancipatory praxis.[81] Faced with a physical menace, an ethical dilemma, or an intellectual impasse, the determination to act can often have a salutary, clarifying, releasing effect. One moves ahead only by moving ahead, and often it is only in the motion that one discovers capabilities and directions. Logical contradictions may become more "soluble" under concrete conditions of praxis. One must have the courage to act upon convictions, to take the risk of a venture into the unknown—not foolishly, of course, but wisely, responsibly. The lack of objective certainty with respect to the horizon and consequences of an action, and the recognition that every act is ineluctably conditioned by, and relative to, specific circumstances of time and place, must not of itself be allowed to have an immobilizing effect since there simply is no human action on any other terms.

This ancient pragmatic wisdom has been rediscovered and restated in modern times by thinkers as diverse as William James, John Dewey, and Ernst Troeltsch. I am especially attracted to Troeltsch because he struggled creatively with the very question of the relationship of God and history with which this project is concerned, and he did so in a fashion that is strikingly relevant to the postmodern temper. In the aftermath of the First World War, when the foundations of modern Western bourgeois culture showed unmistakable signs of crumbling, he stressed the necessity of having the courage to act in situations of objective and intellectual uncertainty, for action can clarify and resolve things when theoretical questions remain irresolvable; and he called for the creation of a new synthesis of cultural values, the beginning of a process of building a new, postbourgeois society. His prophetic words went unheeded and he died before he could contribute to their realization.[82] Gertrude von le Fort, one of Troeltsch's students prior to the war, wrote a novel in which he served as the model for one of the central figures, a professor, who makes this characteristically Troeltschian statement:

> We cannot assure ourselves of the ultimate mysteries except by a bold leap into their depth. This leap is an enormous daring; it is an entirely personal decision, but *we can act on it* despite the dangers and the apparent uncertainty that are involved in it, because it is no blind accident that we entertain such and such ideas about the ultimate mysteries, for these ideas are effected in us by the divine life itself.[83]

"We can act on it." We can act because we experience a kind of empowerment to act, an empowerment that only retrospectively is capable of being clarified reflectively. In this important sense, praxis precedes theory, action precedes thought. But action also gives rise to thought; indeed, it must give rise to thought if it is to be distinctively human action, that is to say, action which is creative, purposive, and responsible as opposed to being instinctual and blind. If we are unable to articulate, both metaphorically and conceptually, what it is that empowers us to act, what calls us forth into action and shapes our acts, then we leave ourselves open to being driven by base instincts, self-serving ends, and vain conceits.

God, History, and Freedom

The specific theoretical question I am attempting to address in this project is how we might learn to rethink the relationship of God and history in light both of the postmodernist challenge and of the empowerment experienced in a particular kind of praxis, which I am designating as "emancipatory," "liberating," or "transfigurative."

It is clear, in the first place, that this relationship can no longer be thought of in terms of the logic of divine sovereignty and the mythos of salvation history. A way of thinking must be found that is noninterventionist, nonmiraculous, and noncausal in its understanding of divine providence, nonlinear in its teleology, and nonsuprahistorical in its eschatology. In making this assertion, however, I do not naively embrace a simple abandonment of classic ways of thinking about the relationship of God and history; rather, I would like to accomplish a critical retrieval, a deconstruction and reconstruction of the tradition. The notion of a total break with tradition, its utter rejection as worthless, is a naive denial of our historicality. What actually occurs in our relationship to the past is what Hegel called "sublation" (*Aufhebung*),[84] which involves a process of both annulling and preserving, of both passing over and taking up. In this process, what is evil, false, destructive, and oppressive in the past has the possibility of being "refined away," allowed to die or be put to death, while what is good, true, salvific, and liberating has the possibility of being preserved, raised to new life in new forms. This is surely not an easy or automatic process; rather, if what is to be preserved is not the evil of the past but the good, critical judgment is required as well as hard labor. Nor is the point to suggest that we can really "do better" than Augustine, Thomas, Calvin, Schleiermacher, Barth, or any of the other great theologians of the tradition with respect to the question of God's saving presence in history. That would be an absurd pretension; it is simply that we confront this question in a new context, and we have a duty, therefore, to rethink it and all the other difficult questions. Our perspective is as relative as every other, and someday our thoughts will have to be deconstructed too, if they are worth remembering at all.

How, then, is the relationship of God and history to be rethought? Gilkey poses the issue in terms of the quest for a "centered vision," a "relative absolute," which will integrate the two great themes of classic and (post)modern theism.[85] The absolute is available only in and through relative symbols, experiences, and commitments, but it is nonetheless present in them. Often today we experience it more in negative than in positive terms: certain things, such as blatant racial and sexual oppression, are, we say, absolutely intolerable. We may know indubitably what is wrong but not how to set it right or even what "the right" is except in the most abstract sense. We can and do live and think on the basis of relative manifestations of absolute meaning, recognizing that what is true for us is still only relatively true, refusing false dichotomies that insist on having absolute certainty, total presence, or nothing at all.

There is much to commend this approach, but I think it finally remains trapped in a conventional categorial opposition (absolute vs. relative, infinite vs. finite, divine vs. human, etc.), which is no longer especially helpful, no matter how highly qualified. This approach also abstracts from the concrete situation of praxis. It starts with a normative conception of the opposites, each in and for itself, and then introduces a qualifying relationship. But it may be that the relationship is constitutive from the outset, in which case the very distinction between absolute and relative is artificial and misleading. My proposal is that "God" and "history" are essentially co-constitutive categories—"God in history" and "history in God." (The "in" of their coinherence, I shall argue, is not simply symmetrical, since history is dependent on God in a way that God is not dependent on history.) The congruence of God and history occurs precisely at the point of praxis—not an indiscriminate, amorphous praxis, but praxis of a particular sort, namely, free, liberating, emancipatory, transfigurative praxis. Freedom involves an activity of shaping, configuring, centering, presencing; it is an activity in which we experience and know ultimacy, but always only in an unfinished, open, plural process. God is present in history in the myriad shapes of freedom. This is the thesis in its barest expression. Now I shall anticipate its three main steps.

God: Triune Figuration

The first step is to establish a process view of God for which the world in general, and human history in particular, are an essential moment of the divine life. The true infinite, according to Hegel, overreaches and encompasses the finite rather than simply standing over against it as a "beyond." God is self-mediated through an other that is not godself, a mediation by means of which God becomes a concrete, living God, or Spirit (*Geist*).

"Without the world God is not God."[86] Hegel's Absolute is not static substance but dynamic, living, infinite (inter)subjectivity, absolute precisely in and through difference and relationship.

Many of these themes are also present in process philosophy, and I shall be drawing on the theological literature related to Whitehead and Hartshorne—the work of Cobb in particular, but also that of Gilkey, Ford, and Ogden. Their work has proved to be exceptionally fruitful, and I am indebted to it for many important insights. But it does seem to me that certain dilemmas created by the process view of God can be avoided by returning to Hegel's original vision, which understood God to be the more primordial category than process and creativity itself. Hegel did this by maintaining a distinction between inward and outward moments of divine mediation (or, in classical terms, between "immanent" and "economic" trinities). The dialectic of identity-difference-mediation within the divine life is the condition of possibility for there being a world that is different from God yet constitutive of God (just as God is constitutive of it). Hegel may also offer richer, more appropriate categories of historical and cultural analysis than does the formal language of process metaphysics.

Hegel must be pushed further, however, in the direction of maintaining the moment of *real difference* between God and world, and thus of taking with complete seriousness the ambiguities, struggles, contradictions, and unfinished character of history in which the divine as well as the human destiny is being worked out. In this respect the left-wing, Marxist-humanist-deconstructionist reading of Hegel is an important corrective to right-wing speculative metaphysics; my intention, however, is to hold to the Hegelian "middle" as far as possible.

In order to understand both divine mediation and historical process, I shall introduce the categories of "figure" and "figuration" from contemporary philosophical hermeneutics and literary criticism, especially as it is found in the recent work of Paul Ricoeur and Hayden White.[87] With them, I want to extend the category from a literary to a historical frame of reference, since it can be used to describe the characteristic historical activity, which is not that of thinking or conceiving (although these are presupposed), but rather that of forming, shaping, configuring. Figuration as I propose to use it is a category both of historical praxis and of historical interpretation.

The notion of figuration can also be applied by a revisionist trinitarian theology to name the founding or constitutive moments both within the divine life and of the God-world relation, thus avoiding the inadequate language of divine "persons" (inadequate not only conceptually but also because of its exclusively masculine imagery). Following a hint from Karl Barth,[88] I propose to speak of the three divine figures as "the One," "love," and "freedom." God as the One is the God whose being-within-self is self-constituting (the eternal dialectical process of identity and difference known by the tradition as the immanent trinity and designated by the symbol "Father"). God as love constitutes the world as different from godself, enters into relationship with it, suffers its alienation and annihilation, supremely so (for Christians) in the death of Christ on the cross. "World" (a symbol that extends and broadens that of "Son") specifies the element in which difference becomes actual and alienated; world history is constituted by endless difference, both productive and destructive. God as freedom both preserves and overcomes the difference, sublates it, transfigures it. Freedom is precisely presence-to-self in, through, and with otherness; it is intrinsically communal, social, synthetic. "Spirit" (the only traditional trinitarian symbol I propose to retain) is one of the richest images of freedom and the fullest of the divine figures, suggesting the process of mediation which is the divine life as a whole. To say that God is Spirit is to say that God is the Free One, or, more precisely, "the One who loves in freedom." I propose to adopt this magnificent Barthian formulation and develop it in ways that go both beyond and against Barth himself. It is a reformulation of the classic trinity of knowledge, found in both Augustine and Thomas Aquinas, in the direction of a trinity of praxis. This trinity of praxis comprises what was known by the tradition as the "economic" or "worldly" trinity.

History: De-Configurative Process

The objective here is to find a way beyond the tragic vision of history that has dominated both the modern and the postmodern sensibility, but to do so only by working through tragedy and recognizing its force and legitimacy. Hegel's philosophy of history is perhaps the best example of a post-Enlightenment philosophical attempt to do just this, and Troeltsch's theology of history the best example of the historicizing and relativizing of religious consciousness without abandoning faith in the divine.

Hegel's philosophy of world history (his "metahistory" or "poetics of history," as Hayden White calls it)[89] offered a tragicomic vision of always incomplete cultural syntheses, guided by the activity of reason (or the divine idea) in history. Hegel's logical categories functioned as a "deep structure" that generated alternative paradigms by which historical experience could be interpreted, but the contents of that experience and its concrete historical shapes were not deducible from the deep structure in a priori fashion. Although profoundly aware of the presence of evil, passion, self-interest, and violence in human affairs, Hegel understood world history to be precisely "the progress of the consciousness of freedom"; and he proposed, in a famous metaphor, that the idea of freedom and human passions "are the weft and the warp in the fabric of world history."[90] My proposed theology of history is at heart an adaptation of this brilliant Hegelian vision to a postmodernist context. Instead of speaking of a single, more or less unified and progressive history of freedom, I believe today we must speak of a plurality of partial, fragmentary, always ambiguous histories of freedom, struggling to survive, and sometimes prevailing, against the forces of domination and oppression.

It was precisely this ambiguity to which Ernst Troeltsch was sensitive in his theology of radical historicality.[91] I am especially attracted to his categories of individual totality, creative compromise, cultural synthesis, and in particular that of "configuration" or "shaping" (*Gestaltung*)—shaping the new, the future. By means of these categories, Troeltsch sought an alternative to the linear teleology of the old salvation history model, but without losing the conviction that history has an orientation to the future and a structure that gives it meaning. Troeltsch's "teleology" envisioned a process of shaping ever-new cultural syntheses through creative compromises in response to concrete historical situations. Such syntheses are relative, fragmentary, and ambiguous, and the work of creating them is an open and unending process. Setbacks and reversals occur as well as advances, and total annihilation or destruction remains a possibility. Troeltsch understood the act of shaping as in some sense the actualization for a particular moment of the divine ground of life, but he never was able to work out the idea of God in a satisfactory way.

Our situation, of course, is quite different from that of Hegel and Troeltsch, and while learning much from them we must at the same time turn to recent work in the philosophy of history from analytic, structuralist, narrativist, and deconstructionist perspectives. History as a method, a form of knowledge, has been deconstructed, shown to be the exercise of something very like literary imagination. And history as a process "defigures" as well as "configures"; all historical shapes are dissolved and replaced in the flux of time, and someday both human and cosmic history as we know it will come to an end. Any theological claims about the meaning and purpose of history must take this postmodern sensibility into account.

Freedom: Transfigurative Praxis

Troeltsch's category of "shaping" and his work in ethics and cultural values already pointed in the direction of praxis. I want to develop this by drawing upon the contributions of hermeneutics, critical social theory, neopragmatism, and the political and liberation theologies in order to test the following hypothesis: the praxis that shapes and synthesizes in ways oriented to the fulfillment of humanity is always "emancipatory" in one sense or another, and that which gives the paradigm for such shaping and empowers it is God's redemptive, transformative presence. For Christian faith, with its focus on the life and death of Jesus of Nazareth, this presence assumes a distinctive twofold shape: the shape of the *basileia* (God's ruling, world-shaping, community-forming power as envisioned in Jesus' parables of the kingdom), and the shape of the *cross* (God's self-divestment unto death by which the annihilating power of nothingness is overcome). These two shapes are superimposed, as it were, to disclose a way of being in the world communally through self-giving love; together they compose what I shall call *the divine gestalt*,[92] which lures, empowers, and shapes human activity in the direction of a transfigurative praxis. This gestalt sets humanity free from past historical syntheses that have outlived their usefulness, from the tendency toward entropy and repetition, from political and socioeconomic oppression, from institutional and systemic dehumanization, from personal alienation and despair. On the one hand, emancipatory praxis is the bearer of God's redemptive gestalt, without which the latter would be a historical abstraction, a suprahistorical miracle, a dogmatic assertion. In history this praxis, the shaping of new and liberating syntheses, on both large and small scales, is never ending, for new forms of oppression arise, new possibilities for evil emerge, just as old ones are destroyed or ameliorated. On the other hand, God's shaping, saving presence is what transfigures and empowers the human emancipatory project. Without such transfiguring and empowering, humanity "on its own" is subject to despair and cynicism or to idolatrous illusions. God is self-actualized in and through emancipatory historical praxis, and the latter is given a foundation that enables it to go on in the midst of conflict, suffering, setbacks, and limits.

The divine gestalt is, very simply, the shape of freedom. It exists in the world liminally, at the margins of the dominant world-formations. Its discernment requires the "hard labor" of human spirit. But like a tiny seed, it has incalculable transformative power, the power to move mountains.

The Beginning of the History of Freedom?

Might we be so bold as to suggest that the end of salvation history offers the possibility of the beginning of the history of freedom? The mythos of salvation history, with its logic of triumph, its linear teleology, and its suprahistorical eschatology must be allowed to die out in order to salvage its enduring conviction that God acts redemptively in history, a conviction from which might be fashioned a new theology of the history of freedom. Precisely this is the task of a postmodern revisionist theology.

One might argue, with Hegel, that the ancient, medieval, and modern worlds slowly achieved a consciousness of freedom. The task of the postmodern world is to put this consciousness to practice. In this sense the turn from the modern to the postmodern is a turn from the primacy of theory to the primacy of praxis, as Marx clearly stated in his final thesis on Feuerbach;[93] it is a turn from the "end" of the history of philosophy to the beginning of the history of the realization of freedom, as Hegel also recognized.[94] The relationship of theory and praxis reverses with this turn; further insight into what freedom *is* will be gained only from and through historical praxis. Conceptual or logical rationality now is supplemented by a discursive or dialogical rationality that is capable of bringing about, ambiguously and brokenly, something that might be called "communicative freedom."[95]

The great challenge of the postmodern world—having inherited from modernity a theoretical grasp of what freedom might mean, but also having glimpsed through the terrors of our time the possibility of utter annihilation, of abject bondage to nothingness—is to take up the history of the praxis of freedom with renewed determination and courage, recognizing how high the stakes are. The future is what we make of it. We know that there will never be a historical consummation of the praxis of freedom, and that God will not rescue the world from its folly. But we also know that we are empowered by God to shape earthly communities of freedom and solidarity—finite, fragile, fragmentary—that image in their very plurality the heavenly kingdom of freedom. In this world there are not one but many shapes of freedom.

CHAPTER II

God:
Triune Figuration

Every constructive argument entails presuppositions; there
are no pure beginnings in the process of thinking, speaking,
believing, or even doubting. I propose to start with that reality
which has become most problematic for postmodern consciousness, namely the reality of God, and then to address the themes
of history and freedom. What I am presupposing by this
procedure is the importance of reopening the question about
the relationship of God and history in light of the collapse of the
salvation history paradigm, and the appropriateness of introducing the theme of human freedom as a focus in rethinking the
relationship because it points to a dimension of transcendence,
of transformative and emancipatory power, in historical
experience. If these presuppositions are valid, then obviously it
will be necessary to speak about God, history, and freedom and
their correlations in some fashion or other. The order in which
these elements are addressed is ultimately not of great
importance since the intelligibility and truth of my thesis can be
judged only when the case has been presented as a whole, that is,
when the circle of correlations has been completed at the end of
the work.

The argument is not intended to be inductive in the sense that
if certain truths about the nature of history or the experience of
freedom are established, then the reality or necessity of God can
be inferred. By beginning without any foundations at the most
difficult point of all, namely, the point of speaking about God, it
will be clear that this is not what is intended. Those readers for
whom the God-concept has become problematic if not unthinkable are invited, therefore, to engage in a thought-experiment
with an open mind. And those readers for whom the reality of a

transcendent supernatural God is a conviction of faith are invited to suspend belief for a while in order to consider new ways of thinking about God.

By starting at this point, however, I do not wish to give the impression that the argument is intended to be deductive any more than it is inductive. I do not intend to postulate the "triune figuration" of God as an ontological foundation or premise for what is subsequently said about history as a "de-configurative process" and freedom as a "transfigurative praxis." To be sure, triune figuration is the divine creative source, the *poiēsis,* of which all human thought is mere image and *mimēsis;* but it is equally true, as I shall argue later on, that our language about God is a kind of "fiction," an imaginative envisionment, issuing from and amid our human *poiēsis* and *praxis,* our historical interpretations and ethical projects.[1] In brief, there is no privileged starting point, either inductive or deductive. We are in the midst of a hermeneutical circle no matter where we enter our figural dialectic; and what is decisive, as Heidegger has pointed out, "is not to get out of the circle but to come into it in the right way"—that is, to work our way through it in disciplined fashion.[2]

Not only do I propose to start with the idea of God; I propose to start, and indeed to focus, on the *triune* God—that is, on the very aspect of the classic doctrine of God that may be the most inaccessible or offensive to modern and postmodern sensibilities. I do so because I think that, properly understood, the trinity introduces process and historicality into God, and my purpose is to show that God and history are correlative themes: the only God we know is a God who is in history and who takes history into God. To establish this, however, requires a deconstruction of the classic doctrine of the trinity.

1. Hegel's Contribution to Trinitarian Speculation

Aporias of the Classic Doctrine

Although not in the strict sense a biblical "doctrine" (if there are such things as biblical doctrines at all), the trinity does seem to be firmly rooted in biblical, especially New Testament, symbolism for God. God's revelation and saving activity seem to be experienced in a threefold pattern: as creator, redeemer, and sanctifier of the world, or as origin, sustainer, and goal of human existence. The names of the trinitarian "persons" predominate as symbols of these constitutive functions in early Christian literature: Father, Son, and Holy Spirit; and by the fourth century the dogma of the trinity was officially sanctioned as one to which every Christian must give assent.

Yet from the beginning, conceptual difficulties plagued this doctrine, difficulties which even the greatest theologians were unable to resolve completely. I shall attempt to identify four of these aporias, then briefly consider the trinitarian proposals of Augustine and Thomas Aquinas before turning to Hegel's speculative revision. I make no pretense of giving an account of the history of the doctrine of the trinity; my intention rather is to focus on the contributions of a few truly original thinkers, assuming that the fundamental issues will come more clearly into view through their work.

First, it was an unquestioned presupposition of classic theism that God is "simple," without real parts, external relations, or properties of any sort that depend on something other than God.[3] God is completely independent of the world, but the world is utterly dependent on God. Moreover, God must be timeless and changeless, since anything that is in time is temporally divisible, and anything that undergoes changes has parts that pass away.

Under these circumstances, it was difficult to grasp how distinguishable actions such as creation, redemption, and sanctification could be predicated of God, or what meaningful distinction might be intended by symbols of the deity such as "father" and "son." The biblical language about God seems to historicize divinity, representing God as an agent who acts through temporal and spatial modalities. This implicit historicization was, however, resisted by transferring the distinctions, relations, properties, and so forth, entirely *within* the godhead, where they lost their historicality and were detemporalized, despatialized. The "immanent" or "preworldly" trinity then was accorded ontological and epistemological primacy over the "economic" or "worldly" trinity, even though the latter, rooted in the economy of salvation, was undoubtedly the experiential foundation of the former.[4] Furthermore, under the influence of Thomas Aquinas, treatment of the immanent trinity was preceded by a treatise "on the one God" in which the essence common to the three "persons" was set forth in a metaphysical conceptuality that did not presuppose revelation. This separation of the two trinities, the primacy accorded the immanent trinity, the precedence of both by a metaphysical discussion of God's simplicity, and the consequent dehistoricization of God, is the second of the aporias that I have in mind.[5]

In the third place, the very pattern of "threeness" that was transferred into the divine life *appears* to be arbitrary and artificial, as Cyril Richardson has pointed out.[6] Three seems to be required because the New Testament presents us with three dominant symbols of God (although its symbolism is still in a fluid state); the task of theology is then to accept this biblical revelation of God's threeness and, in effect, to provide more or less convincing rationalizations of it. There are, in Richardson's view, proper distinctions within the godhead to which the trinitarian symbols point without actually being these distinctions. But the distinctions on his view are *binary* rather than threefold: above all, the distinction between God's absoluteness and relatedness, to which a number of other oppositions are related, such as veiled and unveiled, one and many, eternal and temporal, rest and motion. These oppositions, Richardson asserts, pose an irresolvable, paradoxical antinomy in the godhead, which cannot be composed by reference to a third, mediating term.[7] Although I disagree with Richardson's attack on trinitarianism, as will become evident below, I believe he is correct in pointing out that no true and distinctive place was found for the Holy Spirit in early Christian thought; trinitarian speculation showed its severest strains at the point of accounting for the third trinitarian figure. This matter can be settled in my view, if at all, not by appeal to scriptural authority but only by rational reflection on the nature of spiritual being as such and the being of God in particular.

Finally, the whole conceptual framework of classic trinitarian theology was misleading. Two of the three predominant names of God in early Christian piety, "Father" and "Son," reflected the bias of a patriarchal culture and encouraged anthropomorphic ways of thinking about God; and the three names, rather than being construed as symbols or figures of divine relations, became "persons" of the godhead sharing a common "being," "essence," or "substance." To be sure, the Latin term *persona,* and its Greek equivalents, *prosopon* and *hypostasis,* did not mean "person" in the modern sense of a self-conscious ego, but referred rather to the role played by an actor (symbolized by his or her mask, *persona*), or to a functioning entity, an individuating principle. Yet, despite this fact, the introduction of *persona* terminology into trinitarian theology had the inevitable effect of literalizing talk about God along personifying and familial lines. Thus the Father was said to "beget" or "generate" the Son; the Son, in turn, is "begotten" and "spirates" the Spirit, who "proceeds" from both. It is as though three personal agencies are at work (or at play) within the godhead, although we are told that these agents are "essentially" one and the same, and that they do their work "indivisibly." Moreover, the division of labor is unclear: Father and Son share the work of creation, Son and Spirit the work of salvation. An inner tension is present in the figure of the Father, who on the one hand is the sovereign, awesome Lord of the cosmos, but on the other hand loves and cares tenderly for his children. Confusions such as these were sufficient to obscure the profound truth that was nonetheless present in the doctrine of the trinity.

Augustine

This truth was grasped by the great theologians, but they were unable to resolve the confusions satisfactorily, despite brilliant speculative attempts such as those undertaken by Augustine in his treatise *On the Trinity (De trinitate).*[8] In Books 8-15 of this work, he devised a model for understanding the triune structure of God's being that has shaped theology ever since. The model describes a subject that constitutes itself as subject by a twofold act: an act of self-distinction, through which the subject becomes objective to itself or enters into relation with a real object, and an act of self-relation or return to self. Thus the three constitutive elements of the model are a subject, an object, and the relationship between them. Already a certain tension or incongruence is noticeable in that two of the trinitarian elements appear to be conceived as *points* or *terms* of relations, while the third element is *pure relationality*. Yet Augustine sometimes gave the impression that the second element is more an act or relationship *constituting* an object than the object itself, or, perhaps better, that it is both relationship *and* object. When the trinitarian analogy is the simple act of love (he that loves, that which is loved, and love itself), or an act of sense perception (the attentive mind, the visible object, and vision itself),[9] then the second moment is clearly an object or the term of a relationship. But in the case of the cognitive analogies, which are closer to the divine trinity than sense perception or external relations, the second element is a relationship constitutive of an object. Thus, for example, in the case of human self-knowledge, we have the mind, the knowledge by which the mind knows itself, and the love whereby it loves both itself and its own knowledge. Or in the case of the mind as such, it is composed of memory (by which it remembers itself), understanding (by which it knows itself), and will (by which it loves itself).[10] The latter analogy is the one that most fully illumines the three persons of the godhead: the Father is the divine memory or interior self-relatedness, the Son is the understanding by which God knows godself, and the Spirit is the love by which Father and Son are conjoined.[11] To this trinity of knowledge, which had such an important influence on Thomas Aquinas (and indirectly on Hegel), Augustine added the trinity of love based on the scriptural affirmation that "God is love" (I John 4:16). "And therefore they [the divine persons] are not more than three: one who loves him who is from himself [Father], and one who loves him from whom he is [Son], and love itself [Spirit]."[12]

Certainly Augustine himself was aware of the tensions and inadequacies in these trinitarian analogies. He pointed out that they are mere "traces" (*vestigia*) of the incomprehensible God, yet such traces "are not vainly sought in the creature" since the whole of creation is an image or mirror, a *speculum*, of the Creator; these images range from the lowest physical patterns and relations to the highest, which is mind (*mens*), although God is above the mind.[13] Augustine was also aware of the inadequacy of the terms *substantia* and *persona*, which had been defined as normative by the church in the trinitarian controversy although they are not found in scripture. He was concerned about the terminological confusion between Greek and Latin with respect to the substance-person distinction; and he hinted that what is really intended by the word *persona*, which despite its inadequacies must be used to thwart heresy, is "relation," for something can be predicated of God only according to substance or according to relation.[14] Finally, he pointed in a distinctly modern direction when he said that the triune God cannot be *called* the Father or the Son, except metaphorically. But the trinity *can* be called the Holy Spirit, because the Spirit is a certain unutterable communion of the Father and the Son. All three "persons" are spirit, and all are holy.[15] We might say that the only true and proper name of God is "Spirit," although Augustine himself did not quite draw this conclusion, nor did he provide an adequate conceptual basis for it.

Thomas Aquinas

Augustine was the original genius behind all trinitarian speculation. Thomas Aquinas, in Questions 27-43 of *Summa theologica*, part 1,[16] provided a systematization and rationalization of Augustine's insight by which certain aporias were resolved and others created. According to Thomas, the godhead is constituted by two "processions" or inward activities, those of intellect (knowledge) and will (love), these being the only constitutive actions of the spiritual world.[17] These two processions generate within God four "real relations" (*relationes realiter*). Relative terms indicate a reference to something. If this reference is "in the very nature of things" (as, for example, those entities which by nature are connected with and attracted by one another), then such relations are "real"; but if the reference "is only in the understanding of the mind which links one thing with another," then we have a logical relation (*relatio rationis*). Now it is clear that the relations within God are in this sense "real" since they are not products of our rational understanding, and the trinitarian persons "by nature" refer to each other; but these relations do not compromise God's absolute simplicity because God is not composed of parts or relations that are *external* to God. With reference to the world of creatures, God has no real relation but only a logical relation, since he creates the world not by necessity but "by mind and will," that is, rationally and freely. As far as God is concerned, world-relatedness is, so to speak, only in the divine mind; it does not belong to the essence of the divine persons to be so related. But of course the creatures have a real relation to God because in their very nature they are dependent on God.[18] This is, as we have said, one of the foundational tenets of classic theism, and nowhere was it stated more clearly than by Thomas.

The two processions generate four relations of origin because each procession is composed of a "causal" relation ("fatherhood" in the case of the procession of intellect from the Father and "spiration" in the case of the procession of will from the Father and the Son), and an "effectual" relation ("sonship" in the case of the Son's having been begotten by the Father and "procession," that is, "spirithood," in the case of the Spirit's having been spirated by the Father and the Son).[19] But why should the four relations generate three persons? There is, in fact, no logical or rational necessity for it; this is a truth of faith, not of reason, since by reason alone we can know only the unity of God's essence but not the trinity of persons. The divine persons were defined by Thomas as "subsistent relations of origin" (not simply terms of relations as Augustine's model suggested with reference to the first two persons at least). Given the two processions and the four relations, only two persons are logically required since the

Father can (and does) love the Son as well as know the Son directly, without the Spirit. In fact, Thomas said explicitly that when love is taken "essentially," it means that "the Father and the Son love each other not by the Holy Spirit, but by their essence." But when love is taken in a "notional" or "characteristic" sense, it means "to spirate love," that is, to make, give, "breathe" or "pour out" love. Since scripture tells us that the Holy Spirit is the gift whereby God's love is poured into our hearts (Rom. 5:5), and since this means that the Spirit is "love proceeding," we can say that the Father and the Son love each other and us by the Holy Spirit, which is the bond of union between them and us, and in this respect a third distinct person of the trinity (that person whose distinctive relation is one of giving, proceeding, effecting, not causing).[20] By this brilliant artifice, Thomas thought it possible to demonstrate the "fittingness" of the trinity of persons, if not prove it conclusively. But given his basic model, it is difficult to shake off the impression that Spirit is really a superfluous "third party." If Augustine's trinity finally culminated in the Holy Spirit, which is the most proper name of God, Thomas's could get along without it.

The double procession from the Father issues not only in internal and nontemporal relations but also in external and temporal "missions," whereby God's word and love are sent into the world. These missions serve as the link between the immanent and economic trinities for Thomas, although he used the word *trinity* only of the former. The most fundamental work of mission is that of creation, which is the "procession" or "emanation" of creatures from God. To create is of the very essence of God and is common to the three persons, but it belongs to them in a certain order: the Father creates *through* the Son, and what is thus created is *governed and swayed* by the Holy Spirit.[21] If creation is of the essence of God, indeed if it signifies "the divine action, which is God's essence with a relation to the creature," it is unclear why this relation should be only logical and not real, as Thomas continued to insist.[22] The whole Neoplatonic motif of *exitus et reditus,* emanation and return, that underlay Thomas's vision of sacred history and the construction of the *Summa theologica*[23] might have opened up the possibility of affirming the coinherence of God and world, and of historicizing the concept of God in a fashion anticipatory of modern consciousness. But with the tradition Thomas continued to hold that the works of the trinity *ad extra* are in no sense constitutive of the divine life, which is internally and everlastingly self-complete.

Hegel: The Logical Deep Structure

Hegel was the third great original thinker in the history of trinitarian speculation. He does not appear to have been directly familiar with either Augustine or Thomas Aquinas.[24] This is all the more remarkable since he combined certain Augustinian and Thomistic elements in a way that helped to resolve several of the aporias of the classic doctrine: the arbitrariness of the triadic pattern, structural inconsistencies in the model, the lack of real relations to the world on the part of God, the inadequacies of the category "person," and the place and role of the "third person," the Spirit. Although his trinity remained distinctly rational, and though he maintained God's immanent, logical self-relatedness apart from the world (in both respects in accord with the Augustinian-Thomistic tradition), Hegel denied God's simplicity, thus breaking with the fundamental tenet of classic theism: God as absolute spirit is a complex, dialectical, triadic process of self-actualization through time and history. This process is rooted in what I shall call Hegel's logical deep structure.

G. R. G. Mure describes the nucleus of Hegel's thought as follows: "Hegel holds, and believes it to be the single task of philosophy to show, that reality is not a contingent aggregate, nor an endless generation and evanescence, but a necessarily ordered whole wherein the elements ordered are the phases of a single timelessly self-constituting activity which is mind or spirit [*Geist*]."[25] This self-constituting activity takes the form of self-manifestation in and through the dialectic of thought—"a progressive cycle of unreserved self-definition by thesis, antithesis, and synthesis, wherein each antithesis is the completely mediating and determinant negation, at once the contrary and the contradictory opposite, of its thesis, and each synthesis is the coincidence of these opposites in a fuller definition." This process comprises not only the logic but the whole of nature and finite spirit, and it is completed only by the "super-triad" (logic-nature-spirit) that is the whole of Hegel's system; prior to this whole, we encounter only open spirals, not self-completing circles.

Within this system, the logic can be understood as the categorial "deep structure" out of which Hegel's interpretation of the domains of nature and historical-cultural experience is generated. This deep structure functions as a distinctive form of what Kant called "transcendental ontology." It is *ontological* in the sense that it is a doctrine of categories rather than of supersensible entities (as in the case of traditional metaphysics); and it is *transcendental* in the sense that it presents conditions of possibility of experience rather than simply being beyond experience (as in the case of metaphysical transcendence).[26] What is distinctive about Hegel's transcendental ontology as opposed to Kant's is that it makes the claim to ground not only empirical, sense-based knowledge, but the *whole* of knowledge, theoretical as well as practical, aesthetic and religious as well as scientific. Moreover, this logical deep structure was clearly intended by Hegel to be *constitutive* of the experienced reality that it grounds rather than having a merely *heuristic* or *legislative* function vis-à-vis an independently grounded reality. Finally, the logical categories do not subsist in some ideal supersensible realm but are ingredient in the actuality they ground; the categories are *wirklich,* active, actual, ideal-real, not merely ideal.[27] They disclose the telos of actuality to be communicative freedom, which mirrors the perfect freedom of the concept.[28]

This interpretation suggests that Hegel's transcendental *ontology* yields a postmetaphysical, transcendental *theology.* Hegel's God is not a supersensible entity, a "supreme being," a "transcendent" object (which would in his view be a spurious form of infinitude); rather, God is "transcendental" in the sense of being the ultimate condition of possibility for the totality of experience. In this sense, the philosophical first principle and the theological first principle are one and the same: "God" is the "absolute idea."[29]

But to say that Hegel's God is not a supersensible entity is not to say that God is not actual (*wirklich*). God is actual, "absolute actuality" (*absolute Wirklichkeit*), "actual being in and for itself" (*das Anundfürsichseiende*)[30]—but only in and through the reality of the world, not as a separated, supersensible entity. Apart from the world, God is not an actual God;[31] in and through the world, of which God is the ideal condition of possibility, God becomes concrete, living, true actuality—absolute spirit. Hegel's absolute (*das Absolute*) is not something independent, cut off from everything finite, but rather is precisely that which absolves, releasing finite things to exist apart from the absolute yet in communion with it. The adjective and noun *absolute* derives from the Latin verb *absolvere,* meaning to "loosen from" or "release." Hegel generally employed the term in the transitive sense (the absolute "absolving") as opposed to the conventional intransitive usage (absoluteness "absolved of" every limit or relationship), as evident, for example, from his association of it with the act of "releasing" (*entlassen*) in the *Lectures on the Philosophy of Religion.*[32] Existing things stand out (*ex-istere*) from the absolute; the absolute itself does not "exist" but is the releasing, granting power of existing. Thus the absolute is a profoundly relational category for Hegel, just as spirit is an intrinsically social category.

If this interpretation is correct, then in the final analysis we must say that Hegel's system as a whole (if not the logic alone) is a form of "ontotheology"; but, against the criticism of Heidegger and others,[33] this is an ontotheology in which *theos* has been radically revisioned by Hegel's transcendental ontology, his distinctive vision of *ontos.* The true infinite, the divine God, "overreaches" and encompasses the finite, includes finitude, difference, otherness within godself. God is not "a (supreme) being" but "social being" in the most radical sense of having being in communion with the inexhaustible plurality of human and natural being, and taking that plurality up into the divine life. In virtue of the triadic categorial process that is at the heart of Hegel's logical deep structure, universal substance is rendered concrete and is enriched, becomes genuinely "individual" or "subjective" (more properly, "intersubjective") by its determinations in and through natural and historical particularity. The universal is precisely and only a concrete universal.

What is this triadic process at the heart of Hegel's deep structure? In simplest terms, it is the process or activity that constitutes spirit as spirit. Spiritual activity entails at minimum a self-severance and a self-reunion, a passing over into an other and a remaining at one with oneself, a return into oneself, in this passage. Hegel described the triad as the *minimum rationale* because it characterizes the basic structure of being as a dialectic of being and nothing, through which being passes over into nothing and nothing into being; the passage is becoming, the first and most basic synthesis of the logic, which means, as Mure says, that every subsequent category "cannot be anything less than an instance of temporal process." The spring that drives the dialectic and generates becoming is contradiction and negation, but these have their ultimate source and goal in unity. The ground of difference is identity, the telos of severance is reunion.[34]

The most strictly logical or rational articulation of the triad is found in the dialectic of the syllogism, which is the basic movement of thought itself, the essence of the concept as such. The three moments or figures of any syllogism, according to Hegel, are (1) universality (*Allgemeinheit*), that is, the universal substance or rational principle of a statement; (2) particularity (*Besonderheit*), the particular quality or determinate modification of the universal in the case at hand; (3) individuality (*Einzelheit*), the subject about which the statement makes a predication. For example, in the syllogism

> All human beings are mortal
> Socrates is human
> Therefore, Socrates is mortal

human being is the universal principle (U), mortality is the particular quality (P), and Socrates is the individual subject (I). In this form of the syllogism, U is the middle or mediating term, but all true syllogisms can be varied so that P and I in turn assume the middle position. We find, therefore, not a single but a "triple syllogism" at work in the whole of actuality, expressed in the shorthand: P-U-I, U-P-I, and U-I-P.[35]

This syllogistic structure is mirrored in every aspect of Hegel's philosophical system: in the system as a whole (logical idea, nature, spirit); in the science of logic (being [immediacy], essence [reflection], concept [subjectivity] and its many subdivisions); in the dialectics of consciousness (immediacy, differentiation, return; or identity, severance, reunification); in the doctrine of the trinity (Father, Son, Spirit); and in the philosophies of nature, spirit, right, art, religion, and world history. As we approach the specific philosophies of the real, however, it becomes apparent that this "mirroring" of the deep structure is by no means an exact, monotonous, mechanical replication. The completed teleology of the logical categories is reduplicated in history only partially and openly; in history we have only "open wholeness," not self-enclosed totality.[36]

The basic movement of Hegel's philosophy is from the empirical or experiential (experience as it presents itself to consciousness) to the rational or logical, then back to experience as speculatively interpreted or reconfigured. In this movement there always remains, as Mure shows, an *imperfect sublation of the empirical in the rational.* Mure attributes this to a basic contradiction or duality in human experience that cannot be completely surmounted by any philosophy—the duality between the universal and the particular, the infinite and the finite, the eternal and the temporal, the necessary and the contingent, the intelligible and the sensuous, or (in its most basic form) the a priori (the rational) and the empirical.[37] Both the a priori and the empirical require each other as an other. There is no sheerly empirical experience, but only experience construed categorially in and by thought; conversely, there is no pure thought subsisting in distinctionless self-identity, but only thought applied to an "other" that is beyond pure thought, even if this "other" is not finally an alien other but is contained as a moment within the absolute. In being thus contained, the other cannot be utterly sublated or annulled (*aufgehoben*); for the absolute, the rational, in order precisely to be the absolute, must be related to the nonabsolute—the finite, the historical, the empirical, the sensuous, the particular, the contingent, the nonrational.[38] This has important consequences, as we shall see, for Hegel's reconfiguration of the trinity.

Hegel: The Three Moments of the Self-Development of the Idea of God

A prime instance of Hegel's willingness to engage in imaginative variation of the logical deep structure was his recognition that the Christian doctrine of the trinity cannot correspond exactly to the syllogistic and philosophical triads, since the second trinitarian moment must encompass both nature (particularity) and finite spirit (individuality), while the third trinitarian moment entails the return to universality through the infinite (inter)subjectivity of absolute spirit.[39] Moreover, the trinitarian moments may be set forth in a variety of categorial frameworks—logic, consciousness, space, and time—since the idea of God is available not only to conceptual thought but also to the representational language of religion.[40]

At the same time, Hegel drew together the categories of logic, space, and time so as to offer the following summary of the three moments of the self-development of the idea of God. (1) Universality: this is the absolute, eternal, logical idea in and for itself, God in eternity before the creation of the world and apart from the world. (2) Particularity-Individuality: God creates the world of nature and finite spirit (humanity) as distinct from godself, first positing the separation (Adam), then reconciling what has become alien or estranged (Christ). (3) Infinite Subjectivity: through this process of reconciliation, God becomes spirit, the Holy Spirit present in its community, bringing all things into union with God, and God thus returns to self "enriched" and "spiritualized" by what is other than self.[41] The "becoming" of God is the movement from the purely logical or rational, through the natural and historical, to the spiritual—the transition from absolute idea to absolute spirit. The idea contains within itself the impulse to "go forth freely as nature" and ultimately to actualize itself as spirit, that is, as a process of embodied consciousness.[42] Spirit (*Geist*) is Hegel's richest category, for it encompasses or "overreaches" both the ideal and the real, the rational and the actual. It is not the abstract, purely logical idea, but the idea as realized or embodied in nature and history, the idea in the shape of consciousness. Thus, far from being a dualistic, anticorporeal, Platonizing concept, "spirit" was construed by Hegel more in accord with the biblical sense of animating, vitalizing breath (*ruach, pneuma, spiritus*). If God is absolute spirit as well as absolute idea, then God cannot be fully God apart from nature and history.

Hegel offered this compact formulation of the trinitarian process: "God in his eternal universality is the one who distinguishes himself, determines himself, posits an other to himself, and likewise sublates the distinction, thereby remaining present to himself, and is spirit only through this process of being brought forth."[43] This process constitutes "the divine history," "the eternal history, the eternal movement, which God himself is," "the eternal divine history itself."[44] Language such as this indicates a thoroughgoing historicization of the idea of God. Strictly speaking, the expression "eternal divine history" cannot refer to the innertrinitarian life of God since the latter is not yet a historical process; it is rather a dynamic, logical process, which is the ground of history and temporality. The inner life of God becomes historical when the immanent distinctions within God are outwardly posited in the constitution of a world of space-time other than God, and when God enters into relationship with this world and returns to self spiritualized, historicized, temporalized. Thus we may properly speak of an "eternal divine history" only with reference to the economic or worldly trinity, which encompasses the immanent trinity as the first of its moments. The economic trinity is nothing other than the universal, world history of absolute spirit, which incorporates all finite histories within it.[45]

When Hegel used the word *trinity,* he normally meant by it what the theological tradition did, namely, the immanent, logical, or preworldly trinity—in Hegelian terms, the moment of "universality," the *actus purus* of the inner divine life, the process of differentiation and return contained within the eternal idea, for which "the show of finitude . . . has not yet taken place."[46] At the same time, Hegel recognized that the divine differentiation *ad intra* is the condition of possibility for God's relation to the world *ad extra* and that the outward relations reenact the inner distinctions without simply reduplicating or repeating them—in effect a correspondence between, not an identity of, the immanent and economic trinities.[47] Although Hegel himself did not use the terms *immanent* and *economic,* the distinction was important for him because it establishes God's transcendence of the world upon which God also depends for full actualization. It establishes, as Brian Leftow points out, the "sense in which God's necessary properties are prior to, determine and render strongly dependent the world's necessary properties, and so its very existence."[48] As we have seen, God is also dependent on the world—not in order to be but to exist,[49] to have existential spirituality. To achieve the latter, God does not need the precise character of this world but only some world. This world ultimately is for the sake of God, and God is for the sake of nothing beyond godself.[50] In this respect Hegel was closer to the classic tradition than was Whitehead.

The truth of the immanent trinity is most adequately grasped, according to Hegel, in purely speculative, logical categories as the dialectic of unity, differentiation, and return. It is a mystery, but a rational mystery—the mystery of reason (*Vernunft*), of thought itself. The truth of the trinity may also be grasped in the representational language of love and personality. Love entails a union mediated by relationship and hence distinction; to be a person means to be reflected into self through distinction, to find one's self-consciousness in another, to give up one's abstract existence and to win it back as concrete and personal by being absorbed into the other. God as love is "a play of distinctions in which there is nothing serious." But when the understanding (*Verstand*) enters in and tries to count three divine "persons," it falls into irresolvable contradiction because it cannot grasp the speculative truth of identity in difference. Hegel noted that reason can employ the relationships of the understanding only insofar as it "destroys" (*zernichtet*) the forms of the understanding. Thus the task of a speculative doctrine of the trinity is to destroy, that is, deconstruct, the childlike (*kindlich*), figurative (*bildlich*) forms—the "persons" of "Father," "Son," and "Holy Spirit"—in which the doctrine has been representationally expressed. This is necessary in order to release and retrieve the truth of the doctrine, which concerns God's "real relations," not just internally (as Thomas maintained) but externally as well.[51]

As for the external relations, the contingency of nature and history are necessary to the full actualization of the divine idea, since, as we have seen, in order for the absolute to be absolute it must be related to an empirical other that is not absolute and is beyond pure thought, even if it is not an alien other but is capable of being contained within the absolute as an other. This is the truth of the economic trinity.

The economic trinity as Hegel conceived it incorporates the immanent trinity as its first moment (the moment of universality, immediacy, identity); its second and third moments then reenact the inner self-relations of God outwardly. Immanent and economic trinities are thus neither separated nor identified, and they are related to each other asymmetrically. This would appear to be the most adequate way of conceptualizing the relationship of God and world since it understands them to be co-constitutive of and relative to each other, but without either being reduced to the other, and without the relationship between them being understood as merely symmetrical, which it is not. There is both real transcendence and real immanence. But the way God transcends and is immanent in the world is different from the way the world is immanent in and transcends God.

The natural-historical world, which constitutes the second moment of the economic trinity, corresponds to the second moment of the inner dialectic of the divine life, but Hegel made it clear that the created world is not simply identical with God in the moment of divine self-differentiation ("the eternal Son of the Father"). This would entail a crude pantheism, which he consistently avoided. His position was rather that of panentheism: the world exists in God and depends on God (creation is a continuous preservation), but it is not in any present empirical sense identical with God, although its destiny, its telos is "to pass over," "to take itself back into the final idea."[52]

The real difference between God and world is necessary to both. Within the divine life, "the act of differentiation is only a movement, a play of love with itself, which does not arrive at the seriousness of other-being, of separation and rupture." But "it belongs to the absolute freedom of the idea that, in its act of determining and dividing, it releases the other to exist as a free and independent being. The other, released as something free and independent, is the world as such." This releasing or letting-go (*entlassen*) is intrinsic to the "absolving" character of the absolute, which loosens or releases (*absolvere*) whatever exists apart from itself. To be absolute is precisely to release the other.[53] Because otherness is already a (sublated) moment within the absolute idea, the idea is free to allow this its own *other* also to obtain "the determinacy of other-*being*, of an actual entity," without losing itself or giving itself up. It can give freedom and independent existence to the other without losing its own freedom: "It is only for the being that is free [God] that freedom *is*." By this free grant of freedom, the nonserious play of love becomes, we might say, deadly serious—to the extremity of human alienation, suffering, and brutality, the death of Christ on the cross, which is the death of God.[54]

In his last lectures on philosophy of religion in 1831, Hegel suggested that the eternal divine history is reenacted in the history of Christ. "The abstractness of the Father is given up in the Son—this then is death. But the negation of this negation is the unity of Father and Son—love, or the Spirit."[55] In other words, it is the abstract God, the supreme being, the Father, who dies in the death of the Son, and who is, as it were, reborn as concrete, world-encompassing Spirit. This is what Hegel earlier referred to as "the speculative Good Friday"[56] and "the Golgotha of absolute spirit."[57] The worldly mediation of absolute spirit was given special stress in these last lectures, just as it was earlier in the Jena writings, but now it was balanced by the insistence that the condition of possibility for God's self-realization in and through world process is God's ideal self-relatedness. The ground of the difference between God and world is (to borrow from and misappropriate Whitehead's terminology) their "primordial" and "consequent" identity.

2. Accents of Historicality, Difference, Process, and Embodiment

Historicality and Difference

In the preceding section I have presented an essentially "middle-of-the-road" interpretation of Hegel's thought as it bears on the question of the relationship of God and history, believing that the nucleus of Hegelianism is best understood as a system of mediations, and believing too that we are best served by a mediating theology. But the predominant interpretation of Hegel today among postmodernists argues that his system tends to dissolve the particularity of things in an overarching rational synthesis, and that consequently the fragmentary, ambiguous, negative, and contingent character of historical existence must be stressed much more sharply than it was by Hegel himself. Instead of a system of identity, what is called for today, so it is said, is a system of nonidentity, of radical and irresolvable *difference*.

There is an important element of truth in this criticism, for an ambiguity is in fact present in Hegel's thought that accounts in part for the competing schools of interpretation that sprang up immediately after his death and continue to this day. Mure attributes the ambiguity to the fact that Hegel never completely solved the problem of how thought both sublates sense experience and remains in reciprocal relation with experience. Rather he seems to waver between two positions.[58] On the one hand he clearly recognizes that empirically and historically based experience presents an endlessly novel and to some degree unexpected temporal flow that can never be predicted a priori. Without the impingement of this positive content, there would be no reality for us. His references to the embodiment of particular logical categories in particular phases of nature and concrete spirit remain irregular and sometimes inconsistent, and he rarely attempts precise correlations. In the philosophies of art, history, and religion, "The empirical and historical factor is very conspicuously not, and could not be, sublated in the philosophical interpretation without a residue which at once lames and sustains the interpretation."[59] But on the other hand Hegel's conviction that thought and sense have a single source, and that form and content are inseparable, led him sometimes to "the mechanical imposition of the triadic rhythm upon material which can by no stretch of anyone's imagination but Hegel's be conceived as the indubitable content of that form."[60] This lack of caution is more characteristic at the macrocosmic level, such as the philosophy of world history, than at the microcosmic; and of the philosophy of nature than of the philosophy of spirit. It seems that Hegel was more open to this temptation when confronted by a paucity of material, while an increasing wealth of material (as demonstrated by the later philosophy of religion lectures) complicated the correlations, rendering them less precise and more provisional.

A related difficulty is Hegel's tendency to overstress original and final identity at the expense of intervening difference. This is evident from some of his statements about the relationship of God and world. Though posited as free and independent, the world is not autonomous. It has its truth not in itself but in God; its truth is its ideality, not its reality. From God's point of view, it is but a "disappearing moment," "a flash of lightning that immediately vanishes, the sound of a word that is perceived and vanishes in its outward existence the instant it is spoken." It is an "appearance," whose characteristic is "to pass over, moving itself forward, so as to take itself back into the final idea."[61]

In contrast to spurious pantheism and undialectical monism, Hegel defended what he regarded to be the authentic pantheism of Oriental religion and Spinoza, or what is more precisely termed "panentheism." Authentic pantheism claims, not that "all is God" (*alles sei Gott*)—"no one has ever held that"—but that God is "the All that remains utterly one" (*das All, das schlechthin eins bleibt*), and thus is the negativity and sublation of finite things, which have the ground of their being not in themselves but in God. The "pan" of pantheism is to be taken as universality (*Allgemeinheit*), not as totality (*Allheit*).[62] This is an important distinction to keep in mind in light of postmodernist critiques of "totality," a concept often traced to Hegel.[63] But while Hegel's thought clearly is not totalistic or totalitarian, the question remains whether his "universality" allows sufficient autonomy and duration to what is in fact a very long "moment" of difference. We do not, as a matter of fact, see things from God's point of view but from our own. And from our point of view in the late twentieth century, historicality and difference loom larger than Hegel was willing to allow. Do they loom so large as to rupture entirely the Hegelian dialectic of identity and difference, leaving us with an endless generation and evanescence of irreducibly different finite things, the purposeless throw of the cosmic dice? Is the only alternative to spurious pantheism an equally spurious atheism?

I believe it is possible to avoid the extreme solution of a postmodernist "a/theology" while accepting the validity of the left-Hegelian and deconstructionist critique of Hegel's Neoplatonic, Gnostic, and mystical affinities, arguing in effect for the resolution of the ambiguity in Hegel's thought in favor of the first, more cautious and open-ended way of understanding the relationship between logic and history, God and world. Apart from the question whether such a resolution is closer to the "nucleus of Hegelianism" (as Mure believes to be the case),[64] it is the only sustainable option if Hegel's thought is to continue to be a productive resource in the postmodern world.

Several recent works in theology read Hegel in this direction. Wolf-Dieter Marsch for example argues that in the early writings from the Jena period Hegel maintained that the dialectical mediation of absolute spirit with itself through self-divestment and finitization is carried out only in and through the sociohistorical process.[65] As such it has a thoroughly relative, contingent, unfinished character. Later, in the period of the *Logic* and *Philosophy of Religion,* Marsch believes that Hegel transposed this process almost entirely into the logical or immanent trinity, thus undercutting the realism and provisionality of his earlier theory. Although I do not accept this reading of the later writings, for reasons discussed above, I do believe that Marsch captures the strand in Hegel's thought (present in the later as well as the earlier writings) that must be emphasized today. History must be interpreted (in Marsch's terms) as a succession of situations in which estrangement is brought to consciousness, in which God is experienced as absent, in which the loss of life is felt with anguish. But even under such conditions it is possible to anticipate an emancipated life of "identity in nonidentity." It is possible to have faith that God will not let this life go, just as God did not allow Christ to remain in the grave. In the nonidentical, one is permitted to seek identity, just as the Easter witnesses beheld the risen Christ in the crucified; and even today, says Marsch, we must acknowledge that the risen Christ (*der auferstandene Christus*) is still out-standing (*steht noch aus*). What Hegel called "the cross of the present" entails recognizing and enduring the contradiction between communicative freedom and structures of domination and estrangement. But there is a "rose" in this cross, which is reason, dialectical reflection, the capacity of grasping every contradiction rationally, struggling toward its resolution rather than fleeing or denying it.[66] Such dialectical reflection demands of us "hard labor" because we must inquire about God and God's redemptive activity in this unfinished, fragmentary, ambiguous present known as history, not in a transcendent supratemporal beyond, whether paradisiacal or eschatological.

Such a reading of Hegel should make us cautious about speaking of world history as "the progress of the consciousness of freedom."[67] Despite his recognition of the "cross of the present," Hegel's teleology, at least at the macrohistoric level, is too linear and unambiguous to be persuasive in the fragmented, post-Hegelian world. Yet lest we forget the "rose" in the cross, we must recognize that freedom is present in history. I propose therefore to understand history not as "the progress of the consciousness of freedom" but as an open-ended matrix of "shapes of freedom," which cannot be linked together into a linear teleology. In this way the "long" moment of difference or nonidentity in the triune figuration of God is accorded the weight it requires.

A similar reading of Hegel is offered by Eberhard Jüngel.[68] Starting from Hegel's thematization of the death of God, Jüngel argues that the divine essence must be understood as incorporating negation, which enables God's being to be thought of in terms of history, for without negation there is no history. The death of God discloses that God does not "exist" somewhere as a "supreme being," and that the divine essence is not simply "absolute presence." Rather, God's power entails a withdrawal from omnipresence, and God's presence entails a withdrawal from omnipotence. God's being is that of a process of becoming: a going into nothingness and a coming from godself. Jüngel calls for a reversal of priority between immanent and economic trinities. The economic trinity treats God's history as the God who comes to humanity, while the immanent trinity is to be understood as its summarizing concept. Whereas the economic trinity speaks of God's *history* (God's coming to humanity), the immanent trinity speaks of God's *historicity* (God's being as it comes). "We must ponder this if we want to take God's history with humanity seriously as an event in which God is God."

Process: Whiteheadian Concepts of God

The categories of process and becoming are found in the Hegelian conceptual scheme as well as the Whiteheadian. But their implications for the concept of God in the two philosophers are quite different. "While in Hegel the world is for God and God is for nothing beyond himself, in Whitehead God and the world are for the sake of each other, and both are 'instruments' of creativity," which is Whitehead's "ultimate category."[69] God is subject to the categorial scheme, which operates at all levels of concreteness and abstraction, rather than constituting that scheme as something determinative of the world. For Whitehead, God does not transcend the world as the ground of its being but only in terms of God's distinctive function vis-à-vis creative process.

Whitehead was highly critical of the Western, "Semitic" concept of God as a transcendent, personal, creator *ex nihilo*, since such a concept failed in his view to account for "becoming" as the creative advance into novelty. God-talk is intelligible only if it can be shown that God is a necessary element in such an account. Indeed, Whitehead thought this to be the case. The infinite creative possibilities of the universe would remain chaotic and unactualized if there were not a principle of limitation and ordering, which offers to each occasion of experience the aim for its own ideal satisfaction. Moreover, the momentary achievements of value by each occasion of experience would be forever lost in the relentless flow of time were they not preserved in God's everlasting nature. Thus God must be a supreme nontemporal actual entity, which serves two basic and unique functions in cosmic process, that of envisioning the eternal objects, limiting and ordering them to specific occasions (God's "primordial nature"), and that of prehending actual occasions, preserving whatever value and goodness they have actualized from being lost in the endless flow of time (God's "consequent nature").[70]

The Whiteheadian theologians have accepted Whitehead's criticism of classic theism, but most of them have found it necessary to modify significant elements of his doctrine in order to have a religiously satisfying concept of God. They have done this for the most part by shifting from the microcosmic level of successive phases of divine activity in relation to each actual entity to the macrocosmic level of God's role in relation to world-process as a whole, and by conceiving God as personal, a personal society, rather than as an individual, nontemporal actual occasion. This is true in different ways of John Cobb, Langdon Gilkey, and Lewis Ford, who remain closer to Whitehead's original categorial scheme, as well as of Charles Hartshorne and Schubert Ogden, who have introduced a modified version of "neoclassical" or "dipolar" theism.

Cobb's primary modification of Whitehead is his insistence that God must be a society of occasions, a living person, not a nontemporal actual entity. The subjective unity of God must encompass both the primordial and consequent natures, which ought not to be viewed as separable, successive phases of God's being. Thus God can be regarded as "creator," in accord with most religious traditions. But Cobb wants to maintain the primacy Whitehead assigned to creativity vis-à-vis God. God is created by creativity, and God's role is to form or shape the creative process. Creativity as such is simply change itself, becoming, process. Although it is the material cause of actual entities, it cannot explain what or that particular things are. For this, an efficient and a final cause are required, which is God, who grants to each actual occasion an initial aim, without which it would not be anything specific at all, and who preserves it from utterly perishing. Thus God is both an instance of creativity and the "creator" of new occasions of experience. On this mediating view, God is not the ultimate metaphysical principle but is an appropriate object of religious worship because God is "creative good" or "creative-responsive love."[71]

Gilkey rejects certain basic principles of the process vision. Above all, he insists that God is not to be reduced to one metaphysical factor among others; rather, God is to be understood as the source of the whole of existence, including creativity and flux. The freedom of the creature is guaranteed by the self-limitation of God, who produces a free, contingent being that is not God, rather than by the separation of God from creativity and the reduction of God to finitude. Creativity becomes the power of being within God rather than an independent principle, and God is understood to be in dynamic process but not subject to process.[72] God's power of being is what unites destiny and freedom, which are the two poles of the ontological structure of history and temporality. In addition, however, God is the ground of possibility, providentially envisioning, grading, and evaluating possibilities with respect to each actual present. Human freedom occurs at the point of conjunction of given structures of the past (destiny) with novel possibilities for the future, which are actualized in the present moment by an act of free decision.[73]

These three principles—destiny, possibility, freedom—become the basis for a kind of trinity for Gilkey, but he is imprecise about it and it is unclear whether his view really accords with the "classic trinity of being, truth, and love," as he claims, or whether it is really consistent with Whiteheadian doctrine. God's being creates and sustains the continuity of what is past, given, actual (that is, destiny). God's logos (or truth) orders and envisions the realm of possibility, relating it to actuality by way of relevance, an ordered structure of graded options. Finally, God's redemptive love is needed because destiny can readily become fate and possibilities can remain forever unfulfilled. Thus God's redemptive love is the ground of our freedom, that is, our free and intentional unification in the present moment of a given past and a possible future.[74]

A number of questions may be raised about this model. It is not really appropriate to identify God's "being" simply with what grounds the givenness of the past, for it refers rather, as Gilkey himself recognizes, to a continuous divine creativity in which temporal passage occurs in each present moment of existence. God's creative being as "Father" presides over the mediation of destiny and freedom rather than being aligned with just one of these poles. Thus it is not surprising that the place of the Spirit is eclipsed in Gilkey's model, either by the Father's "preserving" and "accompanying" providence, or by Christ, who operates as both logos and love. Finally, basic correlations with the Whiteheadian structure are difficult to work out, although Whiteheadian conceptualities are employed. Gilkey's second moment correlates readily enough with the primordial nature of God, but the third does not seem to be the consequent nature, and the first has no place in Whitehead at all.

Lewis Ford is an orthodox Whiteheadian who attempts to
draw a fairly traditional theology out of process metaphysics.
Among other things, he claims that a trinity is implicit in
Whitehead because of a little-noticed distinction between the
concrescence of an actual entity and its concretum. This
distinction must apply also to God, the supreme nontemporal
actual entity. What we have in God is one nontemporal
concrescence ("Father") in two concretums, primordial ("Son")
and consequent ("Spirit"). What God concresces out of is
creativity as such (which remains metaphysically ultimate) as its
primordial nontemporal accident, an accident because the
particular character of God's primordial envisagement is not
determined by the essential nature of creativity.[75] Aside from the
difficulty of connecting God's "concrescing" out of undifferentiated creativity with what the tradition meant by the first
trinitarian symbol, it seems that the distinguishing of concrescence from concretum is a technical abstraction within the
primordial nature of God that is scarcely capable of establishing
a first moment of the godhead, since the act of concrescing
depends wholly on primordial envisagement (the second
moment) to be anything determinate at all.

The distinction between the second and third moments is
much sharper as Ford draws it. There is a real transcendence of
the world vis-à-vis God because it shares in creative process
directly, apart from God, as well as in relation to God. Now it is
the world's transcendence of God in view of its own creativity
that requires the third moment of God, namely receptive
dependence within God, or "Spirit."[76] But again, a role is
assigned to the Spirit that is not traditionally associated with that
figure, namely, receptive dependence on the world. More
damaging, however, is the fact that the model does not properly
yield a trinity but a quaternity since there are four constitutive
elements, not three: God's transcendence of world (Father),
God's immanence in world (Son), world's transcendence of God
(world as such), and world's immanence in God (Spirit). Or the
elements reduce to two if the first is really an abstraction from
the second, and the third is not viewed as a moment within the

divine life but as an autonomous participation in creative process, in which case we are left, as Whitehead claimed, with God's primordial and consequent natures as distinguishable moments of the divine life.

The conclusion I draw from this brief study of Gilkey and Ford is that it is difficult to extract a trinity from process metaphysics. This of course establishes nothing either for or against its validity as a metaphysical argument. It only suggests that process thought, despite its many helpful insights, is not especially helpful if one's agenda is to retrieve and rethink the trinitarian symbols. Perhaps it is better to acknowledge that process thought more readily yields a dipolar concept of God—God as absolute and related (Hartshorne, Ogden), or as primordial and consequent (Whitehead, Cobb)—and to argue for the truth of the dipolar version versus the trinitarian one.

Process: The Divine Relativity

The dipolar concept is elaborated by Charles Hartshorne, whose basic thesis is that God is supremely relative or "surrelative," within whose relativity is included the divine absoluteness as an abstract essence. His position is in certain respects just the opposite of Hegel's: it is not the divine absoluteness that overreaches and encompasses relativity, but rather the divine relativity that overreaches and encompasses absoluteness. For Hartshorne, absoluteness is not a dynamic, dialectical, relational concept as it is for Hegel, but rather a static, abstract one. To be absolute, according to Hartshorne, is to be "independent of relations," and "relations of which a term is independent are those external to it, thus only nominally 'its' relations." As absolute, God has such independent relations with "intensional classes" such as ultimate possibilities or eternal ideas. Thus what is called the "primordial nature" in the Whiteheadian categorial scheme is what Hartshorne means by God's absoluteness, if I understand him correctly. But the inclusive and supreme reality, of which absoluteness is only a constituent element, is God's surrelativity. In knowing everything, God is related to everything as subject and receives everything as object; and this supreme relativity would be God's "consequent nature."[77]

The difficulty with this position, from both a classic and a Hegelian perspective, is that on Hartshorne's view all of God's relations are to terms outside godself, these relations falling into two classes: external or independent (divine "absoluteness"), and internal or dependent (divine "relativity"). There is no inner dialectic of self-relatedness within God apart from God's world-relatedness, and thus no ideal subjectivity from which God might go out from self into world-otherness and return to self. The encompassing process for Hartshorne is not a trinitarian divine process that embraces the world but a world process that embraces God as generator of relevant possibilities (God as absolute) and receptacle of actual entities (God as relative).

Schubert Ogden has adopted and further developed this dipolar theism. He is able to say not only that God is "supremely relative" (as Hartshorne does) but also that God is "supremely absolute" (which Hartshorne does not seem to want to say). God's absoluteness is the abstract structure of God's eminent relativity—a relatedness that is relative to nothing and is in this sense absolute, changeless. God is the unchanging ground of change; God's relation to all others is itself relative to nothing but is the ground of all real relations. God is eminently social and temporal, immediately related to everything, as the mind is related to the body. God's world-relations are wholly internal to the world, and therefore God is omnipresent; the divine love is "all-embracing," a "pure unbounded love."[78] Defined in this way, God's absoluteness appears to be a merely analytic quality of the divine relativity and not really distinct from it; and, as with Hartshorne, so with Ogden, God appears to have no self-relatedness or self-presence apart from world-embodiment.

Process theology of both the Whiteheadian and Hartshornean varieties tends to become highly metaphorical when it speaks of God's "action" in the world. We are told that God does quite a number of things. God "presents" a past given to each new act of becoming. God "envisions," "grades," and "orders" possibilities in terms of their maximal relevance for each new actualization. God "lures," "persuades," or "calls us forward" into new ideal possibilities for our existence. God "sustains" the continuity of the past and "accompanies" each new self-actualization. Now the question is how God does all of this. What constitutes a divine "act" in history? With the abandonment of the model of divine triumph and supernatural causal efficacy, this remains one of the most difficult questions facing a contemporary theology of history. Gilkey in particular fails to unpack these suggestive metaphors, while providing valuable detail about other matters, such as the interplay of destiny, freedom, and possibility in every concrete occasion of experience. The question is whether and how *God* is at work in this interplay. Cobb and Ogden, on the other hand, do address just this question, and their proposals will prove helpful at a later point.[79]

Process theology is making a valuable contribution to our understanding of God's relativity vis-à-vis the world, to thinking about how God acts in the world, to rethinking the question of evil, and to affirming the open, unfinished character of history. While learning much from it, however, I continue to explore the possibilities of a different conceptual framework. This arises partly from a desire to enrich the conceptual alternatives of theology as much as possible (and until recently the Hegelian conceptual possibilities have not been as fully discussed by theologians as the Whiteheadian ones); but it also arises from my intuitive conviction that a triadic dialectic is better able to account both for reality as experienced and for divine process than a dipolar one. Thus I am drawn back to Hegel even while holding on to the deeper thematization of divine relativity that the process theologians have given us.

Embodiment

In a recent book, Grace Jantzen argues that God's relationship to the world should be regarded as analogous to the relationship between a person and his or her body when this relationship is understood "holistically," that is, as manifesting an inseparable unity of mind and body.[80] God is not separable from the world, having merely external relations with it; rather, the world is "God's body," and God cannot exist without a body any more than human selves can. Jantzen argues for a rejection and reversal of the tradition's insistence on divine incorporeality and timelessness, not only because it has prevented us from understanding God as a living God but also because it has devalued the material and physical world, encouraging merely instrumental attitudes toward it.

The theme of embodiment, like process, historicality, and difference, is an accent of the postmodern temper to which theology must attend. I affirm this accent with the proviso that God must be understood as both incorporeal and corporeal. The tradition for the most part insisted on only the former because of its convictions that God could have no real relations with the world and that the spiritual is higher than the material in the hierarchy of being, whereas Jantzen seems to insist on only the latter because of her holism. As I have argued, God does have ideal being apart from the world, but insofar as God is spirit, God is also necessarily embodied because the spiritual is the unity of the ideal and the real; there can be no spirit apart from nature. But God's relation to the world is not direct and immediate, like our relationships to our bodies. Divine immediacy is preworldly only; in the world everything is mediated, and thus God does not appear or act *directly* in history. By contrast, Jantzen's view of divine embodiment leads her to say that God "can intervene in the affairs of the world if he wants to, and sometimes he does just that."[81]

The question is whether holism is able to maintain a viable distinction between the "inseparably united" elements of mind and body, spirit and matter. What prevents these elements from collapsing into one another in an undialectical monism? Is the material simply a coarse mode of spirituality? Or the spiritual a refined mode of materiality? The bias of postmodernism is toward the latter. The encompassing metaphor in our time is body, which overreaches the distinction between it and whatever we may wish to affirm about selfhood, mind, and so forth. For

Hegel, by contrast, it is spirit (*Geist*) that overreaches the distinction between nature and spirit: it is necessarily embodied by nature, yet is the telos of nature, and its "principle" is the idea, which is reducible to neither nature nor spirit. Hegel's "system of mediation" provides an alternative to Cartesian dualism and to ancient and modern monisms, whether of matter or of mind.[82] It provides a basis for revaluing our concepts of both "spirit" and "body," although insufficient attention has been paid to the second of these tasks by those working in a Hegelian framework.

If, in the case of divine and human being, it is spirit rather than body which overreaches the distinction-in-unity of both, then the question becomes, What are the "shapes" (*Gestalten*) of spirit? How is it configured when it appears? We never have *Geist* without *Gestalt*.[83] This is one of the truths in the theme of embodiment. But the configuration of spirit is never simply bodily and physical; it is also, and more primordially, temporal. The point is not merely that everything physical or spatial is also temporal, but that spiritual being is constituted as spiritual by a primordial consciousness of time. We exist in time by configuring it, and these configurations also shape our bodily and social existence.

3. "Figure" and "Shape" as Metaphors

A detour is now necessary to help build the case for rethinking the idea of God as a process or event of "triune figuration." The detour will attempt to elucidate the related sets of metaphors that are serving as leitmotivs for this study as a whole, namely, the categories of "shape" and "shaping,"[84] and those of "figure," "figuration," "configuration," "defiguration," and "transfiguration." Hence this section will serve not only as a building block for the present chapter but also as a methodological foundation for the following two chapters.

A *figure* is a "form" or a "shape." Our term derives from the Latin noun *figura* and the verb *fingere*, "to form" or "to shape," which comes from an Indo-European base meaning "to knead" (clay or dough)—a nice earthy image, but a shaping of something to distinctively human ends in which the original form of the substance is transformed, such as clay into pottery and dough into bread. The same is true of our word *shape,* which derives via the Anglo-Saxon *sceap* from another Indo-European root, "to cut with a sharp tool" or "to carve"—that is, to shape a humanly significant object such as a statue or an implement out of a natural substance (wood, stone). *Figuration* is a "forming" or "shaping" (both as act and as product); *configuration* is a shape or figure as determined by the arranging of parts; *defiguration* is the spoiling or "disfiguring" of a shape or figure by destroying or disarranging it; and *transfiguration* is a changing or passing over of a shape or figure into something new: it is a "transformation," a "metamorphosis."

The Germanic equivalent of the Latin *figura* and the Anglo-Saxon *sceap* is (in modern German) *Gestalt,* which derives from a Middle High German form of the verb *stellen,* "to arrange" or "to fix," and which has been brought into English by reference to "gestalt psychology." I propose to use it as a loan word, not in the sense of gestalt psychology, but as employed philosophically by Hegel and historiographically by Ernst Troeltsch.[85]

As an English equivalent to "gestalt," I prefer the term with an Anglo-Saxon rather than Latin derivation, namely, "shape." The word *shape* is flexible in the sense that it can refer to both a "figure" (*Gestalt*) and a "configuration" (*Gestaltung*). It has the advantage of being a simpler, less abstract expression than the latter, and it is closer to the concept of praxis than the former. Shaping, whether physical, ethical, linguistic, or cognitive, is decidedly a practical activity, as I shall attempt to show in chapter 4. But the Latin terms provide a way of linking the three central themes of this study: God as "triune figuration," history as "de-configurative process," and freedom as "transfigurative praxis." They also provide an entrée into recent hermeneutical discussions.

Figures of Speech and of Thought

There are many sorts of figures. I shall be concerned principally with four: figures of speech (tropes), figures of thought (the syllogism and its elements), figures of the trinity, and figurative acts by which history is constructed as both a process and a story. The first two are considered in the present section; the third is taken up in the concluding section of this chapter; the fourth is the subject of the next chapter, although a foundation is laid in the present section under the topic of "figuration and historicality." One obvious advantage to the concept of "figure" is its fluidity and range, which opens up suggestive comparisons and facilitates transitions from one mode of discourse to another. In the case of this project, the resources of literary criticism and philosophical hermeneutics can be brought to bear upon the questions confronting a theology of history and an ethics of emancipatory praxis. It is perhaps going too far to speak of a concept of "figuration" in contemporary hermeneutics. Certainly there is no unified concept or theory, although a consensus of sorts may be emerging among those working on the boundary of literary and philosophical theories of interpretation. I shall rely in particular on recent studies by Hayden White and Paul Ricoeur, who provide convenient access to a wide range of discussion.

A figure of speech is a *trope*, a term that derives from the Greek *tropos*, meaning "turn" (or in Koiné, "way," "manner," "mode"). Tropes, writes Hayden White, "are deviations from literal, conventional, or 'proper' language use, swerves in locution sanctioned neither by custom nor logic. Tropes generate figures of speech or thought by their variation from what is 'normally' expected, and by the associations they establish between concepts normally felt not to be related or to be related in ways different from that suggested in the trope used."[86]

Although technically a metaphor is but one of several tropes, all figures of speech or tropes are in a broad sense metaphorical. They create new meaning by a transfer (*meta-pherein*) of meaning, thereby disclosing significant similarities between things that otherwise are dissimilar. Metaphor in this broad sense is the most basic form of the endless interplay of identity and difference that lies at the heart of human experience; as such it is the foundation of poetry and logic, of narrative discourse (whether fictional or historical), of the religious and ethical use of language, and to some degree of scientific and technological usages as well.

White points out, in a brilliant analysis, that traditional poetics and modern language theory identify four principal tropes: metaphor, metonymy, synecdoche, and irony. *Metaphor* (in the strict sense) establishes a similarity between objects that are manifestly different by means of an analogy or simile in which one thing is represented by or likened to another (e.g., "my love, a rose"; or "reason, the rose in the cross of the present"—which is a double if not triple metaphor). *Metonymy* is the strategy by which contiguous entities can be reduced to the status of functions of one another, as when the name for a part of a thing is taken for the whole thing (e.g., "fifty sail" for "fifty ships"). *Synecdoche* replaces the extrinsic part-part relationship of metonymy with an intrinsic relationship of shared qualities that constitutes an integrated whole (e.g., "he is all heart," or "all the world's a stage"). *Irony* is a use of metaphor to negate tacitly in the figurative realm what is explicitly affirmed in the literal (e.g., "blind mouths," "cold passion"); it is a deliberate "dissembling" or "misuse" of language that reminds us of the untruth that is present in every truth, the relativity that qualifies all assertions. The latter three figures are all types of metaphor, says White, "but they differ from one another in the kinds of *reductions* or *integrations* they effect on the literal level of their meanings and by the kinds of illuminations they aim at on the figurative level. Metaphor is essentially *representational*, metonymy is *reductionist*, synecdoche is *integrative*, and irony is *negational*." The "linguistic protocols" generated by them are identity (metaphor), extrinsicality (metonymy), intrinsicality (synecdoche), and dialectic (irony).[87]

This fourfold classification of the figures of speech was worked out by Renaissance theoreticians, employed by Giambattista Vico in *The New Science*, and further refined by modern literary theorists such as Kenneth Burke. White also finds support for it in the work of the structuralists Roman Jakobson and Claude Lévi-Strauss, in the psychoanalytic theories of Freud and Jacques Lacan, and in the developmental theories of Jean Piaget. This confirms, in his view, its "archetypal nature" as a pattern that recurs persistently in Western discourse about consciousness.[88] Tropes and figures are in fact the foundation on which rational, scientific knowledge is erected. This view was shared by Vico and especially by Hegel, for whom cognitive knowledge "was little more than the truth yielded by reflection in the prefigurative modes raised to the level of abstract concepts." White goes so far as to suggest that "Hegel's *Logic* represents little more than a formalization, in Hegel's own terminology, of the tropological dimensions of language."[89] Hegel by no means advocated the abandonment of the tropological but rather its sublation in the logical, and he constantly returned to figurative usages in his philosophies of art, history, and religion.

In his *Logic,* Hegel referred specifically to "the three figures of the syllogism" (*die drei Figuren des Schlusses*), which "declare that everything rational is manifested as a triple syllogism." As we have seen, the three figures vary depending upon which of the terms or component elements of the syllogism—the universal (U), the particular (P), or the individual (I)—occupies the middle position; and they all must, in turn, occupy it in the case of a fully valid argument.[90] Since the three syllogistic figures are defined by their respective mediating terms, the terms themselves take on the characteristic of figures, and it is in this respect that we can see most clearly the link between figures of speech and of thought.[91] Simple metaphor, the trope of sameness or similarity, corresponds to the principle of universality (identity, thesis) in the Hegelian syllogism. Metonymy, which signifies reduction and extrinsicality, corresponds to the element of particularity (difference, antithesis). And synecdoche, which signifies integration, corresponds to the third element, that of individuality (synthesis).

But what of irony, the trope of dialectical negation, the most complex of tropes? Irony occurs when a synthesis, having been completed, is negated, and the "turn" is made to a new thesis in the recognition that every achievement is relative, every synthesis but the thesis of a further phase in the dialectical process, through which in time it will discover its own antithesis. Thus irony transcends the terms of any particular syllogism, but it is incorporated by Hegel's triple syllogism, or the completed circle of syllogisms. The truth is the whole, and the truth lies beyond irony, but it also encompasses irony as the driving force of the dialectic, which prevents any preliminary truth from masquerading as the whole. The question that divides Hegel from postmodernism is whether it is really possible to get "beyond" irony. Can irony be encompassed within a system whose ultimate vision is comic rather than tragic? Hegelian comedy, to be sure, sublates rather than escapes tragedy and is therefore tragicomic; but for most postmoderns, as for the ancient Greeks, it is the purely tragic vision that prevails.

The way beyond irony is to know the truth—an impossible task, we say. But faith's claim to know God is a claim to know the truth, for God is the truth and the whole. But to know God as the truth is to know that God cannot be possessed, for everything that can be possessed is not the truth; it is finite and relative. Ironically, we know the truth only when we know that we do not know the truth. What happens to irony when we appropriate the figures of speech and thought to the trinitarian figures? We can say perhaps that the Father is metaphorical, the Son metonymical, and the Spirit synecdochic, but irony is found in the passage between the two trinities, in the sense that the economic trinity negates (sublates) the immanent and the immanent the economic. Thus irony marks the relationship between God and world. It is ironic that God, having created the world, should suffer at its hands. If the divine suffering were endless and unredemptive, if the round between the two trinities were an eternal recurrence of the same, if the world should kill God rather than God save the world, then irony would have not only a preliminary word, which it certainly has, but also the final word. Faith cannot exclude irony but only hope for its transfiguration through a power greater than irony, which is the power of redemptive, suffering love.

Figuration and Historicality

When we think of a figure, we usually think first of a spatial form or shape. But it is evident that a figure of speech or of thought is not a physical phenomenon, even though it has the plastic power of shaping a worldly work or action. Paralleling or perhaps even underlying the plastic power of the figure, however, is its narrative power, its capacity to shape time as well as space. "Time," writes Paul Ricoeur, "becomes human to the extent that it is articulated through a narrative mode, and narrative attains its full meaning when it becomes a condition of temporal existence."[92] I turn now to this aspect of the matter, with the help of Ricoeur.

Metaphorical reference, claims Ricoeur, is the power of a metaphorical utterance to redescribe a reality that is inaccessible to direct description. Only a tiny portion of reality is directly accessible, namely, that which is temporally and spatially immediate; thus our reliance on metaphor is constant and for the most part not thematized. How, for example, do we redescribe human activity apart from the immediate actions in which we are engaged at this temporal instant? We do so by telling a story, inventing a narrative that imitates or "mimics" the action. The narrative imitates by means of a plot. "Plot, says Aristotle, is the *mimēsis* of an action."[93] Thus narrative is the mode of metaphorical redescription appropriate to history— that vast matrix of human activity which, in virtue of not being immediately present, is "past." Ricoeur's unique contribution to the analysis of narrative emplotment is his theory of a "threefold mimesis" at work in every plot: "a reference back to the familiar pre-understanding we have of the order of action; an entry into the realm of poetic composition; and finally a new configuration by means of this poetic refiguring of the pre-understood order of action." What is of special interest for my purposes is that Ricoeur describes these three imitative or representational functions as three types of figuration: prefiguration, configuration, and refiguration.[94]

In the first place, the composition of a plot is grounded in a preunderstanding or prefiguration of the world of action, which Ricoeur calls "mimesis$_1$." This involves its meaningful structure (the analysis of which is the task of action theory), its symbolic resources (as studied by cultural anthropology), and its temporal character. The latter is a structure of within-time-ness (*Innerzeit-igkeit*), which, as Heidegger has shown, is irreducible, even at the prefigurative level, to mere linearity. Our action constitutes a "dialectic of coming to be, having been, and making present. In this dialectic, time is entirely desubstantialized. The words 'future,' 'past,' and 'present' disappear, and time itself figures as the exploded unity of the three temporal extases."[95] All this is presupposed by and included within narrative emplotment.

"Mimesis$_2$," configuration, is the central or mediating moment in the work of narrative construction, which includes both fictional and historical narrative. Although the differences between these two modes of emplotment are important, their similarities, which often have been overlooked, must be recognized first. According to Ricoeur, a plot mediates in three ways. First, it mediates between individual events or incidents and a story taken as a whole, which gives definition to its integrated components. "Emplotment is the operation that draws a configuration out of a simple succession." Second, it brings together heterogeneous factors, such as agents, goals, means, interactions, circumstances, sudden reversals, fearful incidents, unexpected results, violent effects. In this respect it is a "concordant discordance," and it mirrors what I shall later call the "de-configurative process" of history. Finally, it is a temporal mediation, a synthesis of the heterogeneous elements of time. "Emplotment both . . . reflects the Augustinian paradox of time and . . . resolves it, not in a speculative but rather in a poetic mode." What Louis Mink describes as the "configurational act" consists of "grasping together" the story's incidents, drawing from the manifold of events the unity of one temporal whole. This whole, says Ricoeur, is not a speculative whole in the sense of being framed by a logical system; rather, it reveals itself in the story's capacity to be followed. "To understand the story is to understand how and why the successive episodes led to this conclusion, which, far from being foreseeable, must finally be acceptable, as congruent with the episodes brought together by the story. . . . The fact that the story can be followed converts the paradox [of time] into a living dialectic." The "end point" is the point from where the story can be seen as a whole, and once it is seen it permits a reading of time backward and as a coherent process.[96]

Ricoeur appears to believe that the "paradox of time" can be resolved only in a poetic and not in a speculative way. Certainly there are connections between narrative (poetic) and conceptual (logical) configurations of disparate elements, including the temporal ecstases, into a unified whole; but Ricoeur does not pursue these connections, remaining content to ground the configurational act in the work of the productive imagination, as attributed by Kant to the faculty of aesthetic judgment. The move from aesthetic to cognitive judgments was made by Hegel, whose speculative philosophical construction of history was at the same time a "poetics of history."[97]

Finally, with "mimesis$_3$," or refiguration, we arrive at what has been called by H.-G. Gadamer and others the "hermeneutics of application." It involves a move from *mimēsis* to *praxeōs*, from narrative to action, from text to reader, from sense to reference. This move, reserved for the third volume of *Time and Narrative,* is summarized by Ricoeur in four steps toward the beginning of the first volume.[98] First, the traversal from mimesis$_1$ to mimesis$_3$ across mimesis$_2$—that is, from action *pre*figured to action *re*configured through the *con*figural power of *poiēsis*—does not issue in a vicious circle but an "endless spiral" of increasingly enriched interpretations. Second, the movement in question is one from text to reader: reading takes up and fulfills the configural act of composition, refigures it by actualizing its capacity to be followed, enabling the text to have a transforming effect on the world. Here Ricoeur is able to appropriate the recent emphasis on the hermeneutics of reception and reader-response criticism advanced by theorists such as Roman Ingarden and Wolfgang Iser.

In the third place, this movement necessarily involves us in the world that the text projects and that constitutes its horizon. We gain access to this world, however, only insofar as a fusion occurs between our own horizons and those of the text. Every text, according to Ricoeur, intends something other than itself; language is not simply self-referential. In reaction against the romantic preoccupation with the author's intention behind the text, we should not fall under the spell of the structuralist-post-structuralist preoccupation with language as an internal system of signs; rather, we should seek out the world unfolded by the text in front of itself. "What is interpreted in a text is the proposing of a world that I might inhabit and into which I might project my ownmost powers." Now, both fictional narratives and historical narratives propose or project such a world—a world in which human action has in some significant respect been reconfigured. But they do so differently: fiction primarily by metaphorical reference and history primarily by reference to "traces of the real," although a significant "interweaving" of both types of reference takes place in both fiction and history. One reads literary and historical works (as well as works of many other kinds—religious,[99] philosophical, etc.) in order to enlarge, enrich, and reshape the world that will serve as the horizon for one's own engagement in a newly configured, transfigured praxis. To paraphrase Heidegger, one must learn not only to think and read poetically but also to build and dwell poetically.[100]

Finally, the temporal features of the world we are building and in which we are dwelling must be refigured by "narrated time." In part 4 of *Time and Narrative*, Ricoeur calls for an "impure" phenomenology of time that responds and corresponds to the "aporetics of temporality."[101] It must be impure because only a poetic and not a speculative resolution of the intractable aporias of time (the coinherence yet heterogeneity of the modes of time) is possible. Although this assertion may be subject to dispute, I agree with Ricoeur's accompanying claim that it is only in a history that guards against the forgetfulness of death and finitude that the thought of divine eternity (as a more primordial and infinite temporality)[102] is possible.

4. Triune Figuration: The One Who Loves in Freedom

The Model as a Whole

We are ready now to return from the detour represented by the third section, and to some extent also the second, to the primary agenda of this chapter, namely, the attempt to work out a theology of the trinity that will provide a basis for rethinking, in light of the challenges of postmodernism, the question of how God "acts redemptively" in history. I shall build on the tradition of trinitarian speculation that culminates in Hegel, but I shall also attempt to take account of the accents of historicality, difference, process, and embodiment discussed in section 2, and to work with the metaphors "figure" and "figuration" discussed in section 3.

"God," I propose, is a process or event of triune figuration appearing in three primary figures, shapes, or modes. God is a continuing (con)figuring process, which with regard to essence is eternally complete and self-constituting, but with regard to existence is eternally unfinished and open to otherness, difference. What is configured is in the first instance the matrix of ideal self-relations that comprise the abstract subjectivity of God; and in the second instance, the matrix of real spatiotemporal relations that make up the world in which we live and through which God becomes a concrete, spiritual, existent God. With respect to the latter, God is increased or diminished by what actually happens in the world. God's real existence is at stake in the world but not God's ideal, logical being. The configuring process as a whole is what I interpret the "economic" or worldly trinity to be, including as its first moment the "immanent" or preworldly trinity.

The three figures in which God appears may be understood with the tradition as the "persons" of the trinity: Father, Son, and Spirit. For a variety of reasons I propose to speak of God not as Father and Son but as Spirit. Alternatives will need to be found for the first two symbols, and none of them should be construed as a "person" in either the ancient or modern sense, but as a "figure," a shape of appearing, a "gestalt" of acting, a "mode" of being, a "moment" of relating. It is so obviously misleading to think of God as a fraternity of male beings who are begetting, spirating, and proceeding from one another that it is best to drop this language entirely. The triune God is the one true and perfect person, whose personhood is constituted by relational acts of love and freedom, or who subsists in three modes of being or existence, but who is not three supernatural persons or agents. Karl Barth points out that the expression "mode of being or existence" is the literal translation of *tropos huparxeōs,* which was used in early church debates.[103] Thus the same term, *trope,* which has come to designate figures of speech and thought, was also at one time predicated of God's ways of being.

The three figures of the trinity might more appropriately be understood in terms of the logical figures of Hegelian dialectic, which correspond (if Hayden White is correct) to the tropological figures of speech: universality-particularity-individuality, or identity-difference-mediation, corresponding to metaphor-metonymy-synecdoche. Cognitively understood, the triune God is the dialectical process of identity, difference, and mediation, which constitutes spiritual being as such. But in order to counter the predominant intellectualism of the Western theological tradition, rooted in the Augustinian and Thomistic models of memory, knowledge, and will (a tradition that Hegel perpetuates), I prefer a more personal and praxis-oriented model, whose three figures are "the One," "love," and "freedom." God is "the One who loves in freedom."[104] We may also, I propose, think of the three modes of divine being as "God," "World," and "Spirit." For reasons to be indicated, the figure "God" is intended to sublate (annul yet preserve) that of "Father"; the figure "World" is intended to sublate the traditional figures of the Second Person ("Son," "Logos," "Christ," etc.); and the figure "Spirit" will be rethought as the true and consummate name of God.

Our comprehension of the model at this point may be helped by a figure.

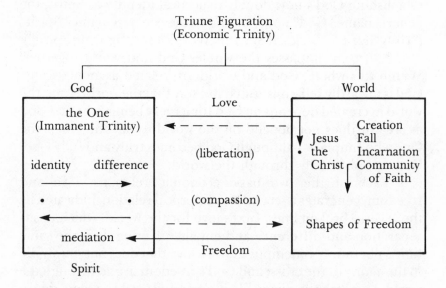

Reflection on this figure suggests the following points about the model, some of which will require further explication as we consider the three figural moments more closely:

1. The economic trinity embraces the immanent trinity as its first moment, and it encompasses both "God" and "world" insofar as these are distinguishable tropes of the total event of "triune figuration."

2. The immanent trinity comprises an inward dialectic of identity, difference, and mediation by which God's ideal "selfhood" or "subjectivity" is constituted, and which is outwardly reenacted (not repeated) in the realm of real difference and historical events.

3. The relation of love from God into the world shows that God is immanent in the world; for Christians this world-immanence or "incarnation" has its focal point in the figure of Jesus as the Christ, but its telos is to become a communal and world-transforming embodiment.

4. The relation of freedom from the world into God shows that the world is immanent in God, returning God to godself, establishing God's now doubly dialectical identity as Spirit, the generic name "God" now yielding to the concrete name "Spirit" ("Holy Spirit," "Ecclesial Spirit," "World-Transfiguring Spirit").

5. Spirit encompasses the whole, God and world together. Within this whole, God and world are related asymmetrically. God is inwardly self-constituted in a way that the world is not; the world as created depends on God for its very being, whereas God as creator does not depend on the world to be "the One," the One who simply is—although God becomes truly and fully God, God as Spirit, only through the world.

6. Each of the two basic economic relations, love and freedom, generates a secondary reciprocal relation, indicated by the reverse broken lines. God's love for the world, which posits separation and difference and entails suffering, is at the same time a liberating, redemptive love, a love that does not simply die in the agony of the cross; and God's freedom in and through the world, by which the divine life is perfected, is at the same time a compassionate freedom, a freedom that is not sheer divine indeterminacy or transcendence but is rather bound to and determined by love for the world. If we like, we may think of these as four relations corresponding to the two processions of classic trinitarian thought. The relations of love and freedom represent the "appropriation" of operations and attributes to the second and third trinitarian figures, while liberation and compassion represent the "perichoresis," the passing into one another of the two figures.[105] The point in any case is to show the dialectical character of these relations; each presupposes, depends on, and contributes to the other.

7. If we appropriate the word "God" to name the abstract identity of the One, what name shall we use to designate the event of triune figuration as a whole? Augustine faced this question and answered it by suggesting that the name of the Christian God is "Trinity," "the one and only and true God," and he addressed this God as "Holy Trinity," "Blessed Trinity."[106] If

we find this too jarring, then, keeping in mind Augustine's further statement that the Trinity may be called the Holy Spirit, but not the Father or the Son, we could name the whole God "Spirit," perhaps using Hegel's expression "Absolute Spirit"—the Spirit that "absolves," lets the world go forth from itself freely and sets it free from every constraining factor.[107] Or if this is too unconventional, then the word "God" will do, since these modes or figures do not connote separable entities but distinct moments of an indivisible divine process. Each includes all and can stand for all. The love of the divine One is a liberating love, oriented to redemption; the freedom of the divine One is a compassionate freedom, riveted to the world; the divine One is the One who loves in freedom. What more can be said? Only that in truth God cannot be named; all our words are but tropes and figures.

The model I am proposing has been inspired by the brilliant conception set forth in sections 28 to 31 of Karl Barth's *Church Dogmatics*. These sections on the reality of God are among Barth's greatest contributions to theological reflection; but they are not without difficulties from the point of view of this project and the postmodern temper. Some of these difficulties will be discussed below; they are related in one way or another to the fact that the controlling metaphor of the *Church Dogmatics* is God's self-revelation in Jesus Christ, the incarnate Word of God, and that by this means Barth sought to redress what he took to be the excesses of liberal theology. The threefold form of the Word of God (revealed, written, proclaimed), and the threefold event of revelation (revealer, revelation, revealedness), control the discussion of the trinity (Father, Son, Spirit) in *The Doctrine of the Word of God*,[108] and they spill over into the treatment of the reality of God in the first half-volume of *The Doctrine of God*. The latter, though it might have gone in a different direction, is determined by Barth's epistemological model, which grants privileged place to the event of revelation in Christ, and privileged authority to the written Word of scripture. As a result of his christocentrism and his stress on revelation as opposed to redemption, the Spirit is subordinated to Christ, and freedom to love, in Barth's trinity.

This is true despite the fact that it was Barth himself who had the insight to introduce freedom into the trinitarian dialectic as the third moment, displacing love to the second moment, and replacing knowledge entirely—so that in place of the Augustinian-Thomistic processions of knowledge and love there stand love and freedom.[109] But in doing so, Barth warns against falling prey to "any sort of dialectic" between love and freedom; rather, we must hold to "the very special dialectic of the revelation and being of God," which establishes a certain order, "the order of revelation." In this order, "the disclosure of God is in fact the first and the last, the origin and the end."[110] Thus, when it comes to the derivation and distribution of the divine attributes, Barth starts with the primary perfections of love (grace, mercy, patience), and ends with the secondary perfections of love (omnipresence, omnipotence, glory), between which are sandwiched first the secondary and then the primary perfections of freedom. God's perfections go from grace to glory. Freedom is clearly the qualifier of love in this dialectic rather than vice versa; it establishes the "unique manner" of God's love, which is "grounded in itself, needing no other, and yet also not lacking in another, but in sovereign transcendence giving, communicating itself to the other."[111]

Identity: The One (God)

God is in the first instance "the One," the one who is primordially self-identical. This One is not, however, a windowless monad; the identity in question is not sheer undifferentiated substance. God is already, in the first moment, a subject-event or person-event, an act or process of self-distinguishing and self-relating that cannot be derived from or traced to anything other than itself. In this respect God is "unbegotten" (Thomas Aquinas), *a se,* from godself. If God is not in this sense self-generating, then it is difficult to avoid the conclusion that God is generated from something other than God, namely, world-process, which may, as a matter of fact, generate many deities. The role of the trope of identity in the triune figuration is to establish the priority of the One vis-à-vis the All. In this important respect I opt with Hegel for the tradition against Whitehead. It is essential that the immanent trinity not be displaced by the economic but rather incorporated in it as a necessary moment.

According to Hegel, the truth of the immanent trinity is most adequately grasped in logical categories as the dialectic of unity, separation, and return, or of identity, difference, and mediation. But it can also be grasped in the representational language of love and personality. Love entails a union mediated by relationship and hence distinction; to be a person means to be reflected back into self through an act of distinction, to find one's own self-consciousness in another, to give up one's abstract being and to win it back as concrete and personal existence by being absorbed into the other. Now God is in the first instance God's own other. As Barth says, in the event by which God is God, God is subject, object, and predicate.[112] This means that God does not depend on an other than God to be a subject, a person. Precisely this is the condition of possibility of God's entering into relationship with an other that is not God in such a way that the autonomy and independence of the other are allowed to stand, are not utterly absorbed into God's own being. It is for the sake of the world, for the sake of the world's freedom, that God's love for the world is a free and unexacted love, and it can be free and unexacted only insofar as in the first instance God is God's own other.

We can appreciate this by analogy with our own experience: if I am not in some sense self-constituting, if I am utterly dependent on others to be the personal identity that I am, then I will either lose myself or destroy others in my intersubjective relationships. What is partially true of us is wholly true of God, and in this sense it is correct to say, as Barth does, that God is not simply a person but *the* person, the one true and perfect person, not merely the ideal but the real person, "not the personified but the personifying person." The divine person is both utterly absolute and utterly related, and the assumption of a conflict between the "absoluteness" and the "personality" of God is false.[113] In fact the distinction between absoluteness and relativity loses its significance if absoluteness means to be both utterly self-related and utterly other-related; to be both is to be utterly personal.

Eberhard Jüngel makes the same point by his suggestive remark that God is not simply absolutely self-*related* essence but also absolutely self*less* essence. It would be a mistake, he says, to play these off against each other. "In love, selflessness and self-relatedness do not contradict each other. Every lover knows that." With respect to God,

> We must speak of a still greater selflessness in a very great, a properly great self-relatedness. A "still greater selflessness in the midst of a very great, and justifiably great self-relatedness" is nothing other than a self-relationship which in freedom goes beyond itself, overflows itself, and gives itself away. It is pure overflow, overflowing being for the sake of another and only then for the sake of itself. That is love.[114]

On this basis, Jüngel strongly affirms Karl Rahner's thesis: "The 'economic' Trinity is the 'immanent' Trinity and the 'immanent' Trinity is the 'economic' Trinity."[115] The "is," however, cannot not be an "is" of simple identity; it is better to say that the immanent trinity is within the economic trinity, and that the economic trinity incorporates the immanent trinity as its founding moment. For, as Jüngel himself states, "God is the one who loves out of himself in that he relates himself to himself in such a way that he derives his being from himself."[116] Jüngel is determined to hold on to this even though his basic thesis is that "God's being is in coming. As the one who is coming, God turns being toward salvation. Thus God is the mystery of the world." But God comes to the world from God; nothing other than God is God's origin, neither being nor nothingness nor process; as such God is the origin of all that is.[117] This is what the tradition meant when it spoke, as in the Apostles' Creed, of "God the Father almighty, maker of heaven and earth."

But how shall *we* speak of God, for whom the symbol "father" has become, or ought to have become, problematic? Unfortunately, this fact is not recognized by Barth and Jüngel, or by most other theologians who have written recently on the trinity (Bracken, Hill, Jensen, Kasper, Mackey, Moltmann),[118] although Hegel knew it long ago.[119] One possibility, suggested by Paul Ricoeur, would be to destroy its idolatrous elements so that "the image of the father can be recovered as a symbol. . . . An idol must die so that a symbol of being may begin to speak." Ricoeur proposes to do this by subjecting the father figure to a critique that displaces and destroys it, but also allows it to return after the dispossession, reinterpreted by other figures and relations that are nonbiological and nonparental. What must be dispossessed, of course, is the patriarchal father figure who both threatens and consoles, evoking the most archaic forms of religious feeling: the fear of punishment and the desire for protection. Ricoeur thinks this destruction and retrieval is accomplished in Israelite and Christian faith, first through the figure of the king or ruler who enters into covenant relations with his people, then through the spouse-like father of the prophets (whose "love, solicitude, and pity carry him beyond domination and severity"), and finally through the conversion of the father from the figure of origin to the figure of new creation by its association with the inbreaking *basileia* or rule of God in the proclamation of Jesus.[120]

It is important to recognize that a process of depatriarchalization is already at work in biblical faith. But it does not go far enough, and Ricoeur is insensitive to this since he is primarily concerned with the atheistic critique of religious belief as advanced by Nietzsche and Freud, not with the feminist critique. From the point of view of the feminist critique, the reappropriation of the forgotten, suppressed, and concealed feminine images of God present in the biblical tradition despite its patriarchal bias is essential: God as mother, midwife, nurse, lover, sophia, to which may be added the widespread goddess-imagery found in ancient religion.[121] Although this imagery is highly valuable for liturgical and political purposes, it too is metaphorical, and we must acknowledge that conceptually it is no more adequate (and no less adequate) to speak of God as "mother" than as "father." A way of speaking of God needs to be found that transcends distinctions of sex as well as those of class, position, nation, and race. One way of doing so is to combine and enrich our images of God (mother and father, king and midwife, lord and lover, etc.), but other strategies are needed as well.

An appropriate strategy for our time, in my view, would be to give up the father figure, not attempting to repossess it after its dispossession. The Gospels themselves suggest this extreme solution with the image of the death of God the father. As Ricoeur points out, this is no longer a killing of the father by the jealous sons as in the Oedipal myth, but rather a dying, a giving up of self, for the sake of others—the very antithesis of the primitive father figure. God is a father who gives up his very fatherhood. "The death of God . . . is the death of separated transcendence. We must shed an idea of the divine as wholly other to reach the idea of the divine as spirit immanent in the community."[122] But this already takes us beyond the first of the trinitarian figures through the second to the third.

What name then shall we give to the first figure? Perhaps there is no appropriate name. My own simple proposal is to employ the generic name *God*. The etymology of this name probably is not of much significance, but perhaps it is worth noting that it may derive from an Indo-European base, *ghau*, meaning "to call out," "to invoke." A child calls out or invokes the names of its parents; thus the parental names of God, mother and father, may be rather close to the root sense of the word God, and it can be used in their stead. The word God, in the singular, generally denotes the One believed to be the eternal, omnipotent creator and ruler of the universe, the beginning and end of all things. It designates the oneness, the unity, the holiness, the sublimity, the aseity of God; if we are unable to say this of God, then nothing else can be said. Using "God" in this sense is rather like the usage of the Hebrew word *Elohim*, which is simply translated *theos* in Greek, *deus* in Latin, and *Gott* or

God in the Germanic languages. The great accomplishment of Israelite faith is that it was the first to attain the true meaning of the word God—the One.[123] As God becomes more sharply configured through the dialectic of differentiation and return, love and freedom, other names are introduced: Yahweh, Logos, Sophia, Christos, Kyrios, Pneuma. All of these, however, presuppose the word God.

Difference: Love (World)

By the act of love, God posits externally the moment of distinction and difference that is already implicit within God; God goes out from godself, creates a world seemingly infinite in extension but strictly nondivine in its perishability and contingency, enters into relationship with that world, becomes immanent within it by suffering its estrangement and negation, and returns to godself by working toward its reconciliation, renewal, salvation. This love is a *free* love since it is not exacted by the creature and is purely gratuitous. The freedom of God indicates that the relation between God and world is in the first instance strictly a divine action, the original divine act of self-distinction, self-othering, self-giving. But it is also true, on my view, that God needs the world to become fully the God that God is capable of becoming—not locked into a self-enclosed unity as the abstract isolated One, but opening the divine self up to encompass genuine otherness, becoming thereby concrete and spiritual, being no longer simply the One but the "All in all" (*panta en pasin,* I Cor. 15:28), "the All that remains utterly one."[124] This "necessity" is imposed not by the world but by God. It is an inwardly imposed necessity and as such is indistinguishable from an act of freedom; the divine necessity is the divine freedom and vice versa.

The divine love is also a love that *liberates,* for it sets the world and human beings free from their self-imposed bondage and reestablishes the rightful relationship between creatures and Creator. This is the reciprocal of the "outward" divine relation of love, the "return" already contained within the "diremption," the reconciliation already anticipated in the moment of estrangement. Speaking from the point of view of Christian faith, Jesus of Nazareth, as the focus of God's act of love for the world, not only suffers from and dies for our sin but also is our historical and risen redeemer—from his "infinite anguish" arises an infinite and liberating love.[125] There are not only scenes of violence in this world but also acts of self-giving love and clearings of freedom, which indeed sometimes are imbedded in the very scenes of violence.

Love, says Jüngel, is the "pacified dialectic" of being and nonbeing, life and death. The meaning of the death of God on the cross of Christ is "the most original determination of God for love." God is love, and love points to the innermost mystery of the divine being. For love is an event of self-relatedness (*Selbstbezogenheit*) mediated by an even greater selflessness or losing of self (*Selbstlosigkeit*). It entails an altered structure of "having," since the lover wants to have the beloved and only in this way himself or herself. God is the event, the history, of a self-giving and thus the end of all self-having.[126]

The death of God also means that we must think "God's unity with perishability" or "mortality." Perishing, Jüngel argues, is necessary to the process of becoming. Over against what he calls the ontological discrediting of perishing, which multiplies its negation into annihilation and allows the shadow of nothingness to fall on all that is perishable, he contends that perishing also contains a positive possibility, the possibility of becoming something new, even for something that is past. In this sense, "the essence of perishability is disclosed as history, which does not permit what has been to remain nothing." History, the telling of a story, means precisely not to lose the possibility of past reality but to preserve it, to re-collect it, to reconstruct it in narrative form. The history of perishability is "the struggle between possibility and nothingness."

The death of God in anguished love means that God is in the midst of this history, this struggle. God's essence is not outside and above it but is precisely in it. "God shares in the struggle between the ontological undertow toward nothingness and the capacity of the possible." Although God creates *ex nihilo* and is the condition of possibility for the struggle in the first place, God is not superior to the struggle; rather, the being of God is revealed "as creative being in the struggle with the annihilating nothingness of nothing." The God who died on the cross of Christ and arose from the dead draws this nothingness into God's own history, defining and determining it, contradicting and resisting its annihilating power.

> God gives nothingness a place within being by taking it on himself. In that God identified himself with the dead Jesus, he located nothingness within the divine life. But by making for nothingness a place within divine being, God took away from it the chaotic effect of its phantomlike attraction. In bearing annihilation in himself, God proves himself to be the victor over nothingness. . . . God is that one who can bear and does bear, can suffer and does suffer, in his being the annihilating power of nothingness, even the negation of death, without being annihilated by it. In God nothingness loses its negative attraction and thus its annihilating effect. Once it is taken up into God's being, it creatively sets for itself a new function. . . . [It] becomes concrete negation which gives to concrete affirmation its critical edge. . . . It becomes the differentiating power in the identity of being.[127]

This is Jüngel's extraordinarily suggestive interpretation of the words of Paul: "When the perishable puts on the imperishable, and the mortal puts on immortality, then shall come to pass the saying that is written: 'Death is swallowed up in victory' " (I Cor. 15:54).

Now the world as such is what is perishable. To say that "the perishable puts on the imperishable," and that God takes the nothingness of perishability into the divine life, can only mean that the world as such is a moment within the divine life. The world is by no means divinized in this process; on the contrary, just the opposite is the case because it is precisely the perishability of the world, its nondivine character, that is taken into the divine life. When the perishable "puts on" the imperishable, it does not cease to be perishable; rather (if Jüngel is correct), its annihilating nothingness is converted into possibility for the new; it becomes "the differentiating power in the identity of being." By taking on the perishable, God's own being is historicized, becomes a being-in-process. The world remains precisely the moment of difference, concrete negation, otherness, finitude, perishability—the continuing struggle between nothingness and possibility—within the triune figuration of God.

When I say "world," I mean the whole world—the cosmos as we know it, the stars and planets, biological life, human consciousness, culture and history. This whole world is the figure, shape, or gestalt of God in the moment of *difference;* it is "God's body." "God's got the whole world in his hands." But surely this must be a heretical statement, not only because it borders on pantheism, but also because it displaces the second person of the trinity, the Son of God, from his rightful place! It is not pantheism, however, certainly not crude pantheism, the sort of pantheism that confuses all things with God and divinizes physical and human nature. The world is precisely *not*-God, and because it is not-God it is a moment within the divine life. The extraordinary thing about God is that God overreaches and incorporates what is not-God within God. God is the identity of God and not-God, the event that takes place between God and world. Thereby God is a God whose being is in process, and what is not-God has the possibility of being saved from its annihilating nothingness. If a label is required for such a view, it is pan-entheism, not pantheism.

But does not such a view substitute "world" for "Christ," thus renouncing any claim to being distinctively Christian? Indeed, one of the challenges of postmodernism to Christian theology is that it resist its often powerful tendency toward christocentrism, the potentially idolatrous fixation on Jesus Christ, the only begotten Son of God, the incarnate Logos, the God-man.[128] There are a number of reasons for this resistance, including not only the well-known conceptual difficulties of classic christology and the sad history of Christian persecution of the Jews but also the much more recent challenges of religious pluralism and feminist consciousness. It is unnecessary to go into all of this here. I will simply observe that giving up christocentrism or "christism" by no means entails giving up Christ, but it does require thinking about Christ differently.

God's loving, suffering, transformative embrace of the world is an inclusive embrace, but like everything else in the world it does not appear everywhere all at once but in distinctive shapes, patterns, configurations. In fact, as I suggested earlier, it appears in the world liminally, at the margins of the dominant world-formations, requiring for its discernment "hard labor." It also appears in a plurality of forms, none of which can legitimately claim finality or exclusive validity; all such claims are parochial and arbitrary because all are tinged with the contingency and relativity of history. But distinctive religious traditions and communities have experienced God's redemptive, suffering presence in the world in distinctive ways, and they have a right, indeed an obligation, to make it known, to proclaim it.

For Christians, the paradigmatic shapes by which God's love of the world is discerned emerge from the life and death of Christ—the shapes of the *basileia* and of the *cross*, which, when superimposed, constitute (so I will argue) the "divine gestalt" by which human history is redemptively reconfigured. This gestalt is normative for, and perceived as such only by, the Christian community of faith, the ecclesial community; but at the same time it is a construal of the whole of history. It is both particular and universal. The same is true of God's presence in history. Those figures in which God is most luminously, revealingly present point beyond their own particularity to the world as a whole. The particular figure of Jesus of Nazareth disappears into his ministry, takes the misery of the world literally into himself, suffers in its place in such a way that his own identity merges with that of the world;[129] he points beyond himself not only to God and God's kingdom but also to the community of brothers and sisters, the little community of table fellowship and the great community of disciples through all ages. His personal, ethnic, sexual, cultural, historical, and religious specificities are taken up into a new corporate, intersubjective embodiment that cuts across all provincial modes of existence and whose telos is simply the world as such. Thus Christ and world are figures of God's love at opposite ends of a continuum, each presupposing and completing the other: Christ is (for Christians) the hermeneutical clue to the world as de-configurative process; and world is the telos of the emancipatory praxis that arises from Christ's life and death. When I speak of "world" as the second figure of the triune figuration, I speak of it in these terms.

Mediation: Freedom (Spirit)

Just as the divine love is a *free* love, so also the divine freedom is a *loving* freedom. It is not simply an abstract volitional freedom, the ability to choose options or actions "voluntarily," without external constraint. It is far more than that; it is a concrete presence-to-self mediated in and through presence-to-others.[130] Thus it presupposes love's positing of distinction and completes love's act of reunion. Love without freedom is an impossibility, and freedom without love is merely capricious choice (*Willkür*). Moreover, just as the "outward" relation of love has its reciprocal in liberation, so also the "inward" relation of freedom has its reciprocal in compassion. The divine freedom is not sheer indeterminacy but a freedom determined by and bound to compassion for the world. Because this compassion is an aspect of the divine freedom, it is not left hanging in the anguish of death and separation, but is completed by overcoming estrangement, negating the annihilating power of death, reestablishing communion by the "subjection" and return of all things, "that God may be all in all" (I Cor. 15:28). In this sense, just as love signifies the immanence of God in the world, so freedom signifies the immanence of the world in God.

Freedom thus means both the perfection of God and the liberation of the world. Freedom as a perfection of God is eloquently articulated by Barth in his discussion of "the being of God in freedom."[131] God lives, loves, and has being uniquely, this uniqueness being God's freedom, the depth in which God is. God's freedom may be construed as both negative and positive, transcendent and immanent, absolute and related. Barth chooses to emphasize the latter while at the same time resolutely rejecting any suggestion that the world should be introduced as a necessary element or divine mode into the life of the godhead. Indeed, it is just God's unqualified world-transcendence that is the condition of possibility of an equally unqualified world-immanence.

> God has the freedom to be present with that which is not God, to communicate himself and unite himself with the other and the other with himself, in a way which utterly surpasses all that can be effected in regard to reciprocal presence, communion and fellowship between other beings. It is just the absoluteness of God properly understood which can signify not only his freedom to transcend all that is other than himself, but also his freedom to be immanent within it, and at such a depth of immanence as simply does not exist in the fellowship between other beings. No created being can be inwardly present to another, entering and remaining in communion with it in the depths of its inner life. . . . [But God can] so indwell the other that, while he is its creator and the giver of its life, and while he does not take away this life, he does not withdraw his presence from this creaturely existence which is so different from his own divine life. Now that it has originated in his will and subsists by his will, he does not detach himself from it in an alien aloofness, but is present as *the being of its being* with the eternal faithfulness of which no creature is capable towards another.[132]

This eloquent statement is compromised, in my view, by Barth's unwillingness to acknowledge that that which is "not God" can and must be a moment within the divine life. If God is so immanent in the world as to be "the being of its being," then the world must be immanent in God as the nonbeing of God's being-in-becoming—for there is no becoming without nonbeing as well as being. In the final analysis, Barth draws back from the economic trinity into the innertrinitarian relations between the Father and the Son. "The existence of the world is not needed in order that there should be otherness for [God]," because "God himself is the Son who is the basic truth of that which is other than God." "There are strictly speaking no Christian themes independent of Christology."[133] Nothing could make it clearer that Barth's christocentrism finally overwhelms and subverts an authentic trinitarianism. The Spirit remains an appendage to, a function of, the inwardly complete relations between the Father and the Son. The Spirit is not really, for Barth, the perfection of God in and through the mediation of God and world, which is the divine freedom.

Freedom signifies not only the perfection of God but also the liberation of the world. This liberation of the world is, as we have seen, the reciprocal of God's love for the world. God loves the world toward an end, which is that of shaping scenes of freedom out of the repeated scenes of domination that make up world history. Within history, these configurations of freedom are fragmentary, ambiguous, incomplete, and the configuring process is as endless as the defiguring one. But precisely within this endless process the world has an ultimate end, which infuses and transfigures the process. This end is the liberation of the world in God, which occurs by means of "subduing" or "subjecting" the world's endless, restless, creative-destructive, annihilating difference in the eternal peace and unity of God. This ultimate liberation is going on all the time; it is not reserved just to some future end. It is rather what gives the world future, new possibility, enabling the fragmentary shapes of freedom to survive and sometimes to prevail against the much more massive scenes of violence and domination. The ground of emancipatory praxis within the world is the liberation of the world in God, and this in turn is the perfection of God's freedom.

What name shall be used to designate the final figure of the triune figuration? The tradition named it Spirit, which, unlike Father and Son, is a retrievable symbol for the postmodern temper. At first this seems implausible. *Spirit* is to say the least a difficult concept, which has long been criticized for being both vague and dualistic, implying a separation of and a hierarchy between the mental and the physical, the soul and the body, the human and the natural, the male and the female, the holy and the profane. The postmodern world is in any event oriented to the body, not the spirit. But what is being rightly criticized here is a lingering Neoplatonism, which has reinforced dualistic, anticorporeal, and misogynist attitudes on the part of Christianity for far too long. I propose rather to use the term "spirit" in the sense employed by Hegel, which as we have seen is closer to the meaning of the biblical terms for "spirit," *ruach* (Hebrew), and *pneuma* (Greek), both of which convey the image of "blowing," "wind," "breath" ("breath of life"). The same is true of the English word "spirit," which derives from the Latin *spirare*, "to blow," "to breathe." Spirit is what is alive, active, vital, moving, and hence in ancient times was frequently symbolized by fire—a material image of an immaterial vitality. It is worth noting that spirit is not a masculine figure. In fact, the word is grammatically feminine in Hebrew and neuter in Greek and English; the personifying translations of it as "he" are completely unjustified. It gives us a way of speaking of God that is not sexist or gender-specific.

Far from being dualistic, then, spirit is a mediating term: it is the ideal manifested in the real, the unity of reason and nature, soul and body, male and female, God and world. It overreaches all these dichotomizing distinctions and levels the hierarchy between them. Spirit is the rational or logical as embodied in consciousness, that is, in existent being qua cognizant, as the German term *Bewusst-sein* suggests. If spirit entails consciousness, then there can never be spirit without the embodying medium, nature. This is as true for divinity as for humanity. God is "Spirit" insofar as God is present to, active in, embodied by that which is other than God, namely, the natural and human worlds. Thus in scripture "Spirit" refers to that modality of divine activity whereby God indwells and empowers the forces of nature, the people of Israel, the ecclesial community, and individual persons. The Spirit is the indwelling power of God that brings the natural and human worlds to consummation by bringing estranged and fallen beings back into everlasting, liberating communion with the one God, whose true and proper name is now Spirit.

If Christ is the figure of God's objective and historical

presence, then the Spirit is the figure of (inter)subjective and .eschatological presence. As intersubjective presence, the Spirit is intrinsic to humanity, the ground of its freedom (the Spirit as Paraclete or Comforter); but as eschatological presence, it is the quintessence of divine freedom, of God's being in-and-for-self (the Spirit as Consummator). The spirituality of God, claimed Hegel, is the truth of Christianity.

> Christian theology . . . conceives of God . . . as Spirit and con-templates this, not as something quiescent, something abiding in empty identicalness but as something which necessarily enters into the process of distinguishing itself from itself, of positing its other, and which comes to itself only through this other, and by positively overcoming it—not by abandoning it.[134]

The triune figuration of God culminates in the third and final figure, which is also the name of the whole God: God as Spirit overreaches and encompasses God as God and God as world; the Spirit is the trinity of one, love, and freedom.

The spirituality of God establishes God's fundamental historicality. We turn now from the question of God to the question of history.

CHAPTER III

History:
De-Configurative Process

Every interpretation of history entails the construction of a narrative, an emplotment of historical events in accord with one or another of the dominant tropes or figures of speech.[1] Even attempts at historical "objectivism" and "realism" cannot escape this exigency, as Hayden White's analysis of the historical imagination demonstrates.[2] Nineteenth-century historiography, according to White, began with the skepticism and irony of late-Enlightenment rationalism (Voltaire, Gibbon, Hume, Kant), then sought alternatives to rationalism in romanticism (Rousseau, Burke, Herder), idealism (Hegel), and positivism (Comte). The great masters of nineteenth-century historiography (Michelet, Ranke, Tocqueville, Burckhardt) all opposed idealism in the name of historical realism, but their realisms took the form of one or another of the modes of emplotment—romance, comedy, tragedy, or satire—and their emphasis on realism obscured the ideological role played by social and political interests, as discovered by Marx. The end of the century saw the collapse of historical realism in the return to a self-consciously ironic mode, which veiled a satirical or a tragic vision of reality under the romantic affirmation of human will-to-power (Nietzsche) or the assimilation of history to art (Croce).[3]

While twentieth-century academic historiography has for the most part remained locked into the ironic perspective, various attacks have been made and continue to be made (by thinkers as diverse as Malraux, Yeats, Joyce, Spengler, Toynbee, Wells, Jaspers, Heidegger, Sartre, Benjamin, Foucault, and Lukács) on the condition of irony, seeking, in White's words, to overcome both "its inherent skepticism, which passes for scholarly caution

113

and empiricism, and its moral agnosticism, which passes for
objectivity and transideological neutrality." White contends,
claiming R. G. Collingwood in support, that the only grounds
for overcoming irony and moving beyond satirical or tragic
emplotments of history are moral and aesthetic.[4]

The moral grounds would presumably require the elaboration of a critical theory of (emancipatory) praxis, and the
aesthetic a cosmology of world-process such as that provided by
Whitehead. But both the moral and aesthetic grounds must be
rooted in a religious vision if skepticism and moral agnosticism
are finally to be avoided. What is required is a theology of
history; and a Christian theology of history must take up the
quest for a way beyond tragedy because its dominant trope
cannot be ironic. Ultimately, its mode of historical emplotment is
comic, not romantic, satirical, or tragic. But it is not simple
comedy: it is a comedy that sublates tragedy and makes use of
irony rather than ignoring or bypassing them. It is, in short,
tragicomic on both microhistorical and macrohistorical scales.
Tragedy is an inescapable dimension of every historical act, since
negative as well as positive consequences flow from it, conflicts
between interests are unavoidable, and every achievement is
partial and transient. Irony is an essential dimension of any
critical consciousness since it entails a recognition of the limits of
knowledge and the problematical nature, the distorting potential, of all predication. But when tragedy becomes the controlling mode of emplotment and irony the dominant trope,
hope is stifled and the very possibility of efficacious knowledge,
belief, or action is undermined.

Among modern thinkers, two stand out as especially helpful
in addressing these questions. Hegel offers an extraordinary
philosophy of history that finds a way beyond tragedy and irony,
while Troeltsch envisions a theology of history that creatively
engages the challenges of modern consciousness and critical
historiography. Although I devote considerable attention to
each of them, I recognize that a simple repristination of Hegel
and Troeltsch is out of the question. Living as we do after
Auschwitz and under the threat of nuclear holocaust, we must

move beyond them both to a consideration of the postmodern deconstruction of history before attempting our own emplotment of history as a tragicomic "de-configurative process." The theological grounds for the claim that God is present in this process, shaping it in the direction of liberation, will be examined in chapter 4.

This, briefly, is the agenda for the present chapter, which is highly selective and makes no pretense at adequately surveying the wealth of literature on historical method and meaning of the past century.[5] My intention is to introduce only what is essential to a particular line of argument, recognizing that many other ways of approaching the issues at stake here are both valid and helpful.

1. Hegel's Metahistory

At the beginning of his earlier *Lectures on the Philosophy of World History,* Hegel distinguished among three sorts of historical writing. "Original history" consists of works by eyewitnesses and participants in the events described; such are the writings of Herodotus and Thucydides and other ancient authors. "Reflective history" (or what we would call scientific history) is the sort of history ordinarily practiced by historians, who no longer belong to what they describe, and who consciously construct a narrative of past events, a "reflective world," in accord with the "maxims, ideas, and principles which the author applies both to the content of his work . . . and to the form of his narrative."[6] In his *Lectures on Aesthetics,* Hegel elaborated a theory of historical writing more fully than he did in the *Philosophy of World History.* History is the prose form closest to dramatic poetry since it is the imaginative construction of a narrative out of prosaic elements of the real but in accord with a poetic envisionment of the ideal, the true. The latter, however, must always be held in check by the historian, who is obligated to allow events to appear in their contingency, mystery, and irrationality.[7]

"Philosophical history," finally, is the explication of the prin-

ciples underlying reflective history and their systematic application to the writing of a "universal" or "world" history from the
perspective of the "spirit" or the "idea" that is "eternally present
to itself" and "directs the events of world history." Today we
might call world history "macrohistory" and philosophical
history "metahistory." The philosopher qua philosopher does
not write scientific or reflective history but engages in
metahistorical reflection at the macrohistorical level on the
conditions of possibility of doing scientific history. Philosophy of
history as metahistory entails reflection on reflection; it is a
doubly reflective process, for which Hegel used the term
speculative. It includes the writing of a "universal" or "world" or
"macro" history, which is not the proper subject of the scientific
historian since it involves gathering the implicitly poetic insights
of the historian into explicit consciousness, transforming them
into a tragic or comic (or satirical or romantic) vision of the whole
process in accord with a philosophical comprehension of the
idea. Such a metahistory functions as the implicit horizon of
every concrete historical investigation and narrative. It appears
when historians begin to press "transcendental" questions about
their subject matter and methods, but it is at just this point that
they cease being merely "reflective" historians.[8]

Philosophical history, then, clearly is not an attempt to write
empirical history on the basis of philosophical preconceptions,
or to bend evidence to fit a priori schemes, although Hegel's
philosophy of world history has frequently been criticized for
doing just this. One may question whether such a metahistory is
either possible or illuminating, but one should recognize that
Hegel never confused it with empirical history, even as he
insisted that once one begins reflecting upon empirical history
something like metahistory is unavoidable.[9]

Reason in History

Hegel's metahistory makes the audacious claim that "reason
governs the world" and that "world history is therefore a rational
process." From the point of view of history, this "conviction and

insight" is a presupposition, but within philosophy it is not a presupposition but a proof, a proof based on the "speculative cognition that reason . . . is *substance* and *infinite power;* it is itself the *infinite material* of all natural and spiritual life, and the *infinite form* which activates this material content." Hegel insisted that the metahistorian's work must have an empirical basis; history must be taken as it is, without introducing a priori fictions into it. But even the accurate apprehension of history entails bringing in interpretative categories, for "truth is not to be found on the superficial plane of the senses." "Whoever looks at the world rationally will find that it in turn assumes a rational aspect; the two exist in a reciprocal relationship." The only alternative to looking at the world rationally is to view it as a product of pure chance and external necessity, as Democritus and Epicurus did,[10] but then in Hegel's view the historical process will lack intelligibility.[11]

To affirm that the world is a rational process is to affirm that it is governed by an ultimate design or end (*Endzweck*), and that this end is in process of being realized despite the quite massive presence of evil ("all that is finest and noblest in the history of the world is immolated upon its altar"). We see this end manifesting itself not primarily with respect to individuals or even nations and cultures but with respect to the whole, the totality of world history, which is simply "the realization of spirit in history." Expressed in philosophical terms, this end is the absolute idea or absolute spirit; expressed in religious terms, it is God's will or God's kingdom (which is God's ruling, redemptive presence in history); expressed in world-historical terms, it is the idea of freedom, since freedom is the very substance of spirit as conscious of itself and present to itself, which is to say that spirit is not a completed entity but is essentially active, engaged in a process of historical becoming. Thus Hegel arrived at his brilliantly provocative insight that "world history is the progress of the consciousness of freedom." This is its end, its design, its purpose, its rationality, and the task of metahistory is simply to comprehend its progression through the axial turns of world history: the consciousness that *one* is free (the Oriental world), that *some* are free (the Greek and Roman worlds), and that *all* are free (the Christian and Western European worlds).[12] The realization of freedom is at the same time the realization of God's presence in history.

The Historical Field as Synchronic Structure

This realization, however, is by no means a simply developmental, linear process. This is true despite Hegel's tendency to speak quite dogmatically on occasion of world history as "governed by God" and as "nothing more than the plan of providence," which "must always prevail in the end"[13]—a way of speaking that bears more than a passing resemblance to the logic of divine sovereignty and triumph. If this is all Hegel had to say, his philosophy of history would have little relevance today. But in fact Hegel's analysis of what Hayden White calls the "historical field" is complex, subtle, and extraordinarily suggestive. Using structuralist terminology, White suggests that Hegel approached history as both a "synchronic structure" and a "diachronic process."[14] In the first approach, history is "apprehended as a *chaos of passions,* self-interest, violence, dashed hopes, and frustrated plans and projects"; while in the second it "appears to be characterized by mere change." But the objective of the first approach is to generate concepts by which the chaos of passions "could be comprehended as a spectacle of *purpose*"; while that of the second is to generate concepts by which the chaos of changes "could be comprehended as a process of *development.*"[15]

Hegel was profoundly aware of the presence of evil, passion, self-interest, and violence in human affairs, and he described history in the most dramatic terms as "an altar on which the happiness of nations, the wisdom of states, and the virtue of individuals are slaughtered."

When we contemplate this display of passions, and consider the historical consequences of their violence and of the irrationality which is associated with them (and even more so with good intentions and worthy aims); when we see the evil, the wickedness, and the downfall of the most flourishing empires the human spirit has created; and when we are moved to profound pity for the untold miseries of individual human beings—we can only end with a feeling of sadness at the transience of everything. . . . Without rhetorical exaggeration, we need only compile an accurate account of the misfortunes which have overtaken the finest manifestations of national and political life, and of personal virtues or innocence, to see a most terrifying picture that takes shape before our eyes. Its effect is to intensify our feelings to an extreme pitch of hopeless sorrow with no redeeming circumstances to counterbalance it.[16]

In such a state of mind it is very tempting to take refuge in fatalism, viewing history as ultimately absurd, busying ourselves with private aims and interests, retreating "into that selfish complacency which, . . . from a secure position, smugly looks on at the distant spectacle of confusion and wreckage." The only alternative to nihilism or complacency is to seek an answer to the question, "To whom, or to what ultimate end have these monstrous sacrifices been made?"[17]

The answer to the question is not to be found by endless reflection on the panorama of sin and suffering. Rather, the latter must be viewed as the means for the realization of a principle or goal that is not given to sense perception but is knowable "by a transcendental deduction of the categories by which it can be inferred."[18] For Hegel, as we have seen, this transcendental deduction yields as the principle and end of history the "idea"—the absolute or divine idea, God's self-actualizing concept, "the eternal inner life of God," which is at the same time the idea of freedom, the realization of spirit (both divine and human spirit) in history. This idea as such is purely universal and abstract. It is "a possibility or potentiality which has not yet emerged into existence. A second moment is necessary before it can attain reality—that of actuation or realization, whose principle is the will, the activity of humanity in the world at large."[19] Thus Hegel was led to the key proposal that there are two principles of history, the first being the *idea*, the divine idea, the idea of freedom, which inwardly impels history toward its end, and the second, human activity or *passion*, which is the historical bearer or instrument of the idea.

> These two are the weft [*Einschlag*] and warp [*Faden*] in the fabric of world history. The idea as such is the actuality [*Wirklichkeit*], and the passions are the arm which serves it. These are the extremes, and the middle point at which the two coincide and in which they are united is ethical freedom [*sittliche Freiheit*].[20]

The fabric metaphor with its image of the weaving together of crossed threads shows that this is indeed a structural analysis of history. Just as there can be no fabric without both weft and warp but only loose threads,[21] so there can be no history without the interweaving of both divine idea and human activity. The German term used by Hegel for "weft," *Einschlag*, means that the threads are driven back and forth by the shuttle across the threads running lengthwise in the fabric (the "warp" or *Faden*): this is Hegel's vivid metaphor for the empowering, driving, shaping, "crossing" presence of God in history. The pattern that results from the interweaving, the actual cloth of history, is what Hegel called "ethical freedom"—the fabric of social, political, and cultural institutions that constitute history as a "second nature," a realm in which human beings can dwell, a realm of freedom (as opposed to the necessity of the realm of nature).[22]

But in the case of history, as Hegel envisioned it, the threads are qualitatively distinct from one another, so the question immediately arises how they can be interwoven without the weft canceling out the warp. How can the divine idea drive back and forth across the passions of history, shaping them toward an end without violating the very instruments that bear it, without robbing them of their subjective freedom, will, or autonomy? "How is it possible for the universal or the rational to determine anything whatsoever in history?" Hegel attempted to elucidate this paradox with a series of examples that show how things may be used against themselves without being destroyed. This is true of natural elements used to build a house designed to shut out the natural elements. The elements "are utilized as their respective natures allow," but they "act together to create a product which restricts their own activity." The same is true of the human passions, "which fulfil themselves and their ends in accordance with their specific nature, and thereby create the edifice of human society in which justice and order are given power *over the passions themselves*." Clearly, human actions "may have implications which transcend the intention and consciousness of the agent."[23]

At the basis of this historical phenomenon is the "speculative" insight into the union of the universal and the particular, a union such that "universal reason exists as an immanent principle within history, in which and through which it fulfils itself." It does so in such a way that "all the expressions of individual and national life, in seeking and fulfilling their own ends, are at the same time the means and instruments of a higher purpose and wider enterprise of which they are themselves ignorant and which they nevertheless unconsciously carry out." This "is what we may call the cunning of reason [*List der Vernunft*]," which "sets the passions to work in its service, so that the agents by which it gives itself existence must pay the penalty and suffer the loss," while the idea itself "remains unscathed" in the background.[24]

Hegel was clearly speaking metaphorically here (this "is *what we may call* the cunning of reason"), and he was in danger of overstating his conceptual claim. Strictly speaking, reason is not an agent, certainly not a cunning agent. To us it may appear that reason acts cunningly, since ends are accomplished in history that are diametrically opposed to the intentions of historical actors, and evil often appears to be outwitted and eventually foiled. But on the one hand the metaphor of cunning is too close to the logic of sovereignty for comfort, while on the other it is evil that may exhibit greater cunning in our time than reason. Perhaps it would be better to say that reason works persuasively, luringly, in the mode of attraction or paradigm rather than of causality; it does so not as agent but by way of its shaping, configuring power. Again, it is not literally true that reason "sends forth the particular interests of passion to fight and wear themselves out in its stead." But so it may appear when we observe, as Hegel shrewdly did, that often when the great figures of history attain their ends, "they fall aside like empty husks."[25]

The primary thrust of Hegel's analysis throughout this section is not to suggest that human beings are mere pawns in a divine chess game but just the opposite, namely, to show that divine reason and human activity (the weft and warp of history) are co-constitutive and mutually engaging. Each depends essentially on the other: without the passions reason has no power, and without reason activity has no telos. The divine reason does not impinge as an external, manipulative force, but works inwardly as the human subject's own intrinsic, emancipatory rationality. "Human beings are ends in themselves only by virtue of that divine principle within them which we have all along referred to as reason—and, insofar as it is inwardly active and self-deter-mining, as freedom."[26]

Hegel's hint here and elsewhere that it may be appropriate to think of the divine presence in terms not so much of the concept of reason but of the idea of freedom—an idea that shapes an intersubjective nexus of freedom (*sittliche Freiheit*), a historical world in which human beings can dwell humanly—is an attractive one since it signals a shift of emphasis from theoretical to practical categories, from *Begriff* to *Gestalt*. I shall attempt to elaborate and defend this shift in the next chapter.

The Historical Field as Diachronic Process

When we turn to Hegel's treatment of the historical field as diachronic process, that is, "the course of world history," we find that what he offers is a typology of cultural shapes rather than a linear theory of historical development or a cyclical theory of historical recurrence, both of which entail causal explanation based on natural laws. Hegel's mode of historical explanation is typological rather than causal. This is a most important point, which is supported as well by his treatment of the history of religions.[27] Hegel was unfamiliar with modern evolutionary theory, but he would surely have rejected it as an appropriate model of historical process, just as he rejected the theories of the organic life cycle with which he was familiar: the transfer of a content to a new form (metempsychosis), or the re-creation of a new life out of the old (the Phoenix myth). Spirit (*Geist*), says Hegel,

> does not merely pass into another envelope, nor rise rejuve-nescent from the ashes of its previous form; it comes forth exalted [*erhoben*], transfigured [*verklärt*], a purer spirit. It certainly makes war upon itself—consumes its own existence; but in this very destruction it works up that existence into a new form, and each successive phase becomes in its turn a material on which it exalts itself into a new formation [*Bildung*].[28]

Or:

> In the case of the spiritual sphere, a higher form [*Gestaltung*] is produced through the transformation [*Umarbeitung*] of earlier and less advanced ones. The latter accordingly cease to exist; and the fact that each new form is the transfiguration [*Verklärung*] of its predecessor explains why spiritual forms occur within the medium of time. Thus, world history as a whole is the expression of spirit in time, just as nature is the expression of the idea in space.[29]

The fact that temporal passage entails a transfiguration into novel forms as opposed to a mere repackaging or rejuvenation of what is old, means, as Hayden White points out, "that the historical process must be viewed, not as mere movement, change, or succession, but as 'activity'."[30] Thus the appropriate mode of emplotting history—which is the story of "spirit in time"—is not naturalistic but dramatic (whether tragic, comic, or tragicomic remains to be seen); and the law of history is not a natural, mechanical, causal law but the law of freedom.

Temporality demands narrativity; activity demands freedom.

Because time entails negativity, the nonbeing of a thing, the key category of history for Hegel is "transition" (*Übergang*); and transition occurs not as evolution, succession, or repetition, but as "transfiguration"—that is, as the creation of a new form or figure out of something that is dead, that has ceased to exist. Novelty results from a genuinely creative act, an act of freedom, and hence it involves discontinuity, rupture, and breaks just as fundamentally as it does continuity and preservation. Spirit passes through a spiral of endlessly varying forms, each of which is sublated (annulled and preserved), and none of which are exactly repeated. Because what is involved is an open spiral rather than a closed circle, the beginning and ending of a spiritual life never coincide.[31]

At the level of world history or macrohistory (which is the proper domain of philosophy of history), Hegel thought it possible to identify "the successive stages [*Stufengänge*] in the development of that principle whose substantial content is the consciousness of freedom." These stages are related to one another not as links in an evolutionary chain but as distinctive cultural types through which spirit passes transfiguratively, moving from one form of the consciousness of freedom to another. The *rational* determination of these stages in their universal form is the task of logic, which defines them variously as the triad of immediacy, differentiation, and reunification, or the dialectic of thesis, antithesis, and synthesis, or the syllogism of universality, particularity, and individuality.[32] But the *concrete* determination of these stages belongs to the philosophy of spirit and may be summarized as follows: at the first, immediate stage, spirit is still immersed in nature and exists in a state of unfree particularity (only *one* is free); in the second stage it emerges partially into an awareness of its own freedom (*some* are free); and in the third stage spirit enters into its purely universal form in which it achieves consciousness of itself as spirit (*humanity as such* is free).[33]

When transferred to the plane of world history, these three logical moments or spiritual stages yield *four* cultural worlds, which are related to one another typologically, not genetically: the Oriental, the Greek, the Roman, and the Christian-European. Why are four worlds generated out of three stages? As Hegel explained it in the earlier lectures, it is because the second stage of spirit, that of separation and partial emergence, is made up of two distinct subphases, the ages of youth (the Greek world) and of adulthood (the Roman). The Oriental world is associated, then, with childhood, and the Christian-European world with old age.[34] Hegel here introduced the unfortunate analogy of the individual life cycle (childhood, youth, adulthood, old age) as a means of illustrating the four archetypal cultural worlds—unfortunate because it suggests a kind of organic evolution. Of course, on Hegel's view, this life cycle entails a spiritual process in which there occur qualitative transitions, not merely a genetic process or physical maturation. The human being is what he or she freely makes of himself or herself.

"All this," said Hegel, "is the a priori structure of history to which empirical reality must correspond."[35] But it is not quite as simple as that. When logic is applied to historical shapes (*Gestalten*), it becomes *typology*, and there is a looser connection between logic and typo-logic (as well as theo-logic) than Hegel sometimes allowed. For example, he himself gave a rather different typology of world history in those lectures which are sources of the material printed as an appendix to the published volume. Here the fundamental theme is not the departure of spirit from nature, and the analogy of the life cycle is dropped. The operative categories are "substantial freedom" and "subjective freedom," and a geographical motif is introduced. Spirit travels from East to West as the ways of relating substance and subject undergo change: the Orient represents the dominance of substance over subject, Greece the aesthetic unification of substantial and subjective freedom, Rome their totalitarian unification, and the Christian West their spiritual-ethical unification.[36]

But what happens to spirit after it arrives in the West? This question gives rise to another possible typology, a postmodern variant on the logical scheme: suppose, following the dialectic of

immediacy (primitive culture), differentiation (Oriental culture), and reunification or mediation (Western culture, beginning with Greece and culminating with Western Europe and
North America), we posit a fourth moment, which is the
breakdown of synthesis and the transition to a fresh beginning in
a new triad—the end of Western-bourgeois hegemony, the
(re)turn to the East, the emergence of the South? These four
stages arguably correspond more closely to Hegel's logic[37] and to
the present course of history than do Hegel's own versions. The
story of freedom is not yet finished; we do not yet know all there
is to know about it but must remain open to new disclosures and
possibilities through future liberating praxis. The teleology of
spirit is an open, inexhaustible affair, but also a fragile,
destructible one. Thus we must also remain open to the
possibility that the history of spirit and freedom will be aborted
in a nuclear holocaust. I do not intend to advance this or that
alternative scheme at the moment but rather to make the point
that a number of different typological paradigms may be
generated out of the same basic logical structure. The a priori
does not establish or control the content of the empirical; rather,
it offers paradigms and principles for its interpretation. Of this
Hegel was surely aware, but his polemic against empiricism and
historicism seems to have militated against ready acknowledgment of it.[38]

A Way Beyond Tragedy?

Is Hegel's emplotment of world history ultimately tragic or
comic? It is not either of these alone. Rather, it offers, in Hayden
White's words, "the transition from the comprehension of the
tragic nature of every specific civilization to the comic
apprehension of the unfolding drama of the whole of history."[39]
It is, however, not merely specific civilizations that are tragic in
Hegel's vision, but also every nation, every social institution,
every work of art or scholarship, every human relationship,
every individual action—for all of these are transient and
conflictual, all are doomed to destruction, none achieves the

self-comprehending totality of spirit. "It oppresses us to think that the richest forms and the finest manifestations of life must perish in history, and that we walk amidst the ruins of excellence." Yet, Hegel continued, "out of death, new life arises."[40] This recognition—that the death of an individual or institution no less than that of a civilization has the possibility of transforming human life and culture into new shapes that open up possibilities for consciousness and praxis that did not exist before—is "the informing insight of the comic vision and the highest comprehension of the historical process to which the finite mind can aspire."[41] This possibility is most clearly glimpsed on the scale of macrohistory, for here we are able to recognize that history is "the progress of the consciousness of freedom," a progress that Hegel believed had come to its consummation in the philosophy that comprehends what freedom and spirit essentially are. From this vantage point it is possible to affirm the primacy of life over death, of good over evil, of purpose over chaos, at every step along the path of history, whether large or small. But from the vantage point of the empirical historian, the emplotment of any given segment of the process must be in the tragic mode. What is concealed from us on the microhistoric scale is revealed on the macrohistoric; and what is revealed macrohistorically does apply, retrospectively as it were, to microhistory. The speculative philosopher shares the Christian comic vision of redemption, not on the basis of special revelation but by means of a rational comprehension of the truth of the whole (which includes the recognition that no single individual can claim to possess the whole truth—rather it possesses us, discloses itself to us).

Attractive as this solution is in many respects, it poses severe problems to a postmodern consciousness. We must insist, for example, that the goal of world history lies not merely in the *cognition* of the concept of freedom but in the *realization* of freedom, a fact recognized by Hegel's disciples on the left.[42] The emancipatory project is far from complete, and we cannot exclude the possibility that it will be utterly aborted by nuclear or environmental devastation or the regression of civilization to a state of barbarism, of which there have been several modern portents. At the very least it experiences frustrating setbacks and suffers slow and painful advances. Moreover, no philosophy can claim to have grasped cognitively all there is to know about freedom; further discoveries of what freedom essentially is will be made through its praxis in possibly quite different cultural paradigms. Thus the emplotment of macrohistory as simply comic must be seriously questioned.

On the other hand, the microhistorical emplotment of actions, works, institutions, nations, and cultures as simply tragic is also questionable. The fact is that momentary configurations of freedom do take place, and partial integrations of experience are attained, again and again in human history, often under the most adverse circumstances. Clearings of freedom take place not just at the end of the dark path of history but along the way, and we can rejoice in their occurrence while recognizing their transience and limitation. The work of art provides a useful analogy: it exhibits a kind of completion, a gathering together of the process of becoming into a "compacted fullness," which occurs not once but again and again. Great works of art are complete and whole, but theirs is an "open wholeness," a momentary perfection, not a totalitarian closure.[43] So it is with history: many ends are attained, but these are open, finite ends, ends that open out to an inexhaustible, unattainable presence. This is the only way we experience presence in history, but we do experience it.

It would be misleading to suggest that Hegel regarded microhistory itself as "simply tragic," although he believed that it could be *emplotted* only in the tragic mode. He distinguished, for example, between "happiness" and "satisfaction" in the following way:

The individual . . . is said to be happy if he has found harmony within himself. It is possible to consider history from the point of view of happiness, but history is not the soil in which happiness grows. The periods of happiness in it are the blank pages of history. There are certainly moments of satisfaction in the history of the world, but this satisfaction is not to be equated with happiness: for the aims which are satisfied transcend all particular interests. . . . The world-historical individuals who have pursued such ends may well have attained satisfaction, but happiness was certainly not their object.[44]

Although happiness designates a "comic" fulfillment of the individual human being, clearly for Hegel it is not a historical category; it may occur but it leaves no historical traces. Satisfaction, on the other hand, while a historical actuality, is tragic rather than comic since the aims that are satisfied transcend particular interests and thus do not constitute individual self-fulfillment. From a world-historical perspective, such satisfactions may indeed be seen to be comic, that is, as contributing to a greater harmonization; but from the perspective of the individual they are experienced as tragic, as unfulfilling. The momentary shapes or clearings of freedom to which I am referring seem to hover somewhere between Hegelian happiness and satisfaction since they designate genuine but incomplete fulfillments: they are less than pure happiness but more than sorrowful satisfaction; my contention in any case is that they really do occur, they do leave historical traces, and these traces can be discerned empirically as well as metahistorically.

In my view, therefore, history must be emplotted *tragicomically* on both microhistorical and macrohistorical scales. Partial realizations of freedom occur within all the dimensions of history, and long-term trajectories are discernible, but it cannot be claimed that history as such or as a whole is a comic process. It is an ambiguous process, which is to say that it is tragicomic. The final comedy is the divine comedy, not a human comedy. The only unambiguously comic vision of the perfection of freedom lies beyond history with the consummation of all things in God. This is the eschatological significance of the symbol "kingdom of God" or "kingdom of freedom." Yet this symbol also has an innerhistorical significance: the gestalt of the kingdom is a factor within history and has the power to transfigure it.

These themes, suggested by a sympathetic critique of Hegel, will be elaborated more fully as we proceed.

2. Troeltsch's Critique of Historical Reason and the Shaping of Cultural Syntheses

Theology and the Science of Religion

Ernst Troeltsch was at once a consummate historian and a deeply committed religious thinker. At the beginning of this century, he brought together the disciplines of history, theology, and ethics with a sophistication, passion, and depth of insight not fully matched by any theologian since his time. Neglected for nearly sixty years after his death in 1923, Troeltsch has recently been rediscovered and recognized as a thinker of first importance for a "revisionist" theology—a theology that is attempting to revision Christian faith in response to the cognitive and cultural challenges of postmodernism, as opposed to avoiding these challenges or simply capitulating to them.[45]

Troeltsch envisioned a new theological program grounded in a "science of religion," which would overcome what he perceived to be the deep and destructive split that had erupted within Protestant liberalism between historical-critical theology and "practical mediating dogmatics."[46] On Troeltsch's model, the science of religion would comprise several component disciplines: a general theory of religion as a phenomenon of human consciousness, analyzed both psychologically and epistemologically; a philosophical history of religion (*Geschichtsphilosophie der Religion*), whose task would be to comprehend the great variety of "historical religious formations" and to furnish a "critical valuative grading" of them; and a religious metaphysics, which would attend to the "real object of faith, the idea of God."[47] Science of religion as a whole would function as a kind of "fundamental theology," furnishing presuppositions and principles to both historical theology (which must employ the methods of history of religions and history of culture) and dogmatic theology (which has as its agenda questions concerning the "absoluteness" and "essence" of Christianity and the "exposition of a normative Christian religious system").[48] In turn, the science of religion itself would be funded by norms deriving from history, as established by a formal and a material philosophy of history, and by a general ethics, which would be concerned with both personal morality and cultural values. Troeltsch himself was able to execute only small parts of this grand program, intended to lay the foundations of a new, "free theology of catholic and protestant 'modernism.' "[49]

Every science of religion operates with epistemological presuppositions. Assuming the nonacceptability of basing one's work on a precritical "doctrine of revelation as a church dogma," Troeltsch argued that the basic choice confronting a modern science of religion—a choice that ultimately is "a matter of personal conviction"—is between philosophical idealism and positivism in one or another of its forms. Idealism "not merely conceives of reality as being grounded in spirit [*Geist*]," but also "considers spirit to be furnished with qualitatively creative powers for the production of specific spiritual values"; while positivism "in the first instance recognizes only assured facts and the ordered connections between them, and then turns these facts over to be processed" according to pragmatic criteria related to "the assertion and completion of human existence itself." Positivism was in the ascendancy in Troeltsch's day (as in ours), but it must be rejected, he argued, because it views religion in purely naturalistic and functionalist terms as "absolutely nothing other than an activity of human thought," a way of ordering and explaining reality in naive, prescientific categories; as such, positivism's treatment of religion will be inevitably reductive.[50]

In opting for idealism, however, Troeltsch was, on the one hand, uncomfortable with Hegel's speculative idealism, which, he believed, "deduces from reason itself the reality of nature and of the history of ideas as being a logically necessary explication of reason." On the other hand, he was unable simply to embrace a Kantian critical idealism, which "abandons radically every metaphysics" and purports to limit itself "to the analysis of the

subjective human reason by which alone reality can be contained
and on the basis of whose fundamental conditions it arises for us
at all." Kantianism is unable to take account of religion as a
qualitatively distinct human activity, oriented to an object with a
reality-status other than that of a moral postulate, and it offers
no basis for interpreting the history of religion in its unity,
variety, and development.[51] Thus Troeltsch found it necessary
to execute a kind of neo-Kantian return to Hegel, who offered
the "finest solution" thus far to the task of a philosophical history
of religion.

> But since his teaching is based on a purely metaphysical
> construction of world reason . . . and on the logical law of the
> dialectics of reason immanent in world reason, Hegel's goal may
> be maintained but it must be reached by other logical and
> methodological paths. Without any metaphysics it is not possible
> at all, but it will have to be a metaphysics of *a posteriori* conclusions
> out of the facts and not a deductive metaphysics of the absolute.
> In particular a substitute for Hegel's dialectic must be found, a
> teleological law of development, this being under all circum-
> stances the final and most important concept of all philosophy of
> history.[52]

As we have seen, the relationship between logic and history in
Hegel's thought is not "deductive" in the sense of imposing an
a priori rational scheme on empirical facts, and his construction
of historical process is typological rather than dialectical or
evolutionary. Yet, despite the prejudiced picture of Hegel that
Troeltsch shared with the neo-Kantianism of his day, he
managed to retrieve some of Hegel's most valuable and
productive insights and to reformulate them in his own
philosophy of history, which was more deeply attuned than
Hegel's to historical relativity and ambiguity, and which
attempted to derive categories of historical interpretation from
the work of the practicing historian rather than from speculative
logic. While embracing, in his own terms, Hegel's insight that
"world history is the progress of the consciousness of freedom,"

Troeltsch was suspicious of any claims about the sovereignty or triumph of divine reason in history, and he moved the discussion of freedom in the direction of ethical values and the shaping of ever-new and incomplete cultural syntheses through a process of configuration and compromise. Finally, while his "metaphysics of *a posteriori* conclusions" leaves much to be desired, it does contain suggestive insights into the question of God's presence in history. For these reasons, Troeltsch serves as a valuable transition from a Hegelian to a postmodern consciousness of history, and he moves the discussion of history into an explicitly theological frame of reference, which is especially useful for our purposes.

The Crisis of Historicism and the Critique of Historical Reason

What Troeltsch referred to as "the crisis of historicism"[53] was generated by the awareness that the claims of religions and value systems to absoluteness or normative truth come into conflict with an inescapable reality for modern critical consciousness, that of historical relativism. Sarah Coakley has pointed out that not only are *relativism* and *historicism* ambiguous terms, but also Troeltsch changed his views during the course of his career and failed on occasion to separate types of relativism that are logically distinct.[54] Throughout, Troeltsch maintained a position that is not relativism in the strict sense but what Coakley calls "relationalism," which holds that truth is relative to a context, and which demands that phenomena be studied in the first instance in their own terms. In one of his early essays, he described his own position as that of *Relativierung* and *Relativität* in contrast to *Relativismus*.[55] The problem, said Troeltsch in *The Absoluteness of Christianity and the History of Religions,* is not that of relativism versus absolutism but rather "how to discern, in the relative, tendencies toward the absolute goal." Or, stated more precisely: "How does one work out a fresh, durable, and creative synthesis that will give the absolute the form possible to it at a particular moment and yet remain true to its inherent limitation as a mere approximation of true, ultimate, and universally valid values?" While Christianity is surely a relative, historical reality, in this early work Troeltsch maintained that it is still possible to affirm, in contrast to other religions, that it is the "focal point and culmination of all religious developments."[56]

As his thought matured, however, Troeltsch supplemented his earlier relationalism by what Coakley calls "relativism proper" or "epistemological relativism," which has the logical structure: "Proposition p is actually true relative to, or in virtue of, framework f."[57] This means that truths and values "are to one degree or another actively constituted by the prevailing framework, context, or paradigm"; they are "intra-theoretic." Thus we must now admit that the validity of Christianity is based only on its specific cultural achievement, not in terms of being measured against other quite different religious frameworks, and we can maintain that it is an authentic "manifestation of the divine life itself" only "for us."[58] But Troeltsch supported a "weak" version of epistemological relativism since in his view the *criteria* for discerning what historical truth or value is are not themselves relative to frameworks. "A truth which, in the first instance, is *a truth for us* does not cease, because of this, to be very truth and life."[59] To be sure, in his last writings Troeltsch "flirted" (in Coakley's terms) with not only a criterial relativism but also with the view that some frameworks are so different that their truth claims are incommensurable or mutually incomprehensible—a view that would bring him much closer to the kind of relativism advocated in the recent debate by such thinkers as Winch, Kuhn, Feyerabend, and Phillips. But as Coakley rightly contends, on Troeltsch's own premises both criterial relativism and incommensurability are inadmissible.[60] In *Historismus* and other late writings, he introduced what she calls a "perspectival reality view," designed to show that an understanding and evaluation of alien cultures and frameworks really is possible, but "only if we dare to believe that all history has an ultimate metaphysical point of unity and identity."[61] At the end of the lecture "The Place of Christianity Among the World-Religions," he suggested that all religions may have a common ground in the Divine Spirit and may be tending in the same direction.[62]

Troeltsch responded to the crisis of historicism by engaging in a critique of historical reason in order to discern what its "formal logic" is, and by then elaborating a "material philosophy of history," whose task would be to shape future historical life on the basis of our comprehension of past and present. Since we cannot leap out of our historical skins, the objective of historicism in the sense of "radical historicality"[63] is "to overcome history with history."[64] The material philosophy of history was to be the subject of the second volume of *Der Historismus und seine Probleme,* which never appeared because of Troeltsch's premature death, but hints are scattered throughout the first volume, and various elements of the project are developed in the lectures prepared for delivery in England and published posthumously in *Christian Thought.* I shall examine the formal logic of history in the remainder of this subsection, and then consider Troeltsch's material philosophy of history in the next.[65]

The logic of the sciences concerned with the "real" must be clearly distinguished from the logic of the "ideal" with its rational categories and triadic syllogisms. Here Troeltsch intended clearly to demarcate his departure from Hegel. Rather than being "deduced" from the logical idea, the principles of selection, formation, and connection by which we arrive at historical judgments are "first employed quite unconsciously in comprehending a living reality that has been established critically or by means of one's own intuition." These principles "emerge with increasing clarity through engagement with the object or surrender to the subject matter, and they finally demand a logical formulation."[66] They are arrived at inductively out of the historical matrix itself.

The first and most important of the categories of historical interpretation, according to Troeltsch, is that of individual totality (*individuelle Totalität*). History does not work with elementary particles, like the natural sciences, but with "life-unities" or "totalities," consisting of "a wealth of elementary psychic processes and natural conditions." These "agglomerations" (*Zusammenballungen*) or "concretions" (*Konkretheiten*) already lie before us as historical wholes or units, each of which is

unique and irreplaceable.[67] Expressed in Hegelian terms, the
historian does not work with "particularity" (the proper domain
of the natural sciences) but with "individuality" (*Einzelheit*),
especially with those individual entities that have achieved
spiritual subjectivity by integrating the individual with the
universal and the particular.[68] Troeltsch's distinction between
elementary particles and individual totalities logically presupposes something like the Hegelian dialectic of universal-particular-individual, a dialectic which, as we have seen, is not
deductively imposed on history but arises out of historical
experience, and which entails a process of temporal becoming.

Individual totalities occur at every level of the historical
process. Initially, of course, they are the so-called individuals or
single human beings who are the subject of epic, legend,
biography. But since historical analysis shows that such
individuals can be understood only in light of a larger
totality—family, ethnic group, class, nation, age, or period, and
finally the nexus of humanity as a whole—"it is evident that the
proper objects of scientific historiography are less and less
single, biographical individuals but rather collective individual-
ities such as peoples, states, classes, social location, cultural
epochs and tendencies, religious communities, and events of all
sorts such as wars and revolutions." But even at the collective
level we are concerned with an individual totality, a compacted
wholeness, which can be extracted from the flux of events,
although at its margins it blends into the totality of human
events. The delimitation of such a totality, determining what its
boundaries are, is always a matter of historical judgment—not
merely a subjective judgment but one that corresponds insofar
as possible to the objective shape of events.[69] Although Troeltsch
did not take specific note of the fact, an "individual totality,"
whether subjective or intersubjective, is precisely a historical
shape, figure, or form—in Hegelian terms, a *Gestalt*—and it is
connected, therefore, with another of Troeltsch's key interpretative categories, *Gestaltung*, which is a form or figure
determined by the shaping or synthesizing of parts—a "configuration." Every individual totality is such a configuration. The

task of the historian qua "scientist" is to discern and analyze the configurations of the past; the task of the historian qua ethically responsible human being is to help shape new and productive configurations (or "cultural syntheses") for the present and future.[70]

Practical Teleology, the Shaping of Cultural Syntheses, and Metaphysical Faith

Troeltsch's thoughts on matters relating to what he called "material philosophy of history" are incomplete, unsystematic, scattered, and occasionally inconsistent—but also highly suggestive. I have attempted to identify three predominant motifs that seem to recur as Troeltsch attempted to sketch his own "metahistory" in conscious opposition to Hegel's, while at the same time he was clearly influenced by it.

1. Practical teleology. The most important conclusion from a formal logic of history, Troeltsch believed, is that a contemporary philosophy of history cannot be a systematic, teleological construction of the stages of the actualization of the final end of history ("the progress of the consciousness of freedom"). The realism and empiricism of historical science, together with a sense of catastrophic cultural decline, prohibit such holistic constructions.[71] An empirical view of historical development traces sequences and breaks, continuities and discontinuities, and similarities and differences in the shaping of events and cultures, but it discerns no dominant direction, only new formations, their maturation and eventual decay. Its emplotment of history is essentially tragic.[72]

What, then, remains as the task of a material philosophy of history? Its fundamental task is to obtain from history itself the "criterion" or "ideal" for a new unity of culture, a contemporary cultural synthesis. In this respect, it does retain a teleological aspect, but not in the sense of an "objective construction of world process in terms of a final and eternal end." It is not a rational but a "volitional teleology, which forms and shapes the future out of the past in the present moment"[73]—a task that must be repeated

again and again in each new age and context, recognizing that
only partial and contingent solutions are attainable. We might
also describe this as a "practical teleology," since material
philosophy of history is oriented to praxis, to the ethical
transformation of existing conditions; its goal is the very
opposite of a purely contemplative attitude toward history,
which is quietistic in its ethical implications. Troeltsch had Ranke
in mind here, and he might have said of Ranke what Marx said of
Feuerbach: "The philosophers [of history] have only *interpreted*
the world in various ways; the point is, to *change* it."[74]

But change it to what? Practical teleology finds itself involved
in an inescapable hermeneutical circle for which there are no
final ends and answers. It must start with empirical historical
research and its formal logic, which constitute the objects of
investigation as individual totalities, each of which has a relative
value. These values must be measured first in their own terms,
immanently, but then also with reference to a "universal nexus
of value," which every interpreter employs, if only unconsciously or silently. Such a universal nexus, while arising out of
the historical situation of the interpreter, is at the same time
enriched and corrected by being brought into contact with past
horizons of meaning. We attain universal criteria only from a
full wealth of historical experience, intuition, and interpretation. Thus we find ourselves involved in a profound dialectic of
past, present, and future. Every evaluation of the past both leads
to and is informed by the reconfiguration of the present with an
orientation to the configuration of the future.[75]

2. The shaping of cultural syntheses. The theoretical difficulties
involved in establishing criteria by which a teleology of praxis is
to be oriented are ultimately irresolvable, but lapsing into
dogmatism, skepticism, or quietism is an unacceptable alternative, and in fact, so Troeltsch insisted, a practical solution is at
hand. We need only to notice what is going on all the time in
history: new cultural syntheses, on both large and small scales,
are continually being created, generated out of two sources—
rational norms and ethical ideals, on the one hand, and
individual historical exigencies and actions, on the other. What

occurs in each new synthesis is a creative fusion of the ethically and rationally universal with the historically individual. While such fusions are new and spontaneous, at the same time they entail a reforming and further development of what has already been shaped in the great nexus of historical tradition; they create out of what has been, not out of nothing.[76]

The syntheses thus generated are not timeless, universally valid and absolute; rather, they are relevant to the moment at hand. What is involved is "damming and shaping [*Dämmung und Gestaltung*] the historical stream of life" for a period of time by welding together the cultural values of a given epoch in a fragile synthesis.

> The task of damming and shaping is . . . essentially incapable of completion and essentially unending; and yet it is always soluble and practicable in each new case. A radical and absolute solution does not exist; there are only working, partial, synthetically uniting solutions. Yet the stream of life is always surging upward and onward. History within itself cannot be transcended. . . . The kingdom of God and nirvana lie outside all history. In history itself there are only relative victories; and these relative victories themselves vary greatly in power and depth, according to time and circumstance.[77]

Troeltsch's implicit point is that the activity of configuration (*Gestaltung*)—of shaping the new or the future (*Neugestaltung, Zukunftsgestaltung*)—lies at the heart of the historical process and is always at work; without it, the "historical stream of life" would dissipate into a formless, chaotic flood. Despite the relativity of values, the weakness of individuals, the systemic character of evil, and the ambiguities of every situation, it is within the power of human beings to create fragile syntheses that achieve momentary, "relative victories" over chaos or tyranny. These victories are won for the most part through the path of "creative compromise"—compromise between the utopian demands of an ideal and the conditions of actual human life. Compromise is often regarded as something despicable, and indeed a distinction must be drawn between good and bad compromises; but "the fact remains that all intransigence breaks down in practice, and can only end in disaster."[78] Compromise is a necessary component of the fragmentariness, ambiguity, and evil of all historical situations. Consequently, no historical synthesis is complete and final.

Despite important differences, there are some striking similarities between Troeltsch's theory of historical configuration and Hegel's image of the fabric of history. For both, a synthesis or weaving together of two factors is involved—the ethically-rationally universal and the historically individual, or the ideal and the real. For both, the latter factor consists in the laws and forces of nature, the passions and interests of human agents, the matrix of historical effects, the constraints of a given situation. Hegel defined the former as the "idea of freedom," while Troeltsch described it as the idea of "free personality," although he acknowledged that this is a specifically Western cultural ideal.[79] For both thinkers, what is created by the synthesis is a social whole or nexus that enhances individual life—a nexus of cultural values (Troeltsch) or of ethical freedom (Hegel), the specific shape of which depends on time and circumstance.

Troeltsch rejected, however, any overarching teleology of freedom: although specific cultural trajectories may be discernible, it cannot be said that history as a whole is moving toward its consummation or has even arrived at a clear consciousness of what its goal is. The future is open and uncertain; in each new circumstance, we have the obligation and opportunity to shape the future. *Zukunftsgestaltung* is the leitmotiv of Troeltsch's material philosophy of history.[80] If the future is not shaped in the direction of personally upbuilding, socially emancipatory cultural values, then it will be shaped in other, destructive, disfiguring, dehumanizing directions. It is up to us what we make of history or what we do not make of it.

3. Metaphysical faith. But what, finally, empowers us to act? On what basis can it be determined, finally, whether values are emancipatory or dehumanizing? What gives us the courage to face the future in light of past failures and present ambiguities, which threaten to overwhelm us? The answer to this question also led Troeltsch in the direction of Hegel's philosophy of history, but with qualifications. Although historical development at the empirical level seems to be purposeless and tragic, there is also, he said, a "deeper movement," which, while appearing empirically in only a deficient and broken way, can be discerned, excavated, and reintegrated by a historically engaged will. This act of will involves a "metaphysical faith" by which one is able to believe in "a continuity operating in the deepest channel of events"—a continuity "often enough obscured and distorted by the contingency and accidents, the stupidity and weakness, the crimes and malice, the overextension and neurasthenia" of actual history, but which can be "extracted and rendered visible from the empirical course of events for an engaged and believing will." What is extracted and made visible is, ultimately, the "inner impulse and drive of *reason*," which must be attributed to "the final *divine ground,* the inner movement of the divine spirit in the finite spirit."[81] In the process of shaping new syntheses, there takes place an "in-breathing of a new soul and a new spirit," which is the manifestation for this particular moment of "an inner life-movement of the All or of divinity." Such claims entail a religious faith, and it is just this faith that helps to distinguish authentic configurations of value from mere subjectivism because it is expressive of the sense of being grasped and pulled by something that transcends the subject. Creative acts of synthesis frequently have, therefore, a religious, revelatory quality.[82]

Here, of course, we are at the boundary of all science, but this faith does constitute, Troeltsch claimed, "the conclusion and final horizon of all history." Apart from it, we are consigned to pessimism and skepticism when confronted by the repeated tragedies of history, as was the case with Simmel and Spengler; or we will simply entrench ourselves behind the objectivity and rigor of empirical research, as most historians do (in Troeltsch's day as well as ours).[83] Faith views the content of history as "the expression and revelation of the divine ground of life and of the inner movement of this ground toward the total meaning of the world, which is unknown to us. It apprehends the cultural ideal emerging out of each momentary situation as a representative of the unknown absolute." But this must be a scientifically disciplined faith, which is protected from a romantic enthusiasm for totalities, or a logical enthusiasm for unity, by attending to the actual details of history with precision. The struggles and conflicts of history are not in fact logical contradictions, nor is their resolution logical; rather, it is "the surlogical [*überlogisch*] unity of each individual synthesis." We must transpose ourselves into the factual matrices of history in order to derive the synthetic idea from them rather, than from logic. In this fashion we are indeed able to affirm a faith in the "rationality of the actual"; but it is the actual that determines the rational rather than the reverse.[84]

These cautionary words are not alien to a Hegelian perspective if, as we have claimed, Hegel recognized the difference between the logical and the typological (which would be a form of the "surlogical" in Troeltsch's terms) and knew perfectly well that empirical facts cannot be derived from logical relations. Logic functions hermeneutically as a "deep structure" by which experience is to be interpreted, not deduced. If logic is based on life and elucidates life, as was the case for Hegel, then it is correct to say *both* that the actual determines the rational and the rational the actual. The question, however, is what constitutes "actuality" (*Wirklichkeit*). For Hegel, it is not merely what is empirically-scientifically given, the "real." Rather, it is what is true and whole and consummate, or, following a clue from Troeltsch, "what ought to be" (*das Seinsollende*).[85] The rational is the actual, and the actual rational, not in the sense of what is but of what ought to be. An axiological-eschatological dimension is thereby introduced which keeps history open for the future and serves as a reminder of its permanently unfinished character. Both rationality and actuality are eschatological concepts. Troeltsch is extremely helpful in pointing Hegelian thought in this direction.

Troeltsch's metaphysical faith issued in what Coakley calls a "metaphysical perspectivism" designed to combat "unlimited relativism" or "spurious historicism" (*schlechter Historismus*).[86] This perspectivism is to be based on a "revised Leibnizian monadology" according to which each "I" bears within itself all other "I's" and encompasses within itself potentially a consciousness of the All or of the universe. Thus agreement is possible between culturally relative value systems since all human beings ultimately stem from the same ground in the universal life (*Alleben*) and sense themselves to be part of one another. For this reason, too, "objective and spiritual values can be distinguished from those based on merely brutish and environmental factors since the former derive from the divine universal spirit [*göttlicher Allgeist*] whose vital life encompasses finitude within itself and in which individual beings participate." Troeltsch summed up his case as follows: "Relativity of value makes sense only if there is an absolute that is vital and creative within the relative. Otherwise it would be a matter of mere relativity, not of a relativity of value. The latter presupposes a life-process of the absolute in which the absolute itself can be grasped and shaped from every point of view and in a fashion corresponding to each point of view."[87]

Troeltsch's Idea of God and of Divine Providence

We may wonder why Troeltsch found it necessary to repair to Leibnizian monadology to articulate what appear to be such distinctly Hegelian ideas about God—ideas which, in Troeltsch's hand, despite their elusiveness, are highly suggestive as far as the question of God's presence in history is concerned.

Without the idea of God or something like it, Troeltsch claimed, there can be no formation of ethical criteria. But if God is understood as timeless and unchanging, the criterion will have the character of an eternal, unchanging ideal—an absolute substance or an absolute law. Troeltsch called this "rationalistic monism" or "Spinozism," and he thought that there was "a good deal of this Spinozism in Kant's transcendental deduction of causal monism as well as in the 'concept' articulated by Hegelian dialectic." I have attempted to argue that such a reading of Hegel is highly misleading, and that it was precisely Hegel who introduced similar criticisms against Kant and Spinoza. The question, however, is whether Hegel followed through with complete consistency on the implications of his own conception of God as "absolute spirit" in contrast to absolute substance. If God is indeed absolute *spirit,* then there is an intrinsic openness to the divine life, which is something other than a purely rational process, and world history can never be brought to closure. With this observation in mind, the following statement by Troeltsch is worth pondering:

> If [by contrast with rationalism] we opt for Heraclitus and the prophetic-Christian idea of the never conceptually exhaustible productive vitality of the divine will, . . . then any possibility of the construction of the totality of world occurrence as well as of our tiny planetary history disappears; but we do attain the life-depths out of which, along with the inner mobility and change of God himself, the change and mobility of truth and ideality become intelligible—together with a nonetheless persisting engagement in a final truth and unity, which only God knows, if we may call God's knowing "knowing." This is the sphere of *metalogic.* Then any compulsion to designate this or that human truth or ideal construction as absolute disappears; but we do maintain the possibility of grasping the divine life in the relative truth and the relative ideal. . . . We live in a constant movement toward the absolute; but the absolute itself exists only for itself in the unity of its life-fullness and cannot be conceived because it is no concept at all.[88]

Although much of what is said here is very helpful, the assertion that God cannot be conceived must be questioned. The problem is that Troeltsch wants to "grasp" the divine life without conceiving it, to speak of the "productive vitality of the divine will," the "universal divine spirit," the "life-depths," the "inner mobility and change of God," the "All-life," the "life-process of the absolute," and so forth, without unpacking these metaphors. It is not enough to say that speaking of God in this way is part of the risk of faith. Without engaging in the thought, the conceptual thought, to which the symbols and intuitions of faith give rise, all sorts of fantastic notions can and do come flooding in. Conceptualization certainly need not be understood to produce a "universally valid rational system, whose fundamental claim is to make everything necessary and calculable, objective and secure." Rather, in a system like Hegel's something like *conceptual play* is at work for the purpose of generating hermeneutically productive construals of experience and paradigms for thinking about what transcends experience ultimately.[89] To be sure, God is not a concept, but this does not mean that God cannot be conceived—so long as we recognize the relativity and incompleteness of every concept. In fact, I am attracted to the possibility of conceiving God with the help of the central category of Troeltsch's philosophy of history, that of *Gestalt(ung)*, which is a category of historical praxis rather than of logic, even though it may have a foundation in logic. God as absolute spirit is the dynamic, self-manifesting shape or figure that empowers the creative, synthesizing, emancipatory configurations of human life and culture, which are at the same time the self-shaping of God. The shape of God is the shape of free love. These conceptual possibilities will be explored in the next chapter.

Troeltsch's own more systematic thinking about God was pursued in his posthumously edited *Glaubenslehre,* based on lectures delivered in 1911 and 1912.[90] In general he attempted to move in the direction of an ethical dipolar theism (God as the unity of will and essence, *Wille und Wesen*), affirming the idea of divine personality while rejecting the doctrine of the trinity, refusing to resolve the "antinomies" present in the divine life in the form of either a consistent monotheism or a consistent pantheism, while drawing upon elements of both. His constructive view might be described as that of a "process panentheism," but he would probably have rejected those labels as well.[91]

For our purposes, his treatment of God's "world-rule" or providence is of greatest interest. Typically, he said that all speculations about how God's rule operates, how it relates individual things to its purposes, how it takes into itself the relative dependence and freedom of creatures, are "worthless." Faith in divine providence has nothing to do with the teleological concepts, or lack thereof, of natural science.[92] This faith is based on the fact that we experience novelty in the world-process, we recognize the possibility of a creative reconstitution of persons, and we sense an individual direction to life. In fact, the idea of an immediate divine rule is present in every religion. To express this idea today, it is better to speak, not of a *Wunderglaube*, a faith in and based on wonder or miracle, but of an *Unmittelbarkeitsglaube*, a faith in and based on immediacy, the immediacy and particularity of God's providential rule. This immediate divine presence does not violate the general nexus and the continuity of events both natural and historical.[93]

In addition to its relation to the general nexus, each individual event also possesses a particular grounding, appropriate to it, in God's creation and world-rule (an idea akin, perhaps, to Whitehead's notion of a relevant ideal for each occasion of experience). In each event with which we are familiar, we have an impression (*Eindruck*) both of the whole of God's world-rule and of the immediate presence of God. Our impression of the latter is concerned first of all with the ever-new creation of our inner lives, with personal direction and prayer; but from there it extends out to the whole world and considers "the especially important nodal points of world development as creative acts" deriving from divine providence, as does the destiny of humanity as a whole. In sum, our faith in God's immediate presence means that "we can speak of a creation of life, a creation of humanity, a recreation of the inner life, an influx (*Einströmen*) of divine powers in outstanding individuals, and finally of revelation and redemption."[94]

This faith in divine immediacy, Troeltsch emphasized, must be distinguished from the caprice of the divine powers found in polytheism and the absorption of individuals into a unity of substance found in pantheistic and mystical religions. It is fully present in the faith of prophetic Judaism and primitive Christianity, and traces are found as well in Stoicism, Neoplatonism, and later forms of Buddhism.[95] It is a purely religious faith that cannot be explained either metaphysically or scientifically. Rational thought, Troeltsch was convinced, will always link events together according to the principle of logical necessity; its impulse is to go as far as it can and if unchecked will lead to "a universally regulative monism that excludes everything new, irrational, and immediate."[96]

Again, as we have seen, this is not the case with Hegel's "reason in history," which "interweaves" itself with human passions and actions (which are often highly "irrational") to create ever anew the actual fabric of history. This living divine reason, which is at the same time the idea of freedom, is precisely the instrument of God's immediacy and efficacious presence. It is only a technical, scientific rationality that excludes novelty, irrationality, and immediacy. By appearing to recognize no other kind of reason, Troeltsch conceded too much to the opponents of religion and left himself open to charges of fideism. He had no basis for claiming reason as an instrument of critical, emancipatory praxis, as Hegel did, and this is one of the prices paid for drawing back from the "hard labor" of thinking through conceptually the most difficult of modern theological questions, that of God's presence in history. Troeltsch was not only acutely aware of the severity of this labor but also remained suspicious of the best philosophical tools available for addressing it. But without such thinking, Troeltsch's brilliant insights and intuitions with respect to this question will remain elusive and fragmentary. If we are to be equipped reflectively to confront the challenge of the postmodern deconstruction of history (with which all talk about God's presence either evaporates or requires to be totally rethought), we must achieve something like a post-Troeltschian retrieval of Hegel. Hegel and Troeltsch together provide a basis for a postmodern theology of history. Yet this basis alone is not enough; they cannot substitute for the hard labor now demanded of us.

3. The De-Construction of History

My purpose in this section is to focus on two recent developments in the philosophy of history, which I am calling "narrativist constructions of history" and "poststructuralist deconstructions of history." Since narrativist constructions also presuppose a kind of "destruction"—namely of conventional historical realism and perhaps also of extratextual reference—the term *de-construction* can serve to identify both of these movements if the constructive as well as the destructive component is stressed, for example, by hyphenating the word. Both narrativist and poststructuralist approaches emerged in part from the breakdown of the analytic philosophies of history that reigned supreme from the mid-forties to the mid-sixties; and the latter, in turn, were at least in part a reaction to the revival of idealism in the work of R. G. Collingwood and his disciples (such as W. H. Walsh and T. M. Knox). Collingwood represented the awakening of a new interest in philosophy of history, and his influence continues to be felt, so it is helpful to start this section by looking briefly at him.

Our underlying question concerns the implications of the postmodern de-construction of history for a theological construal of historical process. One immediate implication is that the "weak," noncriterial relativism we found in Troeltsch becomes considerably stronger and decidedly criterial. If truths and values are actively constituted by a prevailing framework, context, or paradigm, it seems difficult to deny that the criteria for measuring truth and value are also relative to frameworks. This need not lead to the extreme position of incommensurability between frameworks, but it does mean that even when we understand and appreciate the criteria that are operative in other frameworks, we do so from our own perspective and in our own terms. Our terms and criteria are capable of being modified as they enter into dialogue with other world views, but we cannot assume that Troeltsch's all-embracing metaphysical perspectivism is already in place; it is, rather, something that is in process of being generated and constantly reshaped through dialogue. The implication of this for philosophy of history is that every construal of historical process is very much a relative, finite construct, one among many competing attempts to make sense of this or that range of historical experience, memory, evidence, texts, and so forth. To paraphrase Hegel (and modify his meaning), the only rationality that we find in history is the rationality that we bring to it—although the fact that we are continually bringing rationality to it (even if it is the rationality of irrationality) is not without significance. This kind of relativism seems to be a common assumption among all the parties to the current discussion of history. Theology will have to learn to live with it and accept it—and perhaps eventually even welcome it.

Recent Idealist and Analytic Approaches

Collingwood's influential work *The Idea of History*, written in the late 1930s but not published until 1946,[97] attempted to establish that history is a special form of thought, scientific in character, concerned with the actions of human beings in the past, proceeding by means of interpreting evidence, and undertaken for the sake of human self-knowledge.[98] Beyond this, Collingwood made three important and controversial claims. (1) History is the knowledge of mind. Human actions are not mere happenings but the expressions of thought, and the object of history is to discover these thoughts and understand them. It is not only a knowledge of what mind has done in the past but also a redoing of it, the perpetuation of past acts of mind in the present. History is the life of mind itself.[99]

(2) The work of the historian is autonomous and constructive. It is not dominated by memory and authorities but always goes beyond them critically and constructively, employing the "a priori imagination" to create a "web of imaginative construction," a constructed picture of the past, the test of which is its coherence and continuity, not its correspondence to presumed fixed points or data. Collingwood drew specifically the analogy between the historian and the novelist; both produce works of imagination, but the historian has the additional obligation that his or her picture should be "true," to which end certain methodological rules must be scrupulously followed.[100]

(3) History is the re-enactment of past experience. To discover a past thought, the historian must think it again for himself or herself. Insofar as we re-enact a thought, it becomes our own in a

linkage that transcends time. The gulf between the past and the present is bridged not only by the power of present thought to think of the past, but also by the power of past thought to reawaken itself in the present. In their respective immediacies, the thought of a past agent and the thought of the historian who rethinks this thought are different, but in their mediation they are the same. Thought "in its mediation" refers to its logic or argument, which can be developed and reproduced "either in Plato's mind or mine or anyone else's."[101]

Collingwood's third claim (which presupposes the first) goes a long way toward neutralizing the relativism of the second, and it has been widely criticized for issuing in an identity philosophy that robs history of genuine difference and overlooks the presence of irrational factors such as desire, passion, contingency, and accident. Despite this, the notion of "rethinking," or better, of "re-enacting," has played an important role in modern hermeneutics; and Collingwood's second point has been retrieved and further developed by current narrativist theories.

Analytic philosophy attacked Collingwood's basic assumption that history is a special form of thought and an autonomous science—an assumption he was presumed to share with (the mostly German) "speculative" philosophies of history, which distinguished the so-called human sciences (*Geisteswissenschaften*) from the natural sciences, and which drew a corresponding distinction between two modes of knowledge, understanding (*Verstehen*) and explanation (*Erklären*). The underlying assumption of analytic philosophy, by contrast—one it shared with the neopositivism of the Vienna Circle—is the unity of all science and the universal applicability of empirical method. On this basis Carl Hempel advanced his famous thesis that explanation in history does not differ substantially from explanation in the rest of science because all occurrences in history are governed or "covered" by general laws of universal applicability.[102]

Almost immediately, as Paul Ricoeur points out, partisans of the "covering law model" took up "the apologetic task of minimizing the discordances between the requirement of this 'strong' model and the specific features of historical knowledge.

The price was a 'weakening' of the model so as to ensure its viability."[103] Qualifications of one sort or another were introduced by such post-Hempel analysts as Morton White, Ernest Nagel, W. B. Gallie, William Dray, Patrick Gardiner, Charles Frankel, Alan Donagan, and Michael Scriven,[104] until the point was reached where the covering law model was severely compromised or even abandoned on analytic grounds. For example, Donagan concluded that explanations of historical actions are precisely not dependent on general laws but only on "law-like" statements that suffice to connect one happening with another and apply only to individual cases.[105] Scriven went further in contending that the "general laws of history" are only "probability truisms," and that the deductive method of Hempel entails only "probability inference." Nothing is gained for historical explanation by quoting truisms. Rather we "explain" historical events by means both of inductive judgments and of narrative structures comparable to the dramatic plot in a play or novel, structures which provide a kind of "depth plausibility" for events happening the way they do.[106]

Narrativist Constructions of History

1. Analytic Critiques. It was analytic philosophy, then, which first suggested that the distinctive logic of historical accounts is similar to that of narrative or dramatic fiction—a suggestion developed on a full scale for the first time by Arthur Danto in his *Analytic Philosophy of History* (1965). In an introduction to a new edition published twenty years later under a new title, *Narration and Knowledge,* Danto says that he was influenced not only by a growing consensus among analytic philosophers but also by the revolution in the philosophy of science caused by the work of N. R. Hanson and Thomas Kuhn; and he summarizes his general thesis as follows:

Narrative sentences . . . give descriptions of events under which the events could not have been witnessed, since they make essential reference to events later in time than the events they are about, and hence cognitively inaccessible to observers. . . . My

general point . . . was that narrative structures penetrate our
consciousness of events in ways parallel to those in which, in
Hanson's view, theories penetrate observations in science.[107]

He goes on to criticize what he regards as the illicit projection of
these narrative structures onto the fabric of history itself—a
confusion of *history* with a *historical text,* whereby the role of an
event in a narrative becomes the explanation of its occurrence.[108]
I find this to be an odd criticism, for it seems to presuppose that,
in addition to historical narratives, there are real (scientific?)
explanations of historical events. What is "history," ultimately,
other than the construction of historical texts—not only the texts
of later interpreters but also the (perspectivally quite different)
living texts of present agents, the constructions that we place
upon our own immediate experience, the agendas by which we
live individually and corporately? There simply is no fabric of
history that is not a product of this or that narrative weaving.

Just this is implicit, I think, in Louis O. Mink's claim that
historical understanding is an act of judgment in the Kantian
sense of the synthetic function of "grasping together" or
"comprehending" elements of experience in a meaningful structure. Contemporary agents constitute history by such acts of
judgment just as later historians interpret it. Thus according to
Mink, history "is not the writing, but the *rewriting* of stories," the
original stories having been written, or told, by participants and
observers—"original history" in Hegel's sense. The writing of
history or "reflective history" appears once the "game" of history is
over. The analogy (introduced by W. B. Gallie) of following a game
in progress is, in Mink's view, misleading. The historian rather
traces the lines of a story *backward* in order to establish an intelligible
pattern of relationships; "when we *tell* the story, we retrace forward
what we have already traced backward," thus eliminating the
contingency present in the actual occurrence of events.

This tracing and retracing of story lines requires, according to
Mink, a "configurational" act, which is one of three modes of
comprehension, the others being the theoretical and the
categorial. Comprehension in general is the act "of grasping

together in a single mental act things which are not experienced together . . . because they are separated by time, space, or logical kind." The configurational mode of comprehension differs from the other two because it puts its elements "into a single and concrete complex of relationships," and it is this that characterizes the narrative operation as practiced by writers of both fiction and history. The "comprehensive syntheses" at which historians aim have a practical, educative function: historians "are in a preeminent way the stewards of the funded wisdom of the race," and historical judgment "seems very like Aristotle's *phronēsis,* a kind of sagacity or 'practical wisdom.' " Although Mink does not express it quite this way, the historical syntheses configured in the historian's rewriting of stories have as their telos the writing of our own stories, the shaping of contemporary cultural syntheses in Troeltsch's sense.[109]

The most sophisticated interpretations thus far of historical texts (and implicitly also of historical process) in terms of "narrative configuration" have been advanced by Hayden White and Paul Ricoeur. And since their work is also more suggestive than that of other recent philosophies of history for theological interest (but without in any sense being explicitly theological), I shall focus attention on it.

2. Hayden White. We have already encountered White's brilliant book *Metahistory*[110] in our sections on the concept of figuration (ch. 2.3) and Hegel (ch. 3.1). His general thesis is that the historical work is "a verbal structure in the form of a narrative prose discourse that purports to be a model, or icon, of past structures and processes in the interest of *explaining what they were by representing* them."[111] He unpacks this definition by distinguishing among several "levels of conceptualization" in the historical work, and by showing how, at each level, various representational options are available among which the historian must choose consciously or unconsciously. The great advantage of this "ideal-typical" analysis of the structure of the historical work is that it relativizes all conceptualizations of historical method, whether "scientific," empirical, idealist, analytic, structuralist, deconstructionist, even narrativist, and dethrones all normative claims, whether aesthetic, ethical, religious, humanist, atheist. For it shows that every interpreter of the past makes conceptual decisions on ideological grounds at a metahistorical level. But just as every method and every validity claim is relativized, so each one is legitimated in the sense of being permitted to make its case in terms of its representational persuasiveness, with privileged epistemological position granted to none.

According to White, chronicle and story represent the "primitive elements" in the historical account, since they involve the selection and arrangement of data from the unprocessed historical record.[112] Judgments, however, respecting the meaning of the story come into play only at the next higher level of conceptualization, namely, "emplotment." Emplotment "is the way by which a sequence of events fashioned in a story is gradually revealed to be a story of a particular kind." The kind of story that it is helps to shape its meaning. White, following Northrop Frye, identifies four archetypal modes of emplotment, which seem to recur repeatedly in literature: romance, satire, tragedy, and comedy. Each of these has its own distinctive and typical dramatic resolution of the fate of the protagonist(s), and the fundamental logic of a narrative (historical or fictional) will be controlled by one or another of them, even though mixed types frequently occur. In romance the hero achieves a final liberation from the world of experience; for satire, as a drama of diremption and captivity, exactly the opposite is the case. Comedy offers hope for at least a temporary redemption of humanity from evil and a reconciliation of social and natural forces; while tragedy gives intimations of even more terrible conflicts, although a kind of reconciliation is achieved in the form of the recognition of and resignation to unalterable conditions.[113]

A further conceptual level in historical work is what White calls explanation by "formal argument." Here an explanation of what happens in a story is provided by invoking principles of coherence and combination, laws of cause and effect, and so forth. These principles or laws are grounded in "different metahistorical presuppositions about the nature of the historical field." At this level, according to White, history remains in a state of "conceptual anarchy" similar to that found in the natural sciences in the sixteenth century, suggesting that history is still a relatively young discipline or that the historical field by its nature resists strict scientific construals. White is convinced that the latter at least is the case; and, following Stephen Pepper, he identifies four basic paradigms for giving a conceptual account of historical reality: formist, organicist, mechanistic, and contextualist. Formism aims to identify the unique and unrepeatable characteristics of objects within the historical field; organicist world hypotheses are integrative, synthetic, holistic, and teleological; mechanistic ones are reductive and nomological; and contextualism proposes merely that events can be explained by being set within the context of their occurrence (it modestly brackets the problem of constructing a narrative model of historical processes through time). Among academic historians, the formist and contextualist models have prevailed while the others are viewed with suspicion. But White insists that there are no apodictic epistemological grounds for preferring one mode of explanation to another. The grounds rather are to be found in ethical, ideological opinions, often precritically held.[114]

This brings us to the final level of conceptualization, that of "ideological implication."

> There does, in fact, appear to be an irreducible ideological component in every historical account of reality. That is to say, simply because history is *not* a science, or is at best a protoscience with specifically determinable nonscientific elements in its constitution, the very claim to have discerned some kind of formal coherence in the historical record brings with it theories of the nature of the historical world and of historical knowledge itself which have ideological implications for attempts to understand "the present," however this "present" is defined.[115]

"Ideology," then, is "a set of prescriptions for taking a position in the present world of social praxis and acting upon it (either to change the world or to maintain it in its current state)."

Following Karl Mannheim, White identifies four basic ideological positions: anarchism, conservatism, radicalism, liberalism. With respect to the question of social change, conservatives view it through the analogy of "plantlike gradualizations" and liberals through that of "adjustments" to a mechanism; both are opposed to the necessity of structural transformations, as endorsed by radicals ("reconstituting society on new bases") and anarchists (the abolition of "society," substituting for it a new "community"). Similar differences emerge with respect to temporal process: gradual evolution, distant utopia, imminent utopia, idealization of a remote past. Although there are other, "authoritarian" positions as well, these four represent value systems that claim the authority of "reason," "science," or "realism," and thus are cognitively responsible. Everything else is ultimately grounded in these ideological commitments, according to White: "The ethical moment of a historical work [is] reflected in the mode of ideological implication by which an *aesthetic* perception (the emplotment) and a *cognitive* operation (the argument) can be combined so as to derive prescriptive statements from what may appear to be purely descriptive or analytical ones."[116]

Historiographical "styles" result, according to White, from particular combinations of the modes of emplotment, argument, and ideological implication. He tries to show, quite ingeniously, that there are "elective affinities" among these modes, affinities that also correlate with one or another of four basic "linguistic protocols" or figures of speech that underlie all discourse: metaphor, metonymy, synecdoche, and irony. This can be illustrated by the following table:[117]

Figures of Speech	Modes of Emplotment	Modes of Argument	Modes of Ideological Implication
Metaphor	Romantic	Formist	Anarchist
Metonymy	Tragic	Mechanistic	Radical
Synecdoche	Comic	Organicist	Conservative
Irony	Satirical	Contextualist	Liberal

Metaphor establishes analogical similarities; metonymy reduces entities to being functions of one another; synecdoche envisions integrated wholes; and irony negates in the figurative dimension what is affirmed in the literal. In a prefigurative "poetic" act based on one or another of these protocols, the historian constitutes the domain of analysis and "predetermines the modality of the conceptual strategies he will use to explain it." Of course these modalities do not exist in airtight compartments, and the elective affinities among them are not rigid or necessary. In fact, the greatest historians and philosophers of history achieved dialectic tension through nonaffinitive combinations.[118] The four typological sets and their affinities, as established by White's formal analysis—namely, figures of speech, narrative emplotment, formal argument, and ideological implication—do not determine any particular historical style but rather provide suggestive categories by which a particular historian's strategy can be identified and assessed.

In sum: the construction of a historical narrative is rooted in a largely preconscious aesthetic intuition of how language "figures" thought and reality, and it issues in specific (if often uncritical) ideological or ethical commitments. Which is more basic, we may ask, the aesthetic or the ethical? At the end of his work, White says that "we are driven back to moral and aesthetic reasons for the choice of one vision [of history] over another." Despite his attraction to the aesthetic and the profound influence on him of literary analysis, the moral choice appears finally to be the more critical one for White. On purely aesthetic grounds, there is no reason to seek a "way beyond irony" (which is the most sophisticated of the tropes), but on ethical grounds there is a reason, which has to do with a vision of human emancipation and the urgency of a transformative social praxis. White does not say this directly. He says only that the "formalism" of his approach to the history of historical thought makes use of irony in order to provide grounds for a transcendence of it; and it needs to be transcended because of its "inherent skepticism," "moral agnosticism," and pretensions of

scholarly objectivity and neutrality.[119] A moral urgency trans-
fuses White's aesthetic sensibilities.

But what grounds the ethical? On what grounds can we say
that a vision of human emancipation is the "truth" about human
being? I think White is correct to insist that there are no higher
theoretical grounds, no "extra-ideological grounds," on the basis
of which to choose among competing views of history and
human existence.[120] Just this is the "crisis of historicism." But this
crisis also marks the "turn to praxis," for it is only by acting, by
engaging in projects of emancipatory praxis, that we shall
discover whether the vision is "true." Praxis alone has the power
to resolve the impasse of historical relativism.

But praxis also discloses the horizon of something else, a
religious dimension to human existence, a condition about the
historical world that renders it a possible place in which to dwell
humanly. This religious dimension, when thematized conceptually, becomes a "theology," a theology of history. Such a theology
is not, of course, an "extra-ideological" ground of truth; rather,
it becomes part of the ideological matrix on which narrative
construals of the past and ethical commitments of the present
are based. It is my view that the ideological matrix is incomplete
without the religious dimension—that the aesthetic, the ethical,
and the religious are interlocking components of a feasible
world view. White's various modes of emplotment, argument,
and implication raise profoundly religious questions, but he
does not discuss them as such.

Nevertheless, we can make use of White's hermeneutic model
to analyze religious and theological options. Any Christian
interpretation of existence must find a way beyond irony, which
if unchecked will issue in skepticism or nihilism, and its basic
mode of emplotment cannot be either satirical or tragic,
although it must incorporate tragedy, not bypass it. Its basic
vision is comic, or better, tragicomic, although one finds versions
of Christianity that are romantic. Religious discourse employs all
the figures of speech, but one or another is likely to
predominate; yet if irony predominates consistently, it is likely to
destroy religious belief. We can find theologies that illustrate

each of the modes of argument and of ideological implication identified by White. The theology of the history of freedom I shall set forth in chapters 4 and 5 employs a tragicomic emplotment of the Christian story, works with an organicist model of historical reality modified in the direction of formism and perhaps also contextualism, and embraces both radical and liberal ideologies, favoring one or another on strategic grounds relating to emancipatory praxis. Beneath this, of course, is a particular construal of the essential meaning of Christian faith, which I cannot justify in advance on the basis of appeals to authority or privileged experience, but only argumentatively in terms of its representational persuasiveness within a community of discourse. The same is true of any theological proposal.

3. Paul Ricoeur. The introduction of ethical and religious questions establishes a point of contact with Ricoeur's analysis of the complex connections between narrativity and temporality. We have discussed in some detail his theory of a "threefold mimesis" at work in every narrative emplotment: prefiguration (a reference back to the preunderstood world of action), configuration (the realm of poetic composition proper), and refiguration (a reference forward to a newly configured world of the text in which human beings might dwell).[121] We have observed that Ricoeur, like White, establishes a connection between narrative construction (configuration) and ethical action (prefiguration and refiguration). But for Ricoeur this does not involve a shift in conceptual levels of explanation as it does for White, but rather a movement implicit in the text itself—the movement from *mimēsis* to *praxeōs*, from narrative to action, from sense to reference, from meaning to truth, from text to world.

Assuming now that historical texts exhibit a narrative form and construct an integrated temporal sequence of events, a "plot," it is important to ask what differences, if any, attach to historical as opposed to fictional narratives. If history merely constructs and projects a fictional world, then it can impose no empirical checks on the imagination of the artist, and it can provide no historical basis, no resources rooted in tradition, for ethical decisions and religious claims. This would clearly be a devastating impoverishment.

Despite his deep conviction regarding the "ultimately narrative character of history" in all its forms, Ricoeur also insists that there is only an indirect derivative connection between history and narrative, and that history itself is a "mixed" form of discourse. History cannot be regarded as simply a species of the genus story (W. B. Gallie). A "break" between the two is found at the point of both epistemological procedures and noetic intention. With respect to the first, history is essentially inquiry or research, and its explanatory methods have an autonomy vis-à-vis the explanations immanent in a narrative plot. "Singular causal attribution," as analysts like Donagan have argued, is the characteristic mode of explanation in history, mediating between explanation by covering law and understanding by emplotment. Moreover, as the *Annales* school of French historiography has pointed out, the objects of inquiry or "historical entities" are distinct from the subjects of narrative action;[122] and the long time-spans of historical time differ from the singularity and contingency of narrative time and the compacted presence of lived time. In brief, the historian works with *quasi*-plots, *quasi*-characters, and *quasi*-events. With respect to noetic intention, history refers to an already structured, extant, objective cultural world, and not to the immediate, subjective experience of living agents or the imaginary world of the artist.[123]

Both historical and fictional narrative are oriented to praxis, that is, to a "refiguration" of the human temporal condition.[124] Refiguration, says Ricoeur, means "the power of revelation and transformation achieved by narrative configurations when they are 'applied' to actual acting and suffering."[125] History and fiction produce "poetically" a resolution to the aporias of time—the tension or discordance between the immensity of cosmic time, which is a succession of indifferent instants, and the lived time of individuals in its compacted presence, burdened by the past and anxious about the future—a resolution that speculation is powerless to contribute. But history and fiction do so in different ways, and indeed the difference between them deepens with the passage from configuration to refiguration. History is oriented to reconstructions of the past—which is represented in the present in the form of documentary traces, calendar time, and the succession of generations—by reinscribing lived time upon cosmic time. Fiction, by contrast, invents imaginative variations with respect to the cosmic reinscriptions effected by history, unconstrained by the reality references of the latter. Its reference is metaphorical rather than through "traces of the real."

In fiction, the imaginary *"empowers* the common temporal experience, lightens the burdens of the debt toward people of the past, and thus liberates in human acting and suffering the possibilities that were blocked or aborted."[126] In brief, fiction "derealizes," breaks the bondage of the real, thus opening up new historical possibilities. When one *acts* on the basis of an imaginative variation, a new direction is wrought into the reality of history, and history itself changes. But the converse also holds: what is changed must be actual human history, the actual past, the actual human condition. Thus to accomplish its aim, fiction must borrow from history just as history borrows from fiction. To put it in Hegelian terms, the ideal must be riveted to the real, and the real to the ideal. Where they intersect in the "crossed-reference" or "interweaving" of history and fiction, we discover what Ricoeur calls "human time" and Hegel "the expression of spirit in time."[127]

We also discover at this point, I shall argue, God's presence in history. It is found in the interweaving of actual condition and new possibility, of prefiguration and refiguration, of real and ideal, of fact and fiction. The fabric of history, of human temporality, is constituted by this interweaving. But yet—the fabric as we know it is not whole and it does not exhibit a uniform pattern. It is rather a crazy patchwork, with holes and loose threads that threaten to unravel. The "plot" of God's saving presence in history is much more complex than once we thought.[128] The story is labyrinthine and unfinished: we are in the midst of it; all of our constructions are fragmentary and ambiguous; "salvation history" is at best a highly discordant concordance. Instead of traces of God's presence in history, we may experience only traces of an absence, as we are reminded by the poststructuralists.

Poststructuralist Deconstructions of History

What is deconstructed is not simply our various construals or constructions of history but ultimately history itself. History is displaced by something else, which is not "history" in any recognizable (Western, rationalist, empirical, narrativist) sense. For example: in place of history we have abyss (Derrida), or genealogy (Foucault), or fiction (Taylor), or unreason (Gillespie). The operative trope for each is irony, and the mode of emplotment is either satiric (Derrida and Taylor) or tragic (Foucault and Gillespie). This thesis is undoubtedly oversimplified, and it is narrowly focused on one issue and a few thinkers; but it helps to make the point that postmodernism poses a far more severe "crisis of historicism" than anything Troeltsch envisioned. It is a crisis in which the very category "history" disappears, to say nothing of the categories "God" and "freedom." If we are foolish enough to continue speaking of "God in history" and "shapes of freedom," we must attempt to work our way through this cognitive purgatory, not avoid it, for what gives it such force is the real purgatory—the disintegration and terrors—of the postmodern world. A far harder labor is required of us than anything Hegel envisioned. Clearly we are not equal to the task, but at this point there is no turning back.

1. History as Abyss: Derrida.[129] In a programmatic essay that opened the current deconstruction debate,[130] Jacques Derrida undertook to "decenter" discourse by establishing that there is "no origin, no end, no place outside discourse from which to fix, make determinate, and establish metaphysical boundaries for the play of linguistic signifiers."[131] Language is a closed system of signs, and every sign is but an interpretation of other signs. Derrida views Western thought as having been "governed by the positing of a metaphysical presence which abides through various fictive appellations, from subject to substance to *eidos* to *archē* to *telos,* transcendentality, conscience, structure, man, or the ultimate fiction of God."[132] The effect of deconstruction is to decenter this referential structure, empty the world of any metaphysical presence, leaving only "an endless labyrinth without an outlet."[133] History is this labyrinth, a labyrinthine abyss,[134] whose only "structure" is that imposed by the "structurality" of texts.

The consequences of this decentering, according to Lentricchia,[135] are, first, an unqualified "free-play" of signifiers, unrestrained by any reference to a signified; and second, a "hermeneutical violence" by which one chain of signifiers is substituted for another. The first of these consequences points in the direction of a "new hedonism," an orientation to pleasure, joy, and freedom generated by allowing language to play with itself endlessly—a nihilistic play precisely because of its formalism, its assumption of the absence of any objective frame of reference. This is the direction taken by some of the American Derrideans.[136] The second consequence points in a different direction, the one taken (despite a certain ambivalence) by Derrida himself, who has said that his purpose is not so much to deny the center as to show that it is a function of signification, nor is it to deny the signifying subject but rather to situate it. It is situated within the historicity of discourse, which is now called "intertextuality." What does this situatedness reveal? It reveals, according to Lentricchia,

> the nonontological reincarceration of the signifier within cultural matrices which, though themselves subject to difference and change, nevertheless in their moment of power, use the signifier, take hold of it, establish dominance over it in order to create truth, value, and rationality, and then violently set these *in place* as norms, coercive contexts for expression, meaning, and sanity that claim for themselves eternality and universality, even though these norms will themselves be displaced in time by new structures of domination.[137]

Thus violence and domination rule the abyss, and it is all too easy to withdraw from it revulsively into an aestheticism of linguistic play, leaving the social world to fend for itself. Of course one has no alternative other than to play the power-game oneself, so one does play it (in the academic or literary or commercial world, or wherever one is situated) to the best of one's personal advantage. The only stable "value" appears to be self-interest, self-preservation, self-advancement—that is, narcissism. Anything else is pious illusion.

2. *History as Genealogy: Foucault.* The second direction indicated by deconstruction, leading to a "hermeneutics of violence," has been brilliantly elaborated by Michel Foucault. In the first chapter,[138] I attempted to show how, for Foucault, history is displaced by "archeology" or "genealogy"—terms that seem to have closely related functions. Archeology unearths "discourses" in their specificity and irreducibility,[139] whereas genealogy traces the distinctive "descent" and "emergence" of events. Genealogy, says Foucault in his essay on Nietzsche,

> must record the singularity of events outside of any monotonous finality; it must seek them in the most unpromising places, in what we tend to feel is without history, . . . not in order to trace the gradual curve of their evolution, but to isolate the different scenes where they engaged in different roles. . . . Genealogy . . . rejects the metahistorical deployment of ideal significations and indefinite teleologies. It opposes itself to the search for "origins."[140]

With respect to origins, it is an illusion to suppose that they reveal the purest essence or identity of things, and in their place genealogy is concerned with what Nietzsche called "descent" (*Herkunft*) and "emergence" (*Entstehung*). The analysis of descent displaces the self as an empty synthesis and attaches rather to the body, exposing it as "a body totally imprinted by history and the process of history's destruction of the body." Emergence is produced through "a particular stage of forces," their eruption, interaction, and struggle. Only a "single drama" is ever staged in the process of emergence, "the endlessly repeated play of dominations," "the staging of meticulously repeated scenes of violence."[141] Genealogy becomes, then, as we have said, a hermeneutics of violence. To what end, however, this unrelenting violence is exposed by Foucault is not clear. There seems no prospect of ameliorating or reversing it by raising our consciousness of it; we are fated only to repeat it; the genealogist's work seems at most to be an expression of cold fury, a despairing protest at the futility and sadness of it all. Perhaps it is only that we are required to be uncompromisingly honest about the human condition and the Western "logocentric" structure that conceals it—to create, for the sake of integrity if not redemption, an "internal disturbance."[142]

But another hermeneutical possibility may be resident in Foucault's genealogical archeology. It has at first, he says, a negative work, namely, to suspend the various strategies for unity and continuity.

> We must renounce all those themes whose function is to ensure the infinite continuity of discourse and its secret presence to itself in the interplay of a constantly recurring absence. We must be ready to receive every moment of discourse in its sudden irruption; in that punctuality in which it appears, and in that temporal dispersion that enables it to be repeated, known, forgotten, transformed, utterly erased. . . . These pre-existing forms of continuity, all these syntheses that are accepted without question, must remain in suspense. . . . We must show that they do not come about of themselves, but are always the result of a construction the rules of which must be known, and the justifications of which must be scrutinized.[143]

Once this has been done, "an entire field is set free," a field "made up of the totality of all effective statements (whether spoken or written), in their dispersion as events and in the occurrence that is proper to them." We are led therefore, concludes Foucault, to "the project of a *pure description of discursive events* as the horizon for the search for the unities that form within it."[144]

Reflecting upon these statements, I am led to the following question: when the field is set free, when all the immanent, finite, humanly contrived unities are suspended (those based on subjectivity, categories, projects, books, *oeuvres*, and so on), when history becomes a series of infinite *dis*continuities, when all that we experience is the interplay of a constantly recurring absence—is it not then possible that something new appears as the ground of history? It appears not as the ground of a totalizing, developmental teleology, but as the ground of those partial, fragmentary, disconnected, transient, tiny, yet transforming configurations that enable history to go on at all in the midst of the vast discontinuities; configurations that enable renewals, rebirths, fresh starts to take place, that prevent human life from disintegrating into sheer meaninglessness, that spark a however modest emancipatory praxis in the midst of the scenes of domination. What constitutes this ground? Can it be a human self-presence, which is finally powerless in the face of the constantly recurring absence and the overpowering discontinuities, any more than it can be a hypostatized, repressive metaphysical presence? If a liberating ground appears at all, does it not signify what we are calling God's presence in history? For Foucault, of course, it does not appear. But perhaps he has cleared the field in which it *might* appear.

3. *History as Fiction: Taylor.* Mark Taylor, as we have seen, explicitly announces the "end of history" as one of the consequences of the "unraveling" of the Western theological network; in its place appears "mazing grace," the "grace that arrives only when God and self are dead and history is over."[145] History has come to its end because the plot of Western history (the salvation history plot) has been deconstructed. That is, it has been exposed in a twofold sense: on the one hand, it is grounded in a specious theological "logocentrism"[146] with its logic of domination, triumph, and saving presence; on the other hand, the plot is not ingredient in actual states of affairs but is purely a product of imaginative construction. These two exposés dovetail nicely for Taylor. The philosophical critique of a teleological history of salvation is reinforced by a narrativist literary analysis which shows that history is in any event a work of fiction. In arguing this case, Taylor draws upon many of the same resources I have discussed in the preceding pages, and I have in

several respects pursued a similar line of argument. The problem from my point of view is that Taylor's case is overstated and thus finally loses credibility.

On the one hand, Taylor overstates the totalizing tendencies of the classic theological model of history. It can scarcely be accused in blanket fashion of "denying" death, ignoring ambiguity, seeking "total presence," imposing "pleromatic conformity," weaving everything into a "seamless web," and so on.[147] The theological tradition does not need to be informed by us that "absolute plenitude and total presence are nowhere to be found." On the other hand, Taylor understates the important distinctions that must be established between historical and fictional narrative, while indeed recognizing that they both employ imaginative narrative constructions. In appealing to Collingwood, White, and Ricoeur, as I have done, as well as to Jonathan Culler, Frank Kermode, J. Hillis Miller, Wallace Stevens, and other literary critics, Taylor stresses only the similarities between history and fiction but not the differences. "To say that history is an 'imaginative construction' is not to imply that it is 'unreal.' The fanciful dimension of history does, however, suggest that 'reality' is, in some sense, imaginative. The careful examination of history subverts the sharp distinction between historical fact and fiction."[148] The question is whether reality is in any sense *not* imaginative, or whether *any* distinction remains between fact and fiction. Although Taylor leaves the impression that history and fiction are not simply identical, he never specifies what the differences are, and the basic thrust of his argument concerning the "end of history" is to demolish any difference. Life is "an endgame in which one tries to kill time by telling stories."[149] It then becomes a question of whose stories are more personally and aesthetically satisfying.[150] Questions of reality, of real historical reference, are brushed aside.

4. History as Unreason: Gillespie. Our very partial survey of deconstructionist interpretations of history ends with Michael Gillespie's study of history in Hegel and Heidegger.[151] Gillespie, a political scientist, is not strictly a deconstructionist in the sense of having been shaped by poststructuralist literary criticism or recent French philosophy. But he has been deeply influenced by Nietzsche and Heidegger and reads Hegel's philosophy of history in a deconstructionist direction.

Gillespie argues that Hegel's absolute, which serves as the "ground of history" because it is the final synthesis of freedom and nature, subjective and objective, noumenal and phenomenal, rests upon a logical illusion (the unity of being and nothing in becoming) or a tautology (absolute knowledge equals self-consciousness). I will not attempt to assess the validity of Gillespie's critique (although I doubt seriously whether it can be demonstrated that either an illusion or a tautology lies at the heart of Hegel's system); rather I want to look at the conclusion he draws from it. The dissolution of Hegel's ground

> points to what is perhaps the real truth, that consciousness is *not* fundamental, and hence that reason does *not* permeate all reality but rests upon an underlying darkness that is the true source of human motion and life. The 150 years since Hegel's death have witnessed the ascendancy of this darkness. . . . Who today after Nietzsche and Freud, after Hitler and Stalin, after Verdun and Dachau can still believe in the triumph of reason? How can we avoid the conclusion that not reason but unreason rules in history?[152]

This conclusion may be correct, Gillespie continues, but it is not necessarily correct. We do not in fact know whether the ground of history is reason or unreason or perhaps a mysterious mixture of the two. We know only that the human condition is an endless striving, which never arrives at its goal but is rather a "circular process that continually finds and continually loses its perfection." Hegel then *may* "provide a distant ray of hope to guide us on our long voyage through the dark night of nihilism."[153] Heidegger's embrace of nihilism as a true revelation of being, while an intriguing alternative, may ultimately only lend support to the malignant spiritual and political forces that it seeks to overcome. Thus, Gillespie concludes, the question of the ground of history remains open and the threat of nihilism ever-present in our time.[154]

4. History as De-Configurative Process

I shall now attempt to draw together into a more systematic statement the hints toward a construal of historical process scattered throughout this chapter. These hints will be elaborated in seven connected steps: (1) the constructive character of historical interpretation; (2) the relative and the absolute in history; (3) the quest for a way beyond irony-tragedy; (4) configurative elements of historical process; (5) defigurative elements of historical process; (6) the ambiguity of historical process; (7) the open teleology of historical process.

The analysis of history contained in this chapter has the character of a "formal philosophy of history," as compared with the "material theology of history" to be developed in the next two chapters. The transition in view is not only from the formal to the material but also from philosophy to theology. Theological and ethical claims, as well as questions of ultimacy, truth, and value, have remained for the most part bracketed in the present chapter, and continue to remain so in this concluding section.[155] The brackets will be removed with the turn from philosophical reflection about history as a "de-configurative process" (ch. 3) to theological argument about the history of freedom as a "transfigurative praxis" (chs. 4–5). Theology is a kind of "fiction" that invents imaginative variations on what history offers as "real." It thus takes one step further the constructive impulse already present in historical interpretation.

The Constructive Character of Historical Interpretation

It is a matter of broad consensus among philosophers of history, if not among historians themselves, that every work of historical interpretation entails a "narrative construction" in one form or another. This construction is the product of the "a priori imagination," which, in Collingwood's terms, weaves a "web of imaginative construction," the test of which is its coherence, continuity, and persuasiveness, not simply its correspondence to empirical data.[156] It may not be going too far to suggest that "history" ultimately is nothing other than the construction of historical texts—meaning thereby both the living, enacted "texts" of historical agents, who make sense of and contribute to their particular historical locus by construing and shaping it one way or another (what Hegel called "original history"), and the subsequent, "scientific" texts of professional historians who investigate and write about a particular segment of the past (Hegel's "reflective history"). Beyond this, as White points out, every historical interpreter makes linguistic, aesthetic, and conceptual decisions on ideological grounds at a metahistorical level (Hegel's "philosophical history").

The ontological status of "history," then, is that of an imaginative construct, made in accord with ideological convictions, which must always be renewed, reenacted, rethought. Its ontological status reflects the peculiar temporal status of the past, which does not "exist" somewhere except in the form of "traces"—artifacts, documents, sedimented traditions and memories, calendar time, the succession of generations—and these of themselves are scarcely what we mean by "history"; rather, they are the materials out of which history is fashioned. Recognition of this fact should guard against apodictic assertions concerning "proper" and "improper" presuppositions and methods of historical interpretation. The latter must be articulated and defended, but the only validity tests are those of representational persuasiveness and ethical implication. Certainly more than one construal of historical process as a whole, as well of specific historical sequences, is valid, and all such construals must be recognized to be relative, finite, partial, and contingent.

We must of course insist, with Collingwood, Mink, and Ricoeur, upon the differences as well as the similarities between historical and fictional narrative. The former, which is based on inquiry or research concerning past happenings, must attend to rules of evidence and develop distinctive explanatory methods, which are not simply borrowed from natural science or narrative emplotment. We must avoid the uncritical, convenient conclusion that history simply "is" fiction.

The Relative and the Absolute in History

Despite the latter distinction, historical interpretation appears to be afloat in a sea of relativism. Indeed, the fate of every interpretation of history is finally to be overtaken by that very process it investigates, the process of historical becoming and change. The only possibility of "overcoming" history is by means of history itself.[157] But this statement means that we are not helpless in the face of historical relativism, even as there is no escape from it.

It is perhaps useful to distinguish between types of historical relativism, as Coakley does in her analysis of Troeltsch. As we have seen, the types she distinguishes are relationalism, noncriterial epistemological relativism, criterial relativism, and contextual incommensurability. The first holds merely that truth is related to a context; the second that propositions are actually true relative to a specific framework; the third that the criteria of truth and value are also relative to frameworks; and the last that frameworks are so different that their truth claims are incommensurable or mutually incomprehensible. Although Troeltsch may have flirted with the last two types, according to Coakley, his mature position is basically that of the second type.

It does appear, however, that once one admits to epistemological relativism, it is difficult to avoid the conclusion that not only propositions but also criteria are relative to specific frameworks. Criteria are instruments of knowledge, and the basic claim of epistemological relativism is that all knowledge is relative to frameworks or paradigms. But if the criteria of truth and value are relative, does not this imply that truth and value themselves are relative?

Yes, of course they are; but this admission does not require us to deny at the same time the "absoluteness" of truth and value. Truth, if it is truth, must be "absolute," that is, open, whole, universal, unconcealing, "absolving" or liberating from whatever is concealed, parochial, closed in. Truth not only is expressed in frameworks but also transcends frameworks, loosens their boundaries, expands their categories, modifies their particular, partial, and fragmentary criteria. If this were not the case, we should have to conclude, as many do, that there really is no such thing as "truth" or "value," only opinions, views, emotions, or mind-sets ("bliks"[158]). It is not inconsistent with our affirmation of the absoluteness and oneness of truth that we should admit to knowing it only partially, in many different forms and categories, according to different criteria. We do not have absolute knowledge of the absolute, but it does not cease for this reason to be the absolute. Or as Troeltsch expressed it: "A truth which, in the first instance, is *a truth for us* does not cease, because of this, to be very truth and life."[159] If we are to speak of a relativism *of truth and value*, and not of mere relativism, he observed, then there must *be* "an absolute that is vital and creative within the relative," "a life-process of the absolute in which the absolute itself can be grasped and shaped from every point of view and in a fashion corresponding to each point of view."[160]

The absolute, then, is not something static and unchanging, but precisely something that is itself relative in the sense that it both shapes and is shaped by specific points of view and situations. We observed earlier in our discussion of Hegel that the word *absolute* derives from the Latin *absolvere*, meaning "to loosen (*solvere*) from (*ab*)," hence "to release," "to set free." The conventional notion of the absolute is of something that itself is absolved from or independent of everything finite and relative. As opposed to this passive or intransitive sense of "absolute," however, we can also think of it as active or transitive in a twofold sense: (1) it releases or sets free from itself everything finite, determinate, historical; (2) it loosens or opens up everything that is limited, enclosed, constraining within the finite and historical (including culturally bound perspectives).[161] Precisely in virtue of this activity, as opposed to a passive aseity, the absolute itself is what is utterly free in and for itself. And because of its utter freedom, it is free also to enter "absolvingly" into every relationship without losing itself, releasing the other to be free and independent, opening relationships up, generating imaginative variations and new possibilities. Thus, what is truly absolute is also truly relative, utterly free and utterly freeing. This further dimension of absoluteness was not recognized until modern times, beginning with Hegel. Its recognition means that we are not required to choose between absoluteness and relativity as though these were abstractly opposed and mutually negating qualities.

Nor are we required, by the admission of criterial relativism, to conclude that cultural frameworks and epistemological paradigms are so different as to be mutually incomprehensible or impermeable. We are in fact able to grasp and appreciate, if initially only in our own terms, the criteria operative in, and the apprehensions of truth and value available to, other frameworks, which implies an openness or accessibility between frameworks, perhaps even a degree of consensus or convergence among them which in no way dilutes their differences; and this in turn implies something about the ultimate conditions of possibility of human discourse and communication, even if we are reluctant to flesh this out in the form of a "metaphysical perspectivism."

My conclusion, therefore, is that even a criterial relativism does not exclude the possibility of knowing and especially of practicing the truth in specific and often quite different historical contexts. I have argued that the test of truth is more likely to be pragmatic than theoretical. The fact that the pragmatic test works reasonably well confirms the absoluteness of truth, its absolving power. Thus while admitting to a more radical form of relativism than Troeltsch did, I am convinced that his stance, oriented as it was to praxis, and affirming the dialectical relationship between the absolute and the relative, remains sound.

The Quest for a Way Beyond Irony-Tragedy

The struggle against the enervating effects of an undialectical, unlimited relativism (or what Troeltsch called "spurious historicism")[162] is closely related to the quest for a way beyond an ironic approach to history with its accompanying tragic (or satiric) vision. We have seen Hegel's warning against nihilistic complacency in face of the "confusion and wreckage" of history, and Troeltsch's warning against pessimism and skepticism in face of the decline and fall of civilizations—warnings recently echoed by Hayden White, who recognizes the danger of "moral agnosticism" on the part of allegedly objective and neutral scholarship. In the kind of world in which we live, moral agnosticism readily becomes a tool in the hands of immoral, evil forces. The stakes are too high to allow us the luxury of not seeking a way beyond irony and tragedy.

But in seeking a way beyond them, we cannot simply avoid them; rather we have no choice but to work our way through them. For, as we have seen, tragedy is an undeniable dimension of every historical action since negative as well as positive consequences flow from it, conflicts between interests are unavoidable, and every achievement, no matter how glorious, is partial and transient, eventually doomed to destruction. We walk, as Hegel said, among "the ruins of excellence,"[163] and the recognition of this fact is surely ironic.

My own attempt to find a way beyond irony and tragedy by moving through them results in a vision of history as a "tragicomic de-configurative process." I have indicated why I do not accept the Hegelian tendency to locate comedy at the level of macrohistory and tragedy at the level of concrete events. Rather, the whole of history at all levels is at once tragic and comic. The notion of "de-configurative process" attempts to capture and expand upon this insight.

Configurative Elements of Historical Process

For Hegel the dynamism of world-process is not a formless flux but an active process of forming. Historical becoming is inherently a process of structuring or shaping, configuring (*Gestaltung*). Hegelian dialectic, as William Desmond points out, "is the principle of the articulation of this structuring."[164] We have observed that in historical process, as Hegel envisioned it, this dialectic appears as a weaving together of crossed threads, ideal and real, universal and particular—the idea of freedom, on the one hand, and human activity or passion, on the other. The former is what inwardly impels history toward its end, while the latter is the historical bearer or instrument of the idea. An interaction takes place between these two factors, generating new and unique but always partial syntheses, concrete historical shapes or figures (*Gestalten*), which we call "events" and "personalities." This is the historical form of the logical dialectic of universal-particular-individual. The universal offers the ideal possibility for a new configuration, while the particular provides the material conditions from which it is fashioned in terms of both data from the past and human energy and motivation. The partial character of each configuration ensures its own eventual dissolution, its defiguration, its return to the soil of history, so that the configuring process is driven on to ever-new shapes in a progressive teleology of spirit.

This Hegelian vision of historical process, which I have elaborated here in terms that go somewhat beyond Hegel himself,[165] was adopted and modified by Troeltsch, according to whom, as we have seen, new cultural syntheses, on both large and small scales, are continually being created in history, generated out of two sources—rational norms and ethical ideals, on the one hand, and individual historical exigencies and actions, on the other. Without this process of "damming and shaping," the "historical stream of life" would dissipate into a formless chaos or be subjected to a harsh tyranny. Fragile syntheses achieve relative victories over chaos and tyranny, for the most part through a process of "creative compromise." But the future is open and the outcome of the process is uncertain.

For both Hegel and Troeltsch, the shaping, synthesizing process has something to do with the creation and enhancement of human freedom, individual and social. Whether there is an overarching teleology of freedom in history is a matter of dispute between them. In this dispute I think we must ultimately agree with Troeltsch: although specific cultural trajectories may be discernible, it cannot be said that history as a whole is moving toward the consummation of freedom, or that it has even arrived at a clear and complete consciousness of what freedom is. It is enough to be able to say that momentary shapes of freedom do occur, and partial integrations of historical life are attained, again and again despite constant adversity, and that we can rejoice in their occurrence while recognizing their transience and limitation. This is the comic element of history. I shall return to it in chapters 4 and 5 where, with the removal of the formal philosophical brackets, I shall attempt to speak more directly about the ground and end of history and the material content of the shaping process.

Defigurative Elements of Historical Process

The term *defigurative* as I propose to use it has both a dialectical and an ethical component. Dialectically it means the breakdown of a configuration or the negation of a synthesis, the deconstruction of a construction. Ethically it carries the connotation of "disfigurement," namely, mutilation, deface-ment, destruction, especially by brutal, violent means. Evil enters the historical process at this point, although evil is not to be confused with dialectical negation as such. The latter might be regarded as one of the conditions of possibility of evil, but evil itself introduces something more, a disruption or despoiling of the process. My primary concern here is with the dialectical component; to do justice to the ethical component would require a separate and detailed treatment.

A careful examination of Hegel's dialectic as applied to historical process shows that he directs as much if not more attention to the deconstructive moment as to the constructive. As we have seen, the key category of history as a whole for Hegel is that of "transition" (*Übergang*), which involves discontinuity, rupture, and breaks just as much as it does continuity and preservation. History does not for Hegel "evolve" in a seamless, uninterrupted progression of forms, each emerging out of the other in an organic-like process; rather the negativity of temporal passage intervenes between forms, occasioning "transformations" or "transfigurations." Moreover, two of

Hegel's three interpretative categories for cultural history are negational or deconstructive. The three are: "formation" (*Bildung*), "over-refinement" (*Überbildung*), and "degeneration" (*Verbildung*); and it is worth noting that most of a culture's life is spent in the second and third stages.[166] Other deconstructive categories can be added from Troeltsch's formal logic of history: originality, uniqueness, breakthrough, and the role of the unconscious, chance, and contingency.[167] The latter three in particular are lacking in Hegel and point to a dimension of history of which we have become much more profoundly aware since Nietzsche and Freud.

William Desmond helpfully explains the prominence of negation and differentiation in Hegel's dialectic and its affinity to deconstruction. An exclusive logic of "either A or not-A" is unable to account for the nature of being as becoming. Becoming "is a process in which a thing in time becomes *other* to its former shape, while yet in this process of differentiation remaining itself." For Hegel, everything is itself and also other, which is to say that its identity is "determinate," defined by an inherent process of differentiation. Univocal language cannot grasp this complex process, but dialectical language can. Dialectic follows the flow of development "by which an initial unity, seemingly simple and hard set, breaks itself up into polarities, antitheses, oppositions."[168]

> The comparison [of dialectic] with deconstruction is striking. Thinking makes war upon itself. It generates itself and drives itself forward by contradicting itself, creating itself anew out of the destruction of its own previous, partial forms. . . . Each configuration (*Gestalt*) of consciousness disfigures itself, each form deforms itself, every construction deconstructs itself under the relentless power of the "negative."[169]

But, continues Desmond, "for Hegel, after deconstruction, dialectic opens up to a moment of reconstitution." Negation is itself possible only on the condition of something positive, a preservation of what has been negated in a new synthesis, which is a "complex unity immanently differentiated, a dialectical unity," which embraces both univocal unity and equivocal differences. It is striking that Hegel defined the absolute as precisely "the identity of identity and difference." The complex unity of the absolute is "absolute because it is *absolving*, freeing, not just dissolving. It absolves us, as it were, from the sense of difference as sheer hostile opposition, the animosity of the mutually negating dualisms said to beset the western tradition."[170]

This suggestive play on the root sense of the word *absolute* points to a Hegelian way beyond deconstruction, a way beyond construction and deconstruction to reconstruction, or, in our terms, beyond configuration and defiguration to transfiguration. For us to follow this path will require moving beyond a formal philosophy of history to a material theology of history. Desmond is helpful as we prepare to make this move. He suggests that Hegelian dialectic is capable of a double interpretation, one tending to closure, the other more open-ended. Dialectical thinking can be seen as either "*encapsulating* the *structure* of a process of becoming" or as "*participating* itself in the active *structuring* of such a process." On the second, "open" reading of Hegel, the absolute is not an "empty conceptual unity of totalitarian thought." Rather it can be seen "as *absolving*, as releasing rather than *dissolving* or *enclosing*."[171] If the absolute is an open, releasing, absolving wholeness rather than a closed totality, then the "progress of the consciousness of freedom" cannot be viewed as a predetermined, overarching, linear teleology, but remains something always to be worked out afresh in history, fragmentarily and ambiguously, from one moment to the next. Desmond suggests that the art work is a microcosmic analogue of the open wholeness of the absolute. So also in my view is the praxis of freedom. These are the concrete, finite shapes in which the absolute appears in history.

We should not, however, move too hastily beyond deconstruction—though move beyond it we must. Deconstruction has the advantage of forcing us not only to opt for the open rather than the closed reading of Hegel, but also to come to terms with

the ethical as well as the dialectical meaning of "defigurative"—
the fact that mutilation, destruction, banality, brutality, violence,
and radical evil disrupt and disfigure our fragile syntheses.
Something like Foucault's hermeneutics of violence is required
to come to terms with the fact that the most noble experiment in
democracy enslaved one people (black Africans) and nearly
destroyed another (native Americans), or that the most cultured
nation of modern Europe unleashed an unprecedented
holocaust of destruction upon the Jewish people. In face of these
and similar atrocities, such as Stalin's purges and the Cambodian
massacres, it is not easy to dispute the claim that the only drama
ever staged in history is "the endlessly repeated play of
dominations."[172] Facing up to this challenge is part of the hard
labor demanded of us.

The Ambiguity of Historical Process

That history is a de-configurative process means that it is
ambiguous. Paul Tillich was among the first to introduce the
category of "ambiguity" into a discussion of history in a central
way. For Tillich, life as a whole in all of its functions is ambiguous
because, under the conditions of existential estrangement, the
essential polarities of finite being (individualization and participation, dynamics and form, freedom and destiny) pull apart and
move against each other. According to Tillich, spiritual life
manifests itself in three basic functions—self-integration (morality), self-creation (culture), and self-transcendence (religion)—
each of which is threatened by a distinctive kind of ambiguity:
disintegration, destruction, and profanization.[173] When spirit
appears in sociocultural and political forms, it has the character
of "history." In the dimension of history, the three functions of
self-integration, self-creation, and self-transcendence generate
a distinctive set of ambiguities: the ambiguities of power
(centralization versus anarchy), of change (revolution versus
reaction), and of end or goal (utopianism versus cynicism).
These ambiguities give rise to the basic question of the meaning
of history, to which the symbol "Kingdom of God" is the

Christian religious answer (there are many other answers as well).[174] Tillich's analysis is carried out with brilliance and in detail, but its persuasiveness depends in part on the extent to which his underlying ontological structure is accepted. Apart from this, however, his basic contention that the whole of finite life, including historical life, is both fragmentary and ambiguous is highly persuasive.

Another approach to ambiguity in history is found in one of Paul Ricoeur's earlier essays, where he argues that there are three levels of interpreting history: progress, ambiguity, and hope.[175] Progress takes place at the level of tools and their products; products accumulate and tools improve, and together they constitute technical progress. When, however, we ask what humanity does with its tools and possessions, progress becomes ambiguous. Ambiguity marks the aspect of history in which events take place, and the categories by which it is described point to the pervasive ambiguity: crisis, apogee, decline, period, and so forth. At this level history is not one but multiple, a multiplicity that cannot be rationally systematized. There appears to be no coherent, overarching pattern, only a confusing interplay—an interplay, to express it in our own terms, of configurations and defigurations, of integrations and disintegrations, of building up and tearing down. Ricoeur's third level, hope, remains bracketed at this point in our analysis.

A detailed study of ambiguity is provided in a recent book by Ruth Page.[176] Ambiguity, she argues, is a combined result of diversity, polyvalence, and change, which are pervasive features of our experienced world. Ambiguity is usually taken to refer to "double meaning," but it is more than that; it points to the fact that things can usually be interpreted and evaluated in a number of different and often contradictory ways. Page seems to think of ambiguity as the inexhaustible, incalculable matrix ("the restless, fruitful and destructive sea") out of which everything is created anew and order is temporarily fashioned. It is not so much the consequence of historical action as its precondition. The value of her contribution is that it requires us to enlarge the category of ambiguity to include not only history but also nature and cosmos.

David Tracy has developed this theme along lines supportive of our analysis.[177] He says that ambiguity is to history as plurality is to language. History is not merely contingent but interruptive; our own Western history is "an interruptive narrative with no single theme and no controlling plot." What "interrupts" it are those terrifying facts that will simply not "fit in," facts that point to a profound contradiction and a radical evil close to the heart of things. "Ambiguity may be too mild a word to describe the strange mixture of great good and frightening evil that our history reveals," but for the time being it is the best we have. The appropriate response is not one of either complacency or guilt, nor of optimism or pessimism, but rather one of resistance, attention, and hope—resistance to ourselves and our own traditions, attention to the suffering of others, and hope founded on conversation.

The themes of suffering and interruption are powerfully elaborated by Rebecca Chopp in her recent study of liberation and political theologies.[178] Her key insight is that suffering *interrupts*—especially massive, public suffering such as that represented by the slave trade and slavery, global warfare, the Holocaust, the repression of basic human rights, widespread and persistent poverty and starvation in the third world, the presence of a sizable underclass in the first world. Suffering interrupts conventional meanings and demands radical solutions. It ruptures our experience and understanding of history—both the classic salvation history mythos and the liberal theory of evolutionary progress. Progress, says Chopp, is "modernity's plastic mask." Suffering is humanity's history, confession, freedom, and fate. Radical suffering, like radical evil, is interruptive partly because of its "nonidentity" character: that is, we lack the ability fully to express and comprehend it; we cannot fit it into an interpretative schema by which we might make some sense of it. It has the character of a surd. Such suffering demands of us what the Latin American liberation theologians have called "a preferential option for the poor" and a "solidarity with suffering," or what Chopp calls "the praxis of suffering."[179]

Chopp's recognition that suffering is interruptive and demands a radical kind of praxis represents an authentic insight; perhaps it is the profoundest lesson of the twentieth century into the meaning of history, a lesson of which we are reminded by post-Holocaust Jewish theologians such as Arthur Cohen and Emil Fackenheim.[180] History is not a seamless web but a ruptured fabric, full of breaks, holes, crises, disjunctions, caesuras, which shake the very notion of history itself. Suffering and evil are not random, accidental occurrences, but take on a systemic character, so that we speak, for example, of interrelated "circles of death" or of a "culture of death"—poverty and starvation, genocide and apartheid, institutional and cultural violence, environmental pollution and despoliation, personal alienation and meaninglessness, psychological anxiety and disintegration. This systemic structure of suffering can be broken if at all only by a determined praxis of suffering. Chopp has learned this, not only from the German political theologians and Latin American liberation theologians who are the subject of her study, but also from the French philosophical deconstructionists. She knows, as we know, that any attempt today to construct a linear, progressive teleology of history with a predetermined outcome would be doomed to failure. It could pretend, at best, to be a history of victors, not of victims. History is in fact an open, uncertain, and ambiguous process, the risks are very high, and the odds are always against those who choose to practice suffering.

But where does this leave us? Does it not tempt us to opt out of history, to give up on the historical process, to adopt a fatalistic, apocalyptic attitude, a belief that history is doomed to destruction, that the only true hope lies beyond history or in a dramatic divine intervention? Some recent theologians have been tempted in this direction, but along this path lie, if not despair and nihilism, then either a this-worldly hedonism or an other-worldly indifference. The other possibility is to turn back to history with a renewed determination, with a sober, almost defiant hope that possibilities for transformation do exist within history despite the terrible interruptions, that the praxis of suffering can issue in the praxis of freedom. Suffering, poverty, and oppression are not ends in themselves; they are abominations, evils, that must constantly be resisted and combated. The praxis of suffering is a negative work; it must be converted into a positive work, the praxis of freedom.

But what is the condition of possibility for such a conversion? Does it not assume an underlying rationality of history? David Tracy insists that we must be suspicious above all of "the optimism concealed in Western notions of reason"—despite the glories of reason. We must resist, he says, "sanguine versions of error, rational consciousness, and the self."[181] Sin is not mere error but inauthentic existence, self-delusion, systemic distortion. Is not, then, Hegel's claim that "world history is a rational process" utterly falsified—indeed precisely by the interruptions of suffering? Are not the only alternatives to "reason in history" either unreason (Gillespie) or chance and necessity (Nietzsche, Foucault)?

I think it is rather the case that reason is present in history under the mark or condition of ambiguity.[182] Just because reason is the highest human achievement, when it falls into estrangement and self-destructive conflicts it becomes the most powerful and malicious instrument of evil imaginable. Reason run amok, put to destructive and deceptive uses, is what gives evil its terrible power. The rationality of the death camp operations was impeccable, as is that of nuclear war-games. The only weapon powerful enough to fight reason is reason itself. It is not, then, a matter of reason versus unreason but of reason versus reason. Perhaps this is why reason must take on the aspect of "cunning"—precisely to unmask and do battle with its own inverted, distorted alter ego. In any event, we must not abandon reason to "technical rationality" or to "systemic distortion"; rather we must claim it, in the form of "discursive rationality," as an instrument of critical, emancipatory praxis, recognizing that the truly rational is not yet what "is" but what "ought to be."[183]

The Open Teleology of Historical Process

Throughout this work, I have been highly critical of overarching, linear teleologies, which seek to identify specific stages of advance (or decline and advance) in the drama of salvation, culminating in a final victory of good over evil at the end of history. Such teleologies simply do not cohere with what we actually know about history or with what we can reasonably expect for the future. Hegel's vision of history as "the progress of the consciousness of freedom" is usually regarded to be such a teleology; but, as we have just seen, his dialectic need not be viewed as encapsulating the structure of a teleological process but rather as participating in and moving with the dynamic structuring process of history itself, which we have called "de-configuration." The absolute of the "open" Hegel is an absolving or releasing absolute rather than a closed totality that dissolves everything in a final static identity.[184]

Such a reading of Hegel brings him much closer to the kind of "practical" or "volitional" teleology that we have found in Troeltsch. Troeltsch warned against any systematic, teleological constructions of stages of actualization of the final end of history. Empirically, there appears to be no dominant direction to history, only new formations, their maturation and decay. But at the same time, Troeltsch recognized, human action is purposive and must be oriented to ends. Further, there must be criteria of truth and value that provide direction to such orientations. We attain these criteria, not merely by way of the exigencies of particular situations, but also from an immersion in the full wealth of historical experience, intuition, and interpretation.

On this basis, our "teleological" responsibility is to shape new cultural syntheses, on both large and small scales, out of past resources, with an eye to present needs and possibilities, and on the basis of a commitment to universal ideals or values. This is a task that must be repeated again and again in each new age and context, recognizing that only partial and contingent solutions are possible, and that our formulation of the ideal is always culture-specific and relative—even the ideal of "free personality," which is formulated in the language of Western culture. Through this continuing process, a certain matrix of historical values may be built up and even institutionalized; but institutions are always fragile and can readily be destroyed or perverted into instruments of domination. Although certain "trajectories of freedom" may be discernible in history, there is never the possibility of a utopia of freedom, though our thinking and acting must retain a utopian dimension. Troeltsch insisted: "The kingdom of God and nirvana lie outside all history. In history itself there are only relative victories."[185] To have such victories is enough; we should cherish and rejoice in them.

Such a teleology is not closed but open. It has the character not of a straight line or of a circle but of a spiral, an open-ended, helical spiral—an image to which I shall return in the concluding chapter. The openness of such a teleology corresponds to the openness of the divine life, which is not an enclosed and finished totality but an "open wholeness." This is precisely what it means to speak of God as "absolute" and as "spirit." As absolute spirit, God is the dynamic, self-manifesting shape or gestalt that empowers the creative, synthesizing, emancipatory configurations of human life and culture, which are at the same time the self-shaping of God. The shape of God is the shape of free love. We are now at the point of bringing together our reflections on "God" and "history" into a theology of history oriented to "freedom" or "transfigurative praxis."

CHAPTER IV

Freedom:
Transfigurative Praxis

1. The Turn to Praxis

Beyond Absolutism and Relativism to Dialogical Praxis

In the introductory chapter, I suggested that the way beyond the unproductive alternative of absolutism versus relativism might be found through engagement in some manner of transformative, emancipatory praxis. The determination to act can have a salutary, clarifying, releasing effect, overcoming the inertia and uncertainty that frequently burden a purely theoretical weighing of alternatives. (This is as true of intellectual action, such as determining to write the first words of a new chapter without quite knowing where it will lead, as it is of moral or social or physical action.) Action does entail a risk, a wager, a venture into the unknown, but at the same time we experience a kind of empowerment to act, which we are able to reflect upon only retrospectively.

Just this turn to praxis is the underlying theme of Richard Bernstein's influential book, *Beyond Objectivism and Relativism.*[1] (The term *objectivism* is similar to what I have called "absolutism," although in another frame of reference I have attempted to retrieve the concept of "the absolute" from objectifying and absolutizing interpretations.)[2] Through a critique of scientific rationality, Bernstein attempts to establish that a hermeneutic dimension is present in the natural sciences as well as the social and human sciences. Hermeneutics then discloses itself to have a fundamentally practical dimension, since all understanding, no matter how abstract, both reflects concrete interests and is oriented to political judgment and practical discourse in the world.[3]

Bernstein's constructive argument is developed through a detailed study of four major twentieth-century philosophers: Hans-Georg Gadamer, Jürgen Habermas, Richard Rorty, and Hannah Arendt. According to Bernstein, "The outstanding theme in Gadamer's philosophic hermeneutics is his fusion of hermeneutics and *praxis*, and the claim that understanding itself is a form of practical reason and practical knowledge—a form of *phronēsis*."[4] Gadamer does indeed refer to "the rediscovery of the fundamental hermeneutic problem," which is that of "application," a third essential element that must be fused with "interpretation" in the total event of "understanding"; and he identifies Aristotle's concept of *phronēsis* as specifying the distinctive kind of knowledge that governs human activity—a kind of "seeing" or "insight" into what is "right" in a given situation of action, which is not reducible to either *epistēmē* (scientific knowledge) or *technē* (skillful knowledge).[5] But this "rediscovery" does not in fact play as central a role as one might expect in Gadamer's work, which is oriented more to the historicality and linguisticality of hermeneutics than it is to praxis, and which is governed finally by an aesthetic rather than an ethical vision of reality, as well as by a respect for tradition rather than a critical transformation of it. The lack of centrality of praxis is reflected by Bernstein's acknowledgment that he has had "to expose some of the deficiencies and tensions" in Gadamer's hermeneutic in order "to reveal the radical thrust of his own thinking, one which points to the goal of nurturing the type of dialogical communities in which *phronēsis* can be practiced and where the freedom of all human beings is concretely realized."[6]

It is just this "radical thrust" that was developed into a comprehensive theory of "communicative action" by one of Gadamer's most original students, Jürgen Habermas. This was part of Habermas's attempt to reconstruct a theory of rationality that would maintain the emancipatory aspirations of the Enlightenment and of Hegel while also attending to the deformations of reason to which Marx, Nietzsche, Freud, and

Foucault have called irrefutable attention. As distinct from the systematic distortions of communication, which are found everywhere, authentic communication or "communicative praxis" offers the possibility of "the argumentative redemption of validity claims through mutual dialogue and discourse"—a dialogue that is unconstrained and predicated on conditions of equality and solidarity.[7] This is a theme of great importance to which I shall return in section 3 of this chapter.

Although Richard Rorty has been quite critical of Habermas's "foundationalist" tendencies, his defense of pragmatism, according to Bernstein, brings him rather close to the substance of Habermas's claim. For Rorty this takes the form of arguing for the willingness to engage in and continue conversations, without making any assumptions about the conditions of possibility for or the outcomes of such conversations.[8] But it is in the work of Hannah Arendt that Bernstein finds the most rigorous analysis of dialogical conversation, which in her view is at the heart of politics. Public, political debate is a form of "action" or "praxis," as distinct from "labor," which is grounded in physical necessity, and "work," which fashions the products of the human world. The essential conditions of debate are human plurality and equality, and its essential form is persuasion, which is at the heart of judgment. Like Gadamer, Arendt attempts to reclaim praxis from *technē*, but unlike him she views authority as incompatible with persuasion; and her key category is neither tradition (Gadamer) nor reason (Habermas) but revolution—that is, "the 'revolutionary spirit' which attempts to found public freedom."[9]

In these four thinkers, Bernstein concludes, we find "the central themes of dialogue, conversation, undistorted communication, communal judgment, and the type of rational wooing that can take place when individuals confront each other as equals and participants." Just this vision provides a way beyond objectivism and relativism, since it responds to the conflict and plurality of the human condition without imposing objectifying or authoritarian claims; rather, it enables us to "discover some *common ground* to reconcile differences through debate, conversation, and dialogue."[10] This is a practical as opposed to a theoretical or metaphysical solution to the fact of relativism. Bernstein thinks that we are driven to find an alternative to the unproductive stalemate of objectivism versus relativism because, on the one hand, we have the growing conviction "that there may be nothing—not God, Philosophy, Science, or Poetry—that satisfies our longing for ultimate foundations, for a fixed Archimedean point upon which we can secure our thought and action"; but, on the other hand, in face of the very real threat of total annihilation, we recognize the urgency of finding *some* basis for communication, negotiation, and solidarity. This is likely to be accomplished by means of a practical rationality, not through a theoretical resolution of differences.[11]

Although agreeing with the primary thrust of Bernstein's remark—and leaving philosophers, scientists, and poets to speak for themselves—I should like to enter a caveat as a theologian that nothing is further from the truth than to think of God as "a fixed Archimedean point." This could only be a *deus ex machina,* not the living God of the prophets and apostles (and even of some theologians and philosophers). But to speak of this God's redemptive presence in history requires turning to praxis for reasons not dissimilar to those adumbrated by Bernstein.

Theology and the Concept of Praxis

Both the European political theologians and the Latin American liberation theologians have insisted on the primacy of praxis in the work of theology. Johann Baptist Metz, perhaps the best known of the former group, formulates the issue quite broadly in his work on "practical fundamental theology":

> Theory and praxis are not dealt with here in the usual order of priority, in which praxis is regarded as the continuation, implementation or concrete application of a previously defined theory. Practical fundamental theology is, on the contrary, directly opposed to a nondialectical subordination of praxis to theory or the idea. In it, great emphasis is placed on the

intelligible force of praxis itself, in the sense of a dialectical
tension between theory and praxis.[12]

One may of course observe that "nondialectical subordinations"
are to be avoided in both directions, and that just as there is an
"intelligible force of praxis," so also there must be a practical
intention of theory, as Metz would surely agree. Yet it is not clear
from the quoted remark or from Metz's work as a whole just why
praxis should be regarded as the more encompassing of the two
categories, the one to be accorded primacy.

Gustavo Gutiérrez comes closer to answering this question
with his proposal that theology is critical reflection on a praxis
that always in some sense precedes it. The foundation of
Christian praxis is simply love, which is "the nourishment and
the fullness of faith, the gift of one's self to the Other, and
invariably to others." "Theology," in relation to this praxis,

> is reflection, a critical attitude. Theology *follows;* it is the second
> step. What Hegel used to say about philosophy can likewise be
> applied to theology: it rises only at sundown. The pastoral activity
> of the Church does not flow as a conclusion from theological
> premises. Theology does not produce pastoral activity; rather it
> reflects upon it. Theology must be able to find in pastoral activity
> the presence of the Spirit inspiring the action of the Christian
> community.[13]

This is not to suggest that it is not necessary, indeed crucially
important, that the Christian community should take this
second, reflective step. After all, human activity is uniquely
reflective and intentional in character; it is activity transfigured
by thought, which makes it praxis as distinguished from instinct,
desire, habit, or mere labor; and thought, once introduced, must
be pursued to the limit in open dialogue. But at the end of his
own magnificent exercise in reflection, Gutiérrez claims that
theology can only be verified by the practice of a commitment to
abolish injustice and to build a new society; and, in a paraphrase
of Pascal, he concludes that "all the political theologies, the

theologies of hope, of revolution, and of liberation, are not worth one act of genuine solidarity with exploited social classes. They are not worth one act of faith, love, and hope, committed . . . to liberate [human beings] from everything that dehumanizes [them]."[14] Who would deny this? And yet creative theology can itself be a work of praxis, an act of solidarity. Surely Gutiérrez's is.

Another approach to the primacy of praxis is to suggest that it is a concept of "concrete totality," capturing within a single concept all the essential dimensions of human being—existential, intersubjective, material, historical, and transcendental. Action involves an objectification of inwardness; it entails the activity of others as well as myself; it utilizes yet transcends material conditions; it takes place within a sociohistorical nexus; and it co-affirms the absolute as the horizon of possibility for any action whatsoever. In brief, the category of praxis brings into play all the dimensions of human existence simultaneously.[15]

This holistic approach to human being as a concrete totality also suggests a holistic theological method, one that is rooted in praxis and understands itself as the theory of a praxis. Such a method would reject both ahistorical universalism and historical particularism, seeking instead what Hegel called the "concrete universal." Such a quest underlies the method of this book. I am arguing that "God" and "history" are correlative, co-constitutive categories. God is self-actualized in and through historical process, and history is shaped by a gestalt that transcends it. Apart from this interpenetrating relationship, talk about God moves in the direction of ahistorical universalism, and talk about history in the direction of particularism, purposelessness, and sheer *différance*. God and history are conjoined at the point of praxis—not indiscriminate, amorphous praxis, but praxis of a distinctive sort, namely, free, liberating, emancipatory, transfigurative praxis. Such praxis is the concrete universal—God and history together in the shapes of freedom.

On the assumption that theology itself can be a work of praxis, and that it should understand itself as a theory of praxis, the theology of history advanced in this chapter and the next is intended to represent a form of "reflective praxis" employing a discursive or practical rationality.

Theology and the Ground of Praxis

Bernstein points to a paradox in the appearance of communities in which emancipatory praxis is genuinely possible, a paradox observed by each of the four thinkers on whom he is relying: Gadamer, Habermas, Rorty, and Arendt.

> Each of [them] points, in different ways, to the conclusion that the shared understandings and experience, intersubjective practices, sense of affinity, solidarity, and those tacit affective ties that bind individuals together into a community *must already exist.* A community or a *polis* is not something that can be made or engineered by some form of *technē* or by the administration of society. There is something of a circle here, comparable to the hermeneutical circle. The coming into being of a type of public life that can strengthen solidarity, public freedom, a willingness to talk and to listen, mutual debate, and a commitment to rational persuasion *presupposes the incipient forms of such communal life.*[16]

Bernstein observes this paradox but does not know quite what to make of it. Are these shared understandings and practices, these incipient forms, simply a historical nostalgia for a long-lost communal ideal such as once existed in Greece? If so, Bernstein knows, with Hegel, that there can be no return to this "immediacy." And, he continues, "Hegel also saw that the various attempts of modern man to impose his will in order to create a new, mediated form of universal community have resulted in a series of grotesque failures." We cannot return to the past and we cannot forcefully engineer a new society. All we are able to do, and *must* do, is

> to seize upon those experiences and struggles in which there are still the glimmerings of solidarity and the promise of dialogical communities in which there can be genuine mutual participation

and where reciprocal wooing and persuasion can prevail. For what is characteristic of our contemporary situation is not just the playing out of powerful forces that are always beyond our control, or the spread of disciplinary techniques that always elude our grasp, but a paradoxical situation where power creates counter-power (resistance) and reveals the vulnerability of power, where the forces that undermine and inhibit communal life also create new, and frequently unpredictable, forms of solidarity.[17]

In support of this analysis, Bernstein points out that Arendt spoke of "the 'miraculous' quality of action, how it can make its appearance against all odds," and that Habermas shows how communicative reason develops "a stubbornly transcending power even when it is violated and silenced again and again."[18]

The as yet unanswered question is how all of this is to be accounted for if it cannot be traced to a long-lost past and if it cannot be attributed to the human will-to-power in the form of social engineering. It is simply there: a "miraculous" quality, a "stubbornly transcending power," a power that seems to be evoked and strengthened when attempts are made to suppress it. It is a power that transcends us as future possibility, and it is experienced as a gift, as grace, as empowering presence, as "a strange empowering kind of power all its own."[19] Bernstein himself draws no religious conclusions at this point. But is it inappropriate to suggest that precisely this is how God's presence and power are experienced in history, if they are experienced at all? When all the immanent possibilities for continuation or renewal are exhausted, when persons and peoples are driven to the depths of defeat and despair, they can and do experience the "miraculous" ability to start over, to build afresh, to maintain a struggle and a vision. History is a process of victories and defeats, of configurations and deconfigurations; yet it is empowered and lured onward by a transfiguring practical ideal, a gestalt of freedom, the image of a communion of solidarity, love, mutuality of recognition, and undistorted

communication. The gestalt that lures and empowers history is
the gestalt of God. It appears as such when the historical field has
been cleared of all pretensions, of all autonomously based
projects and powers, and when human projects and powers are
seen rather to be the bearers, the vehicles of *God's* presence, of
God's strange empowering kind of power.

2. God's Presence: Divine Gestalt

The Interweaving of Divine Presence and Transfigurative Praxis

In this section and the next I shall consider the interaction of
two factors—redemptive divine presence and transfigurative
human praxis—which together generate historical process as a
history of freedom. I cannot avoid considering them in turn, one
after the other; but already this sequential treatment represents
an abstraction from and a falsification of what is essentially a
unitary though complex process. My thesis is that, viewed
theologically, historical process may be understood as a dialectic of
two interacting factors: ideal and real, possible and actual,
universal and particular, transcendent and immanent, divine and
human. We have seen that both Hegel and Ricoeur described this
dialectic by employing, in rather different senses, a similar
metaphor, that of an "interweaving" of crossed threads or
"crossed references," which together make up the fabric of
history—a fabric that, for Hegel at least, takes on the character of
ethical freedom or emancipatory praxis.[20] Troeltsch described the
process with a different metaphor, that of "shaping the historical
stream of life" through creative syntheses of the ethical-rational
(which is grounded in the divine life) and the empirical-actual.[21]

From both Hegel and Troeltsch I have adopted the category
of "shape," "gestalt," or "figure" (*Gestalt*) as more helpful for
conceptualizing God's empowering presence in history than the
category of "idea," although the intended meanings are very
similar. The divine gestalt is, I shall argue, the shape of
love-in-freedom, a shape rendered concrete by certain images
associated with the ministry and death of Jesus, images of

compassionate freedom and liberating love. These images have their roots in the history of Judaism and reverberate in and are enriched by the continuing history of the ecclesial community. On the one hand, it is the shape of love-in-freedom and its multiple images that lure, empower, and transfigure human activity in the direction of emancipatory praxis. Without such transfiguring and empowering, humanity on its own would be continually subject to entropy, despair, illusion, systemic distortions and oppression. But on the other hand, human activity is the bearer, instrument, or vehicle of the divine gestalt, without which it would be a historical unreality, a suprahistorical miracle, or a dogmatic assertion. The gestalt of loving freedom, which is the very figure of God, must *take shape* in concrete historical praxis. Otherwise, it would remain an abstract ideal and history an unstructured, disoriented cacophony of occurrences. The two factors are fundamentally co-constitutive, interwoven. For purposes of analysis, I shall unravel the fabric since its complexity cannot be grasped all at once; but in so doing I recognize that the whole cloth of God in history and history in God, conjoined in the shapes of freedom, is being taken apart in ways that do not do justice to its actual interwoven texture.

Another, more familiar way to establish the same point is to affirm with Gutiérrez that "there are not two histories, one profane and one sacred, 'juxtaposed' or 'closely linked.' " There is no special salvation history but only one human history: "the history of salvation is the very heart of human history." Gutiérrez rightly notes that "contemporary theology has not yet fashioned the categories which would allow us to think through and express adequately this unified approach to history." We must avoid the temptation of falling back into a discredited "distinction of planes" model, while at the same time taking care not to reduce divine saving empowerment merely to human emancipatory potential.[22] What we have is not a distinction of planes, one suprahistorical and the other historical, but a single plane—the fabric of history—made up of distinctive though interwoven threads.

Gutiérrez himself struggles mightily to find appropriate

categories for expressing this complex totality. Two of his most notable formulations follow:

> The liberation of humanity and the growth of the Kingdom both are directed toward complete communion of human beings with God and among themselves. They have the same goal, but they do not follow parallel roads, not even convergent ones. The growth of the Kingdom is a process which occurs historically *in* liberation, insofar as liberation means a greater fulfillment of humanity. . . . But the process of liberation will not have conquered the very roots of oppression and the exploitation of humanity by humanity without the coming of the Kingdom, which is above all a gift. Moreover, we can say that the historical, political liberating event *is* the growth of the Kingdom and *is* a salvific event; but it is not *the* coming of the Kingdom, not *all* of salvation. It is the historical realization of the Kingdom and, therefore, it also proclaims its fullness. This is where the difference lies. It is a distinction made from a dynamic viewpoint, which has nothing to do with the one which holds for the existence of two juxtaposed "orders."[23]

> In human love there is a depth which we do not suspect: it is through it that we encounter God. If utopia humanizes economic, social, and political liberation, this humanness . . . reveals God. . . . The mediation of the historical task of the creation of a new humanity assures us that liberation from sin and communion with God in solidarity with all of humanity . . . does not fall into idealism and evasion. But, at the same time, this mediation prevents these manifestations from becoming translated into any kind of Christian ideology of political action or a politico-religious messianism. Christian hope opens us, in an attitude of spiritual childhood, to the gift of the future promised by God. It keeps us from any confusion of the Kingdom with any one historical stage, from any idolatry toward unavoidably ambiguous human achievement, from any absolutizing of revolution. . . . The Gospel does not provide a utopia for us; this is a human work. The Word is a free gift of the Lord. But the Gospel is not alien to the historical plan; on the contrary, the human plan and the gift of God imply each other.[24]

The emphasis in both these passages is on the interaction or "mediation" of the transformative kingdom of God with the human, historical process of liberation in such a way as to avoid either confusing them or separating them. I thoroughly applaud this emphasis. But the means by which Gutiérrez expresses the relationship-in-distinction of kingdom and historical process remains conceptually loose and misleading. He suggests that, in addition to its "growing" historically within liberation, the kingdom also "comes" from the future as a gift in a nonhistorical or suprahistorical fashion. But insofar as the kingdom is a power, paradigm, or gestalt that is effective within history, it can only work innerhistorically since history admits of no suprahistorical interruptions. Precisely *as* an innerhistorical power or factor, the kingdom must indeed be distinguished from that which it empowers, but not in such a way as to be dehistoricized or to allow an inadvertent falling back into a distinction of planes.

It is another question, of course, whether history as such and as a whole is limited by something that is not history as we know it. There may indeed be another dimension to the symbol "kingdom of God" which points to a transhistorical consummation of all things in God. This is undoubtedly what Gutiérrez has in mind when he speaks of the "coming" of the kingdom as "the gift of the future." But this consummation is not an extension of an innerhistorical process; it is something radically different, something that we cannot work to achieve within history. It is an object of faith rather than of praxis.[25] Insofar as the kingdom "comes" within history, it can only do so by "growing" within the emancipatory human project in such a way as to empower and lure this project to press toward an ideal, a possibility, a gestalt, a way of being communally human in the world in the presence of God, which is the purpose of history but not to be confused with any particular historical accomplishment. The "coming" and "growing" of the kingdom are one and the same. God acts in history by drawing and shaping us toward a never-realized, always open innerhistorical telos.

God's Activity in History

But *how* does God "act" in history? How are we to interpret this commonly used expression? The question is rarely asked whether it is even appropriate to speak of God as an "agent" of historical acts. The terms *action* and *agency* can be construed in a variety of ways, and any one of a number of action theories or metaphors may be at work in a theologian's assertions about the activity of God in the world or history. These theories and metaphors have been helpfully analyzed by Owen C. Thomas in an anthology of essays on this topic which he has edited.[26] Thomas distinguishes five distinct positions; I shall briefly summarize the first three, while discussing the last two in more detail since they provide a basis on which to build a further argument.[27]

1. Personal Action. This position, often associated with G. Ernest Wright's slogan, "God's mighty acts in history," is the one commonly shared by conservative and evangelical theologians. It is based on the analogy of human personal action and assumes that God is a superhuman agent who intervenes directly in the world through the interruption of the finite causal nexus.

2. Primary Cause. This is the traditional Catholic or Thomist approach to the question, according to which God as primary cause acts in and through all secondary causes in nature and history, although in some special cases God acts directly in "miracles" apart from secondary causes. Modified versions have been articulated by Austin Farrer and Etienne Gilson. When the exception of miracle is excluded, this approach is quite similar to that of Protestant liberal theology, as espoused by Rudolf Bultmann, Gordon Kaufman, and (in an early phase of his work) Langdon Gilkey: God acts in and through natural and historical processes without disrupting them.

3. Two Perspectives and Languages. Bultmann suggests another type of approach by his well-known statement: "This is the paradox of faith, that faith 'nevertheless' understands as God's action here and now an event which is completely intelligible in the natural or historical connection of events."[28] This view, when fully elaborated, entails a perspectival understanding of the relation of science and faith and does not offer a theory of the actual relation of divine and finite activity. Science and faith are unrelated, nonconflicting, nonsynthesizable language games, and no grounds are available for adjudicating their cognitive claims, if indeed any are made.

4. *Uniform Action.* On this view, which has been most consistently articulated by Maurice Wiles, God's action in the world is understood to be uniform and universal, while it is the varieties of human responses that give it the appearance of particularity. Thomas is rather critical of this option since in his view it is not clear whether God is understood by it to *act* or to be a cause in specific natural and historical events.

But the basic intention of Wiles's model is precisely to question—in a rather gentle fashion, to be sure—the coherence of speaking about specific divine "acts." This intention is more explicit in recent writings.[29] We may speak appropriately, he says, of "the gradual emergence of our world as a single divine act," the purpose of which may be described as "maximizing the growth of personal freedom and creativity." "Providence" means that such a purpose is in some manner and measure reflected in the world as we know it, but Wiles questions whether we are required to affirm particular acts of God in history. There is indeed a single though complex act "that we may and must affirm to be God's act, namely the continuing creation of the universe." The very complexity of this act includes within it a number of secondary actions or subacts, which traditionally have been attributed to God, but inappropriately so. Wiles provides a careful analysis and critique of each of these: regular patterns of the physical world (their very regularity militates against speaking of them as subacts of God); miracles (empirical evidence is lacking for their actual occurrence); actions by human agents with no conscious intention of furthering any purpose of God (there is no intelligible way of relating divine intention to the human deed performed in such cases); and actions by human agents who do freely intend to further God's purposes (this is the most plausible instance, but if these are truly free human acts it is difficult to grasp how they could be spoken of as God's particular acts). Rather, Wiles concludes, God acts in the world by "making possible the emergence, both individually and corporately, of a genuinely free human recognition and response to what is God's intention in the creation of the world." Just what this means at any particular time is not directly given, but is ours to discover. We may perhaps say that God "acts" by inspiring goals, ideals, the vision of new possibilities. "Inspiring" suggests that God acts as *spirit* or spiritual presence rather than as an individual personal agent. In thinking of God as spirit, the stress "is not so much on active agency as on the experience of being a person by virtue of our self-reflexive relation to ourselves and still more our relatedness to other persons. For there can be a rich communion between persons simply by their mutual presence to one another." In other words, God acts simply by "being there" as the kind of God God is, namely, the one who calls forth, shapes, and inspires human freedom and creativity.[30]

The question remains, however, about how God does this. Wiles has pointed the discussion in a helpful direction by suggesting that the model of an individual personal agent manipulating events is not appropriate, however much we may wish to think of God as in some sense personal. But is God's transformative presence simply uniform, universal, and, as it were, rather bland and shapeless? How does this presence exercise its luring, calling, persuading power? Is there anything characteristic or distinctive about God's being in the world that goes beyond the generic act of creation and is oriented to specific historical circumstances and human activities? Wiles does not really take up these and similar questions. For answers we shall have to turn first to process theology and then to some proposals of our own that will both build upon and modify the discussion among process thinkers.

5. *Process.* Schubert Ogden addresses this question in a well-known article, "What Sense Does It Make to Say, 'God Acts in History'?"[31] Drawing upon the insights of "neoclassical theism" (meaning Whitehead and especially Hartshorne), Ogden argues, in agreement with Wiles, that "the divine Self is effectively related to *all* others in such a way that there are no

gradations of intimacy of the various creatures to it. God is not located in a particular space and time, but rather is omnipresent and eternal, in the sense that he is directly present to all spaces and times and they to him." Although in the fundamental sense, according to Ogden, God's action of creation and redemption is not an action in history at all but is the action in which all historical events are ultimately grounded, it is nonetheless possible, he says, to speak meaningfully of God's action in history in the sense "that there are certain distinctively human words and deeds in which [God's] characteristic action as Creator and Redeemer is appropriately re-presented or revealed." These are "acts of God analogously to the way in which our outer acts *are* our acts insofar as they re-present our own characteristic decisions as selves or persons." On this basis Christians can affirm that Jesus is "the decisive act of God," meaning that "in him, in his outer acts of symbolic word and deed, there is expressed *that* understanding of human existence which is, in fact, the ultimate truth about our life before God." While I am puzzled by Ogden's way of distinguishing between nonhistorical and historical actions of God, his suggestion that God's universal presence is "re-presented" in "certain distinctively human words and deeds" does point in the direction of thinking of God's action in history in terms neither of a generalized influence nor of an individual personal agency but rather of specific shapes or patterns of human praxis.

John Cobb takes a different approach to our question. In his article, "Natural Causality and Divine Action,"[32] he analyzes different senses in which God's activity might be thought of in terms of causality. With the discrediting of the Newtonian idea of efficient causality, which entails the necessitation of the effect by the cause, theologians turned to other ways of thinking about God's causality, namely, as formal, material, and final. While all of these have value, in Cobb's view the question of efficient causality cannot be avoided if we are to have an adequate conception of God's activity in the world. But efficient causality must be rethought by way of "real influence" rather than necessary succession. Most of us have experienced the real causal efficacy of something that has influenced us. But this influence is normally not exercised in the form of an overt "action." A feeling or experience of anger can indeed influence subsequent events, but it does so not by engaging in specific actions upon those events but rather simply by constituting itself as anger.

"Similarly," writes Cobb, "if God acts or functions as an efficient cause, it is not through overt, sensible, observable actions. He acts by constituting himself in such a way that other events, such as human experiences, take account of him." Although this cannot be proved to be the case, we can, according to Cobb, describe elements of human experience that might point to God's influence. Such an element is something that suffuses our purposive activity, namely, an eros, desire, or passion toward the realization of greater rather than lesser values in the historical process. This eros is experienced as something implanted within us by the goal—given not by the past, which provides the "data" or material out of which new values are fashioned, but by the future, which draws or lures us toward itself. This future can be understood as "the universal *Eros* that is God himself."[33] God, then, "acts" in the world by constituting godself as the eros or love that draws all things to itself, luring and inviting a free response without compelling it. God has influence simply by being what God is in relation to human experience and activity.

In this analysis Cobb virtually dispenses with the notion of divine agency or divine "acting" as in any sense analogous to overt human activity in the world. In an earlier treatment of the subject, he introduced a personal metaphor, that of "calling," and specifically argued that God is not merely a set of ideal possibilities but an agency, a subject as well as an object of experience. God is the unitary actuality of cosmic scope and everlasting duration that in every moment confronts us with new ideal possibilities. God does this by "calling us forward," "luring us with new and richer possibilities for our being," impinging upon us as "the power that makes for novelty, creativity, and life." This power "is that of an ideal, a power which is not coercive, but not, for that reason, ineffectual." How God actually exercises this power, and in what sense the metaphor of calling is to be construed, are not explained by Cobb in this text.[34] Presumably the metaphor is not to be taken in a literal auditory sense, but rather more after the fashion of an invitation, summons, or vocational calling. We do not literally hear such a call, although it may indeed come about as a language event, that is, as mediated through human discourse. Thus even if God is a subject, this need not be taken to mean that God's worldly influence or persuasion is exercised through some overt, observable activity on the part of a divine agent.

In a more recent work, Cobb describes God's persuasive power as "a certain type of process [at] work in us," a process that can be understood as "creative unification of a multiplicity of elements into a new whole," a process that brings about a "progressive creative transformation of society" through "creative syntheses." Such a formulation moves process thought in the direction of Hegelian-Marxist dialectic and political theology, the contribution of which Cobb is pleased to affirm so long as one acknowledges that the occurrence of this kind of dialectic in history is a contingent matter with no assurance of a fortunate outcome.[35] This turn in Cobb's thought is a welcome one, but again he does not explain very concretely how God is associated with this process or how it operates in history, other than to insist that only persuasion, not coercion, introduces the possibility of creative synthesis.

Ruth Page, a student of Maurice Wiles, has been influenced by process theology but is critical of the tendency present in some of its representatives to make God into a "world director," more subtly so, to be sure, than classic theism, but a director nonetheless. It seems that God does quite a number of things to ensure that the teleological trajectory of the world is maintained. God gives "maximally favorable conditions" for desirable outcomes, expels "incompatibles" and "disorder," "employs a limited coercive pressure to preserve community and prevent orderly advance from degenerating into meaningless anarchy."[36] To avoid these sorts of misleading expressions, Page explicitly opposes the notion that God in history is "an agent analogous to human actors." Rather God is to be understood "to act through being who he is, for his nature has effects. He consciously makes a difference, but he does not intervene in states of affairs." "The attractiveness, goodness and unoppressive power of God make a difference in what one does in the world, so . . . God acts in that what he is has effects." Certain events may prove to be "revelatory" of what God essentially is, but this is more a function of our blindness than a special "act" of God. In substance, Page agrees with a position she ascribes to G. W. H. Lampe: "Through any event God may call us and make himself known, with the result that that event appears different in quality. But this is the effect of his constant and omnipresent relationship with the world which we so rarely perceive."[37]

Page goes on to elaborate this view in a theory of God's omnipresence *with* (not *to* or *in*) the whole of creation: God relates the whole to godself, enjoying or grieving over it in God's own presence.[38] She concludes her project by proposing that God's presence and relationship should "be understood in personal images and characteristics, not because God is personal in nature, but because this is how we apprehend God in categories we understand and value and can relate to him." For purposes of fuller elaboration in personal images while avoiding the notion of literal divine agency, she introduces "role theory" as an aid in conceptualizing what it means to speak of God's presence: God plays the role of "companion" in the world, a role that evokes a relationship of trust, mutuality, being-with.[39]

While considering this to be a suggestive, helpful proposal, I should like at the same time to introduce a different approach. I agree with Wiles, Ogden, Cobb, and Page that the model of an individual personal agent manipulating events is not only inappropriate but misleading as a basis for conceptualizing God's "activity" in the world. At the same time I am concerned about the rather bland and shapeless character of a universal divine presence, which is not only vague but also open to the possibility of being filled with all sorts of unwanted baggage, pious and impious. I agree that God "acts" by being efficaciously present as who and what God is. But *what* is God? How is God's presence constituted or shaped so as to have an impact on worldly events?

My thesis is that God is efficaciously present in the world, not as an individual agent performing observable acts, nor as a uniform inspiration or lure, nor as an abstract ideal, nor in the metaphorical role of companion or friend. Rather, God is present in specific shapes or patterns of praxis that have a configuring, transformative power within historical process, moving the process in a determinate direction, that of the creative unification of multiplicities of elements into new wholes, into creative syntheses that build human solidarity, enhance freedom, break systemic oppression, heal the injured and broken, and care for the natural. A shape or gestalt is not as impersonal and generalized as an influence or a presence, since it connotes something dynamic, specific, and structuring, but it avoids potentially misleading personifications of God's action. What God "does" in history is not simply to "be there" as God, or to "call us forward," or to assume a personal "role," but to "shape"—to shape a multifaceted transfigurative praxis. God does this by giving, disclosing, in some sense *being,* the normative shape, the paradigm of such a praxis. This is what I mean by the divine gestalt.

God in History as Gestalt

When we think of a figure or gestalt, we usually think first of a physical form or shape—something carved with a sharp tool (the root sense of *shape*), or molded from a pliable mass (the root sense of *figure*), or arranged or structured from parts (the root sense of *gestalt*).[40] Each of these acts has the purpose not just of producing a physical form but of creating an object of human significance—a statue, a piece of pottery, a house or dwelling place. In these acts the project of building up a human world is initiated. Thus it is not surprising that these terms came to be used metaphorically and that we commonly refer to shapes or figures of speech, thought, and action, which have the power to shape a social world of intersubjectivity and institutionality, and a temporal world of narrativity and historicality. These metaphorical gestalten are not empirically visible but they have a real power to shape the world in which human beings dwell.

They occur at various levels of consciousness or awareness. At the most fundamental, preconscious level, they function as the structuring patterns and paradigms that underlie everything that we think and do and say. At the overt, conscious level they serve as the actual shapes in which what we think, do, and say appears in the world. The civil rights struggle of the 1960s produced such a gestalt, which initially functioned overtly as the guiding ideal of the participants in the movement, but which has become woven into the American public consciousness in such a way that later attempts to subvert the gains of that struggle by packing the Supreme Court, for example, have proved unsuccessful.

A gestalt is not a person. A gestalt may appear in the action or speech of a person or found such action and speech, but a gestalt, as such, is not a person, a personal agent. A gestalt, rather, is both transpersonal and interpersonal; it is a complex, doubled, plural unity. Under the influence of Goethe, Hegel introduced the category *Gestalt* into his philosophy of nature in just this sense: it connotes a physical structure that occurs not just once but in the plural, it is a one that is also and already a many. He also applied the category to the concept of life. As opposed to a formal mathematical unity, which is only a unit, a living unity doubles itself; it becomes a species. *Gestalt* is thus closely related to Hegel's concept of the infinite, which is not a mathematical-quantitative infinite but rather a doubled or multiple unity, an individual totality.[41]

This concept of *Gestalt* as plural infinite or individual totality was then transferred by Hegel to a theory of consciousness in the *Phenomenology of Spirit*. The basic structure underlying the shapes of consciousness (*Gestalten des Bewusstseins*) is that consciousness is a doubled or plural unity, both relating itself to and distinguishing itself from an other that is its object. In each of the shapes of consciousness, consciousness undergoes a development by which it is drawn out from itself in relationship to a newly appearing other, and then it finds itself anew in that other, becoming thereby increasingly complex, plural, encompassing, yet focused. Finally, Hegel historicized the concept and used it to designate stages in the history of spirit, which is an intrinsically social, ethical reality. The shapes of spirit (*Gestalten des Geistes*) are not merely shapes of consciousness but shapes of a historical, cultural world. Spirit, "by passing through a series of shapes, attain[s] to a knowledge of itself. These shapes, however, are distinguished from the previous ones by the fact that they are real spirits, actualities in the strict meaning of the word, and instead of being shapes merely of consciousness, are shapes of a world."[42] This means that only present shapes are actual according to Hegel; the previous shapes of spirit are annulled and preserved in the inwardizing "recollection" (*Erinnerung*) of consciousness.

The category *Gestalt* functions in similar ways in Hegel's phenomenology and philosophy of spirit to the category *Begriff*, "concept," in his logic. Just as a *Begriff* "grasps together" (*be-greifen*) into an intelligible unity the disparate elements of a representational image (*Vorstellung*), so a *Gestalt* "arranges" or "places together" (*ge-stellen*) in a worldly shape or figure the disparate elements of an appearing thing, a phenomenon. It is not surprising that Hegel should discover a correspondence between the concepts of the logic and the shapes of spirit as they appear in the histories of art, religion, philosophy, and culture. Whether this correspondence is one of exact, mechanical replication, or whether instead it is modified hermeneutically in each instance is a matter of considerable dispute among Hegel scholars; but it is clear in any case that logic itself as Hegel understood it required the transition from rational concepts to historical shapes: the idea drives toward actualization, theory toward praxis. The divine "idea" is a *Begriff* without a *Gestalt*, but when it appears in the world as "spirit," it must be embodied, take on worldly shape; there is never *Geist* without *Gestalt*.

The central category of Troeltsch's philosophy of history is that of "individual totality" (*individuelle Totalität*), which is precisely what Hegel meant by *Gestalt* (a complex, structured unity), and Troeltsch himself introduced the term *Gestaltung* to explain what is going on in historical process—namely, the "configuration" or "shaping" of ever-new, fragile yet creative cultural syntheses out of the disparate elements of historical life, in accord with rational-ethical values ultimately attributable to the "divine ground of life."[43]

In distinction from Hegel and Troeltsch, but in line with a trajectory found in both, namely, a shift in emphasis from theory to praxis or from "idea" to "gestalt," I argue that the "divine idea" or "rational-ethical values" do not appear in history as a theoretical principle or set of ideals but as a structure of praxis, a pattern or gestalt that guides, lures, and shapes historical process. That is how God *appears* and *works efficaciously* in history. The divine gestalt shapes the historical gestaltungen by which structures of freedom, compassion, solidarity, and wholeness are built up. This guiding gestalt is not a person or personal agent but a transpersonal structure of praxis that grounds personal existence and builds interpersonal relations since it itself is intrinsically relational, social, communicative in character.[44]

But what are the specific qualities, shapes, attributes of this transpersonal structure of praxis? One cannot answer this question abstractly or generically but only in light of a specific vision of God as mediated by a determinate religious community—in my case the Christian community of faith and its vision of the triune God. I have argued that God appears in the world in a specific though complex shape, the shape of love in freedom. The two elements of this shape infuse and define each other in several ways. God's love for the world is a free, unexacted love, and it is a love that liberates from the bondage, distortions, and illusions of the world. The world's freedom in God, which is God's freedom in and through the world, is a loving, compassionate freedom, which maintains solidarity with the suffering and anguish of the world, and engages in the work of building communal structures that are emancipatory, transfigurative, redemptive.

This complex divine shape is not empirically observable or directly identifiable with any particular worldly structure since it is fully embodied only in the totality of the world. Although from the perspective of faith this shape is the ultimate ground of world process, it appears in the world only liminally, at the margins of the dominant world-formations, requiring for its discernment "hard labor," enduring the contradiction between the shape of freedom and the system of worldly domination by "taking up the cross" of suffering, liberating love.[45] It is hidden within a plurality of discernible, worldly shapes of freedom, none of which can claim simply to *be* the divine shape because all are limited by the contingency, ambiguity, and relativity of history. But, again in the eyes of a determinate faith tradition, certain of these worldly shapes have assumed a paradigmatic, normative, disclosive power vis-à-vis all the others. These are associated with the life, ministry, death, and resurrection of Jesus of Nazareth, as well as with certain images of Israel that preceded Jesus and with the "ecclesial existence" that emerged in response to his proclamation.

God was "incarnate," not in the physical nature of Jesus as such, but in the gestalt that coalesced both in and around his person—with which his person did in some sense become identical, and by which, after his death, he took on a new, communal identity. Jesus, as Hegel pointed out, was no Greek god: God appeared in the spiritual, ethical shape of his life rather than in his sensible, bodily nature.[46] Of course, gestalten are embodied in the flesh and blood of real human beings; they are, after all, worldly shapes, not abstract, "acosmic" ideas. But flesh and blood per se are not a shape of freedom; that shape is rather the distinctive being of human being, which is a way of being in the world as a communion of self-conscious and mutually relating subjects. As Hegel also recognized, the problem with the Greek gods was not that there was too much humanity in them but rather too little. By this he meant that for the Greeks divine presence penetrated, as it were, only to the exterior, sensible human shape, which was still "soft enough" to be molded into a likeness of divinity, not to the inner, spiritual-ethical shape of humanity, which is at the heart of what it means to be human.[47] The identity of each human person is constituted by and contributes to the interplay of spiritual-ethical shapes. For Christians the person of Jesus of Nazareth played and continues to play a normative role in mediating the shape of God in history, which is the shape of love in freedom.

Jesus' personal identity merged into this shape insofar as he simply *was* what he proclaimed and practiced. But Jesus' personal identity did not exhaust this shape, which is intrinsically a communal, not an individual shape. We can paraphrase Hegel by saying that the *communal* shape of spirit is the true and final gestalt of God in history.[48]

Three powerful images or figures associated with Jesus have become superimposed to form that complex shape which serves as a paradigm of all Christian praxis, and perhaps of all world-transforming praxis. The first of these is the *basileia,* the kingdom, realm, or rule of God, which is the central image of Jesus' proclamation, especially in the form of parables.[49] It is above all an image of freedom, a realm of freedom, a place or structure or world where freedom, communion, and truth prevail as the defining relationships among human beings instead of bondage, alienation, illusion. It is the power of God that establishes this parabolic clearing of freedom, although God rarely appears within the clearing itself. In order to prevent the image of the kingdom or rule of a king (a hierarchical male image) from hampering the transformations wrought by the parables of the basileia, I will normally let the Greek word stand without translation, hoping that it can be filled with a new meaning.

The world evoked by the parables is a strange world. All the established "economies" that govern human behavior and relations of power are shaken to the foundations by Jesus' proclamation of the "nearness" of the basileia. The logic of domination, violence, reward and punishment that prevails in the everyday world is challenged and replaced by a new logic, the logic of grace, compassion, freedom. The contents that make up this new world are familiar—banquets, wedding feasts, farms and farm workers, vineyards, royal households, merchants and stewards, noblemen and servants, public highways, law courts, the temple—but relations, values, behavior, and consequences have been set strangely askew and intensified to the point of extravagance, paradox, hyperbole. The "dislocation" effected by these surrealistic qualities of the parables is an aspect of their liminality;[50] and it is precisely in the liminal, interstitial spaces opened up by the parables that the gestalt of freedom forms. This is a gestalt that is "in" but not "of" the world; it forms "between" the closed systems that make up everyday life, opening them up, absolving them of their alienation, provincialism, false dichotomies, power struggles.

This gestalt, as it takes shape in the parables of Jesus, points unmistakably in the direction of a new kind of communal existence that is intrinsically open to the other, the stranger, those who are marginalized and oppressed or belong to an alien culture, people, or religion. All of the false provincialisms break down—those based on race, class, sex, ethnic or national identity, religious piety, worldly success; none of these are relevant as conditions of God's redemptive presence, which is utterly gratuitous, open to all.[51] This gestalt of freedom, found only at the margins of the everyday world, is a surreal world without definable limits or boundaries. As such, it is able to serve as a generative paradigm of transformative praxis again and again in human affairs under radically different cultural conditions. Jesus himself exemplified this praxis in his ministry; he not only proclaimed the inbreaking basileia of God but enacted it under the specific conditions of his time and place. He condemned social injustice, religious arrogance, and political exploitation; he challenged the authority of the established religious leaders, pressing for a much more radical reading of their own scriptures; he identified himself with the poor, the powerless, the marginalized, having a table fellowship with them; he included women among his following and they had a special relationship with him; he healed the sick and injured, and liberated those possessed by demonic powers.

What did all of this accomplish for him? Condemnation by the religious authorities on a charge of blasphemy, and execution by the political authorities on a charge of agitation against the *Pax Romana.* This brings us to the second powerful image or gestalt associated with Jesus, namely, that of the *cross,* which is above all an image of love, of anguished, suffering, broken love.[52] We considered earlier the sense in which the death of Jesus on the cross is the culminating moment in the act of love by which God posits a world that is other than God, for it signifies God's unity with perishability, God's struggle with the annihilating power of nothingness, taking that power into godself, converting its absolute negation into dialectical negation, enabling it thereby to become the possibility of the new.[53] This is the significance of the crucifixion of Jesus for God.

But what is its significance for us and for our understanding of history? Of course at the core of its significance for us is precisely its significance for God. But beyond this, the cross has another significance for us: it means that all our historical projects of liberation will fall short and ultimately fail. Jesus' project of announcing the inbreaking kingdom of God failed; the transfigured world of the parables was interrupted and displaced by scenes of betrayal, false charges, political dealings, weakness and vacillation, an angry mob, and an ugly finale on Golgotha. It was not a beautiful death, not a "celebration of freedom" (as was said of Socrates' death), and Jesus died with a question on his lips, "My God, my God, why hast thou forsaken me?" Did Jesus, who had proclaimed the saving nearness of God's basileia and had often spoken of God on intimate terms as *Abba,* experience the abandonment and remoteness of God at the moment of death? Was not this a falsification of the truth of his entire message, a negation of his very being? The shape of the cross is a question mark or a cancellation sign, a large X, which must be written across the shape of the basileia, reminding us that its vision of inclusive wholeness, of a liberated communion of free persons, will forever remain marginalized in this world, unable to dislodge permanently the economy of domination and violence, but only to disturb it, to disclose it for what it is, to reduce its scope and hegemony, and perhaps even to modify it. But above all it empowers people to maintain a compassionate solidarity for and with one another in their struggle against the worldly powers—as Jesus himself did, who died for the sake of all those who had joined or would join his cause, and indeed for those who would not. It reminds us that God will not rescue us from history or provide miraculous victories; rather God suffers silently alongside us, so silently that we may not know that God is there. The shape of the cross crosses, is superimposed on, that of the basileia vision, lending it the realism, clarity, and toughness necessary for its endurance in history as a transformative factor. Freedom is infused with a compassionate, suffering, anguished love.

And yet, because the annihilating power of nothing has been taken into God's being and converted there into the possibility of the new—because it has been historicized, made into a differentiating, generative factor rather than remaining an absolute negation—it is possible for human beings to go on after such defeats as the crucifixion of Jesus. "Out of death, new life arises"; from the "infinite anguish" of the cross there arises an "infinite love" and an "infinite freedom."[54] That death is not simply an end but a beginning, that it has the possibility of transforming human life and culture into new forms that open up new possibilities for consciousness and praxis that did not exist before—this is the profoundest meaning of the cross, which was not only the death of Jesus but the death of God by which God undergoes, incorporates, and transforms death. The meaning of the cross is the victory of life over death, the resurrection from the dead.

From the fusion of the images of basileia and cross emerges a third primary christological symbol, that of the *resurrection.* Through the death that put death to death, the shape of communicative freedom imaged by the basileia passes from the limited ministry of Jesus into the broad stream of human history, becoming a productive factor therein. The cross is the mediating link between the radical freedom of Jesus and "the glorious liberty of the children of God" (Rom. 8:21). As "resurrection," the fused, superimposed images of basileia and cross, of freedom and love, acquire the resiliency and realism necessary to endure in the midst of human tragedy, as well as the power to generate a continually transformative vision of a liberated communion of free subjects. The normative gestalt of God that came to speech in Jesus' proclamation and mission now "comes to stand" in the world as the productive paradigm of worldly praxis. It takes on the modality of "standing in the world" (*anastasis*), which is what "resurrection" means. Jesus, whose identity was first established by the gestalt that formed in and around his person, now assumes a new, communal identity as the "risen" Christ, the "body" of all those who share in and contribute to the transformation of the world wrought by suffering love. Resurrection takes place when basileia community forms under the conditions of the cross.[55]

The divine gestalt present in the proclamation, death, and resurrection of Jesus is closely related to certain normative gestalten or "root experiences"[56] of Judaism—exodus, covenant, prophecy, exile, messianic kingdom—which delineate the shape of God's presence in history as one of liberation, constancy, judgment, suffering, hope. It is also related to the normative gestalt of Christianity, which might be described as "ecclesia" or ecclesial existence—a mode of human existence transfigured in the direction of a nonprovincial, nonhierarchical, nonpatriarchal, nonethnic communion of persons, open to all without any prior conditions whatsoever, liberated from the power of sin, death, and oppressive structures by the grace of God, bound together in a solidarity and mutuality of love by the presence of God's Spirit.[57] The ecclesial community is the "body" of Christ in a more determinate sense: it is the community in which Jesus is explicitly recognized and confessed as the bearer of the divine gestalt. The ecclesial gestalt is never adequately embodied in any empirical church or Christian group; it is rather a critical, productive paradigm of praxis by which the empirical churches are continually judged and transformed. Of course God's presence in history is not restricted to the ecclesial gestalt any more than the latter is restricted to the institutional churches.

Any discussion of the shapes of God in history is unavoidably determinate; shapes are not general but specific. Our discussion reflects familiarity with and commitment to Christian faith and its Judaic roots. But God takes shape in other religions as well, and their claims are as legitimate as ours. The question is whether there is a certain coherence or congruence among these shapes, or whether they are utterly different from one another. Does something like the shape of love-in-freedom appear in other religions as well? This is to pose the question in a frame of reference determined by our own categories, but that seems unavoidable too. In any case, it is a question I cannot yet answer, although the posing of it forces a recognition of the relativity and limitations of my project. What is required is to bring together in a fruitful working relationship the disciplines of constructive theology and history of religions, and that is a task for the newly emerging generation of theological scholarship. I *hope* for a convergence and mutual transformation of the religions through dialogue and shared praxis in the face of common threats, and there are signs today that just this is beginning to happen,[58] but it is too early to know to what degree it will succeed or what forms it will assume.

The complex, Jesus-related gestalt of basileia and crucifixion, of loving freedom and liberating love, fused in resurrection, together with its associated images in Israel, the church, and possibly other religions, is woven into the fabric of history and becomes a powerfully generative factor within it. This gestalt, which is God's presence in history, generates shapes of freedom within the general economy of domination, transfigurative praxis within a de-configurative process.[59]

3. Transfigurative Praxis: Shapes of Freedom

The Meaning of "Freedom"

I have proceeded to this point without specifically attending to the meaning of the third central category in this study of God, history, and freedom. None of these terms is susceptible to any simple definition, and part of the argument is that they come into view together as co-constitutive themes. The question of freedom is almost infinitely extendable and the literature is enormous. I shall briefly consider three basic dimensions—subjective, intersubjective, and objective or actual—and, in order to introduce them, will refer to several suggestive passages from Hegel, who probably reflected more profoundly on the meaning of freedom than any other philosopher, ancient or modern.[60]

"Just as gravity is the substance of matter," wrote Hegel, "so also it can be said that freedom is the substance of spirit."

> Speculative philosophy has shown that freedom is the one authentic property of spirit. Matter possesses gravity insofar as it is impelled to move towards a central point; it is essentially composite, and consists entirely of discrete parts which all tend towards a center; thus matter has no unity. . . . Spirit, on the other hand, is such that its center is within itself; it too strives towards its center, but it has its center within itself. Its unity is not something external; it always finds it within itself, and exists in itself and with itself [*er ist in und bei sich selbst*]. Matter has its substance outside itself; the being of spirit, on the other hand, is presence to itself [*Beisichselbstsein*], which is the same thing as freedom. For if I am dependent, I am beholden to something other than myself, and cannot exist without this external point of reference. If, however, I am present to myself, I am also free.[61]

Human being or spirit "gravitates" inwardly rather than outwardly; it is drawn toward an inward center where it is "with itself," present to itself. This seems to happen, in the first place, by acts of self-awareness or self-consciousness whereby the self makes itself its own object. Self-consciousness presupposes a distinction between the self as subject and as object of knowledge, a distinction mediated by knowledge of objects other than ourselves. The self cannot be "with itself" without being with others; it is intrinsically and from the beginning a social self. In the second place, human beings constitute their presence to themselves, their independence or autonomy, by acts of deliberation, decision, and responsibility. Deliberation is an act of "weighing" (*librare*)[62] arguments, motives, influences, data. The free, self-centered, deliberate person does the weighing and reacts to the struggle of the motives in the form of decisions, the "cutting off" (*de-cisio*) of possibilities, for which she or he must be willing to assume responsibility. Motives, influences, and data are the given reality, the involuntary matrix, the "destiny" out of which decisions arise; and bodily capabilities are the means by which decisions are enacted. We can never escape our physical, social, and historical destiny in a kind of disembodied autonomy, but we are not enslaved to it either: insofar as motives are weighed and decided among, we are beyond them and hence free of them.[63]

We are able to see that freedom, defined this way, is intrinsically rational, for reasoning or thinking entails precisely a process of coming into presence—an inward self-presence or subjectivity or centeredness mediated through relationships to what is other than self; it involves, in Hegelian terms, a dialectic of identity, difference, and reintegration. At the strictly ideal or conceptual level, reason assumes the form of logic; but it is also embodied in acts of consciousness by which spiritual-historical existence is constituted as free, centered existence. Reason appears in history in the shape of freedom. Of course, reason appears in history for the most part in broken, misshapen, distorted, truncated forms, so we must speak of not one but many shapes of freedom, engaged in a continual emancipatory struggle with the myriad forms of bondage and oppression. This link between freedom and rationality is a crucial one for my argument. What is truly rational is truly free, and vice versa; what deforms reason also deforms freedom, and vice versa. God is active in history on behalf of, and present in the shape of, rational freedom and liberating rationality.

Freedom is not only intrinsically rational and subjective; it is also, as we have just seen, essentially intersubjective and social. Human spirit as such is social: a human being is self-conscious, self-constituting, and free, not in relationship to himself or herself alone, but only in relationship to others, through acts of conflict, struggle, recognition, reciprocity, and solidarity. The human center is not a private, isolated center, but a dialectical, communal, communicative, plural center. Communicative freedom does not exist at the outset but is the result of a struggle for recognition by which inequality and domination are gradually overcome. Hegel described the condition thus achieved as "universal self-consciousness" or "universal freedom":

It is that free self-consciousness for which the other self-consciousness confronting it is no longer . . . unfree but is likewise
independent. In this stage, therefore, the mutually related
self-conscious subjects, by setting aside their unequal particular
individuality, have risen to the consciousness of their real
universality, of the freedom belonging to all, and hence to the
intuition of their specific identity with each other. . . . In this state
of universal freedom, in being reflected into myself, I am
immediately reflected into the other person, and, conversely, in
relating myself to the other I am immediately *self*-related.[64]

This communal or social dimension is reflected in the root
sense of the words we use for freedom. Greek *eleutheria*, through
its probable Indo-European base *leudh*, designated those who
belong to an ascendant people (cf. German *Leute*) or are citizens
of a community of free speech and praxis, the *polis*, by contrast
with those who lack citizenship rights (slaves, women, children).
English *freedom* comes from an Indo-European root that meant
something like being "fond of" or "on friendly terms with" the
chief, that is, belonging to his tribe, which is privileged and
powerful. (Our words *friend* and *freedom* are etymologically
associated.) And English *liberty* derives from Latin *liber*, which
probably had the same Indo-European base as Greek *eleutheria*.
The children of a family, specifically the male children who will
inherit the property, were known as *liberi*.

Of course, all of these meanings were flawed; the Indo-European words for "freedom" were formed semantically at a stage
of human consciousness when it was believed that *some* were free,
while many, indeed most others were not free. The contrast
between ascendant and oppressed peoples, master and slave,
citizen and alien, male and female was imbedded in the meaning
of these terms. Freedom entailed participation in a community,
but it was a privileged, exclusive community, a clan or caste. If
the great discovery of modernity has been that *all* human beings
are free, then the challenge is to replace the exclusive
community by the universal community or what Hegel called
"universal freedom."

To accomplish this requires moving beyond the level of

intersubjective intentions to another level, that of objective, institutional structures. Rather than simply living in the world provided by nature, human beings have created a distinctively human world of culture and sociopolitical institutions, ordered by ethical relations, ideally those of justice or "right." "The system of right," wrote Hegel, "is the realm of freedom [*Reich der Freiheit*] actualized, the world of spirit brought forth out of itself like a second nature."[65] This Hegelian image is reminiscent, not only of the *basileia tou theou* proclaimed by Jesus, of which it is a philosophical translation, but also of Aristotle's definition of the *polis* as "the community of the free" (*koinōnia tōn eleutherōn*).

What is this "realm of freedom"? It certainly is not to be identified with any empirical political system or state; rather it appears to be the principle, paradigm, or gestalt that underlies emancipatory sociopolitical structures. In another of his suggestive passages, Hegel wrote: "Freedom, shaped into the actuality of a world, receives the form of necessity, the deeper substantial nexus of which is the system of the principles of freedom."[66] Interpreted along the lines of the present analysis, this means: freedom shaped (*Freiheit gestaltet*) into the actuality of a world yields worldly shapes of freedom (*Gestalten der Freiheit*), which together constitute a sociopolitical nexus, a "system of the principles of freedom," whose paradigm is the ideal shape of freedom—a "realm of freedom," a liberated communion of free subjects in which the freedom and fulfillment of each is simultaneously the freedom and fulfillment of all. This ideal might also be spoken of, in an idiom suggested by Habermas, as "communicative freedom."

I shall now attend to a theory of communicative freedom that attempts to work out the Hegelian vision in a conceptuality adequate to the postmodern situation, and I shall then ask what the worldly shapes of freedom generated by this ideal shape imply about historical process.

Communicative Freedom and Emancipatory Praxis

Jürgen Habermas has said that he began his career with a concern for a "theory of the pathology of modernism" from the

viewpoint of "the deformed realization of reason in history."[67]
Such a project is clearly grounded in Hegel, but it also moves
decisively beyond Hegel with the recognition that reason as it is
actualized in history is always "deformed" by conflicting ideologies
or interests—psychological, social, political, religious—and is
never able to achieve its final ends. Thus Habermas set himself the
task of elaborating a new comprehensive theory of rationality as
the ground for a critical theory of society, a theory that would
provide "a way of redeeming, reconstructing, and rationally
defending the emancipatory aspirations of the Enlightenment."[68]
The centerpiece of this theory is what Habermas calls "communicative action," which is a type of social interaction mediated by
discourse and oriented toward reaching understanding. Because
the telos implicit in this action is free human community based on
unrestrained dialogue, and in order to establish a connection with
the present analysis, I propose a variation on this term, namely,
communicative freedom. The terms are related but not strictly
parallel: "communicative freedom" specifies the *kind* of praxis
implicit in "communicative action."

Anyone engaged in communication with the intention of a
free exchange of ideas and collaborative action will advance
claims that are capable of being vindicated or falsified. For the
sake of the "argumentative redemption of validity claims,"
communicative action must presuppose the possibility of an
unconstrained, undistorted dialogue, a dialogical rationality,
and this possibility must be grounded in the very character of
linguistic intersubjectivity. It is "always already" there despite its
empirical deformations. We can, Habermas argues,

> locate a gentle but obstinate, a never silent although seldom
> redeemed claim to reason, a claim that must be recognized de
> facto whenever and wherever there is to be consensual action.
>
> Again and again this claim is silenced; and yet in fantasies and
> deeds it develops a stubbornly transcending power, because it is
> renewed with each act of unconstrained understanding, with
> each moment of living together in solidarity, of successful
> individuation, and of saving emancipation.[69]

In order to establish that "a communicative ethics grounded in the very structure of intersubjectivity and social reproduction" is a genuine possibility as opposed to mere "relativism, decision-ism, and emotivism," Habermas can appear, in Bernstein's view, to mount a new version of a Kantian transcendental argument for the a priori status of reason, and to do so in a "totalizing" or "holistic" fashion. But Habermas can also be read in another way, as offering an "interpretative or hermeneutical dialectics which seeks to command our assent 'by the overall plausibility of the interpretation that [it gives].' " This dialectics is intended to show, in Bernstein's words,

> that there is a *telos* immanent in our communicative action that is oriented to mutual understanding. This is not to be understood as a *telos* that represents the inevitable march of world history or the necessary unfolding of a progressive form of social evolution, but rather as "a gentle but obstinate, a never silent although seldom redeemed claim to reason," a claim to reason that "although silenced again and again, nevertheless develops a stubbornly transcending power." It is a *telos* that directs us to overcoming systematically distorted communication. It can orient our collective *praxis* in which we seek to approximate the ideal of reciprocal dialogue and discourse, and in which the respect, autonomy, solidarity, and opportunity required for the discursive redemption of universal normative validity claims are not mere abstract "oughts" but are to be embodied in our social practices and institutions.[70]

It does seem that both Bernstein and Habermas understand this telos as a modified version of "reason in history"—that is to say, as a dialogical or discursive rationality that is implicit in all human communicative structures and practices as the transcendental condition of their possibility. Bernstein's second reading of Habermas does not eliminate the transcendental dimension of the argument per se but places it in an interpretative rather than a totalizing frame of reference. This transcendental condition is grounded for Bernstein and Habermas in a nonreligious humanism, whereas Hegel explicitly identified reason in history with the "divine idea." The theological version of this transcendental condition should not allow itself to introduce totalizing claims any more than the humanistic one, or to understand reason as something that marches through history triumphantly;[71] rather, it should understand reason, using Habermas's terms, to work gently and persuasively, yet obstinately and with a stubbornly transcending power, which impels us to move beyond every achieved synthesis, both rational and cultural, recognizing that such syntheses are valid only for a time and that the emancipatory project will never be finished in history.

The claim that this transformative rationality is the divine idea rather than simply a human potentiality requires a theological argument that appeals to precisely the same distinctive qualities of communicative action that Habermas and Bernstein have observed and accounted for on nontheological grounds. The rival claims can be adjudicated only in terms of their interpretative persuasiveness vis-à-vis the experienced reality of communicative freedom. Inevitably, judgments respecting that persuasiveness will reflect one's own prejudices and convictions, one's way of seeing and being in the world. I insist only that the theological account must avoid introducing totalizing claims, and it should not be accused of doing so simply because it is theological. Moreover, because we are talking about a rationality that is imbedded in history and is discursive or dialogical, oriented to praxis, I prefer, as explained above, to avoid the language of idealism and speak of the "divine gestalt" (the shape of communicative freedom, of love-in-freedom) rather than the "divine idea."

We would do well to observe how Habermas—as Martin Jay has shown in a brilliant analysis[72]—attempted to refound the Hegelian-Marxist holistic vision on a more adequate theoretical base, thus diminishing the totalizing tendencies of his work. (1) From systems theory (Luhmann), Habermas adopted the notion of a decentered whole consisting of two levels, one intersubjective and the other functionalist. (2) From psychological learning theory (Piaget), he gained help in reformulating his notion of totality so as to avoid suggesting that history is a universally coherent process of development, but without falling into the opposite view that history is utterly without direction or is a process of inevitable decline. There are in history a plurality of productive factors, and evolutionary processes are not irreversible; but they do represent structural sequences that a society must go through insofar as it is evolving at all. (3) Post-Wittgensteinian linguistic philosophy (Chomsky, Austin, Searle) helped Habermas to recast the Marxist concept of totality in the direction of a theory of "communicative competence" that develops over time through intersubjective interactions (Mead, Durkheim). Its telos is the achievement of an "undistorted speech situation," which, in Habermas's terms, is not "a utopian model for an emancipated society" but is used rather to "reconstruct the concept of rationality" as a "communicative rationality." (4) Finally, sociological modernization theory (Weber, Parsons) suggested to Habermas that modernity is and remains an "uncompleted project," and it encouraged him to develop a "decentered rather than expressive holism" involving an interplay between systemic and lifeworld dimensions of society.[73]

The poststructuralist critics of Habermas (most notably, Michel Foucault) have not been satisfied with these revisionary efforts and remain convinced that any kind of holism must be completely rejected. But the antiholistic particularism and "carnivalesque play" offered by these critics, argues Jay, are utterly powerless against the seemingly inevitable march of history toward the use of increasingly sophisticated and destructive weapons, culminating in "nuclear totalization." "If the human race is to avoid the negative totality of nuclear catastrophe, we may well need to find some positive alternative, . . . [namely] a liberating totalization that will not turn into its opposite."[74]

This alternative, couched as it is in almost apocalyptic terms, seems to call for nothing less than a theological response. Such a response is not provided by Jay, who confines himself to searching for the germ of a defensible concept in the "debris" of Marxist humanism. But one is offered by Helmut Peukert, who has virtually alone developed a "theology of communicative action" on the basis of Habermasian theory.[75]

Peukert contends that "the thesis of the egalitarian and solidaristic basic structure of communicative action is at the same time the central thesis of the whole of theology." The "limit idea implied in communicative action itself" is "the unlimited, universal communication community, the realization of freedom in solidarity through historical action." The question Peukert poses concerns the conditions of possibility for the realization of such a communicative freedom. This question exposes aporias in all previous attempts to found communicative action and requires for its resolution a theological response, a reference to God. The fundamental aporia for Peukert does not merely concern how freedom is to be accounted for in the midst of historical domination, inequality, and violence, although he does briefly consider what he calls "the question of an absolute freedom as the presupposition of finite historical freedom." Rather, the pressing question for Peukert is how it is possible to maintain "anamnestic solidarity" with those who "have been destroyed and annihilated as victims of historical processes." Since death cuts off past subjects from participation in the universal communication community, the very idea of such a community appears to be falsified by the death of those who sacrificed to help make it possible. How can we live with the thought that we "owe everything to the oppressed, the downtrodden, the victims of the prior process of liberation"?

This question, argues Peukert, necessarily introduces a theological dimension into history. It raises the question of that "actuality" (*Wirklichkeit*) which is "absolute, liberating freedom," which "saves those who live in solidarity unto death in death," and which "will make the dead live again." This actuality is God—an actuality disclosed in and required by the very fact of communicative action, which provides the basis for a practical proof of God. The fact that we do participate in and experience communicative freedom carries with it an implicit acknowledgment that those who have gone before us and who have sacrificed themselves on our behalf are not cut off from the universal communication community but are somehow preserved and enabled to share in its fulfillment. The very idea of the universal communication community "as the utmost idea achievable" requires that this be the case, yet we lack the means to achieve it. Only God is capable of overcoming the severance of death, the amnesia of history, and the annihilating power of injustice. The identity of this God is established for Israel by its basic experience of the God who maintains solidarity with the victims, and for Christians by the resurrection of Jesus from the dead, which is the ultimate "empowerment" and "enablement" of anamnestic solidarity.[76]

The poignancy of Peukert's theological argument is reinforced by its context, which is that of attempting to make sense of history after the traumas of Nazism and the Holocaust. Peukert is attempting to elaborate certain hints found in the writings of Walter Benjamin and Max Horkheimer, who brought reflections from the Jewish religious heritage (from which they were alienated) to bear upon their work in critical social theory. Horkheimer wrote:

> The thought is monstrous that the prayers of the persecuted in their hour of greatest need, that the innocent who must die without explanation of their situation, that the last hopes of a supernatural court of appeals, fall on deaf ears and that the night unilluminated by any human light is also not penetrated by any divine one. The eternal truth without God has as little ground and footing as infinite love; indeed, it becomes an unthinkable concept. But is the monstrousness of an idea a cogent argument against the assertion or denial of a state of affairs? Does logic contain a law which says that a judgment is simply false that has despair as its consequence?[77]

This "monstrous," "unthinkable" thought led Benjamin in his last work to pose the question whether the past is closed or open. If it is closed, we are left simply with "enslaved ancestors," "the generations of the downtrodden," "the dead." But "empathetic memory" has the capability of modifying, of transforming what is closed into something unclosed and fluid. Benjamin admitted that such a statement is "theological" and appears to be completely unfounded on the basis of historical materialism, but it is nonetheless unavoidable if one is to maintain solidarity with the generations of the oppressed, which is the only alternative to making empathy with the victor the methodological principle of historical writing. To grasp history as "the history of the suffering (or Passion) of the world" is to introduce an implicit theological claim.[78]

Peukert's attempt to elaborate these hints is strangely formal and somewhat stilted. A theological dogma—the resurrection from the dead—is dropped into the midst of a historical aporia and remains for the most part unpacked. What does it mean to speak of "God's act of resurrection" and to assert that God is the "unconditionally saving actuality" for Jesus and all others, past and future? How does Jesus' resurrection from the dead "empower" and "enable" anamnestic solidarity? Are these and similar statements simply blanket assertions that accompany the package of faith, or are they elusive metaphors that require interpretative rigor on the part of each new generation of faith? Despite the formalism of his theological answer, the question raised by Peukert about the fate of those who have suffered sacrificially in the past is undeniably important. It reminds us that we must be prepared to speak, as we shall attempt to do in the Epilogue, not merely of the history of freedom *within history,* but also of the consummation of freedom *in God.* Only such a consummation can fully redeem the unredeemed suffering of the victims of history. This consummation, I shall argue, is something that is going on all the time and is not simply postponed to the "end" of the temporal-historical process. Nor should the consummation be thought of as in itself unhistorical although it is transhistorical: just as God-in-history does not cease to be God, so also history-in-God does not cease to be history, although its spatio-temporal historicality is changed into the more primordial and infinite historicality of God. Peukert also reminds us that when we do speak of the history of freedom within history, we must avoid any kind of progressivism or triumphalism; the sufferings of one generation cannot be justified by the triumphs of the next, if there are such triumphs.

But we must, nonetheless, really speak of the history of freedom within history, which Peukert is loathe to do. We must affirm that God acts to liberate the oppressed and empower communicative freedom within history as well as in God. It is not enough to hope that all will be raised into eternal life in God, although without such hope communicative action remains aporetic; we must also be able to believe that "a strange empowering kind of power" is presently at work within history. The victims of history are "saved" not simply by being raised from the dead into eternal communion with God but also by experiencing partial fulfillments and momentary clearings of freedom within history. Happiness does not belong to the victors alone; in fact theirs is often the truly unhappy consciousness. We certainly cannot claim to be the first generation to enjoy an authentic liberation and a happiness denied to our predecessors, as Peukert perhaps unintentionally implies. We too are victims, although our victimization may be trivial compared with the victimization of those who have gone before. We can rejoice in the victories and suffer in the defeats of our predecessors as well as our own, affirming the goodness of "what is" while hoping for what is better, the preservation and consummation of all beings in God.

Maintaining anamnestic solidarity with the victims of history, refusing to forget them, insisting on telling and retelling their story, can have a transformative effect within history, even if the final redemption of their suffering is in the hands of God alone. Their story, the gestalt that emerges from it, can serve as a powerful deterrent against the repetition of such atrocities, and thus it can help to save the future for future generations. Is this part of the meaning of the "resurrection of the dead"? If so, resurrection is a powerfully historical category as well as a strictly theological one. It brings what is dead and gone into play once again, both within history and in God. To make sense of this, a theology of resurrection would be called for which Peukert himself does not provide, and which lies beyond the bounds of our present theology of history.[79]

Another kind of criticism of Peukert's attempted theological resolution of the aporias present in communicative action is set forth by Jens Glebe-Möller, who also draws heavily on the work of Habermas and other critical social theorists.[80] While sympathetic with much of Peukert's program, Glebe-Möller concludes that under the conditions of postmodernity it is no longer possible to speak of God as any sort of transcendent, personal power. The word *God*, especially as shaped by the egalitarian Yahweh tradition of ancient Israel as well as by Jesus' proclamation of the kingdom of God, must now be seen as simply the designation of a norm—the last and highest of norms, the "ideal communicative fellowship." It is this norm, not God as a reality distinguishable from human praxis, that enables us to endure guilt and maintain solidarity.

> But [in the face of guilt] are we not then back at the point where only faith in a divine deliverance can rescue us—where, with Peukert, we have to reintroduce the thought of God? I continue to be convinced that we are today unable to think that thought. . . . But *can* we be in solidarity? In the last analysis, we can be nothing else, for solidarity—the ideal communicative fellowship—is presupposed in everything we say and do! No divine deliverance, no formula for release from guilt, is necessary. The only requirement is that we are thoughtful, that we use our minds. *Thoughtlessness* keeps us subject to guilt, to the passive consciousness of guilt. But thoughtlessness is not overcome by some divine deliverance. Thoughtlessness is overcome only by thoughtfulness.[81]

What Glebe-Möller calls "thoughtfulness" might be thought of as a form of "reason in history," which could in turn provide a way of thinking about God's presence in history in noninterventionist terms—and it is such an interventionist theology that Glebe-Möller has in mind when he criticizes the notion of a "transcendent" God who "delivers" or "rescues" us from guilt and "saves" us from death by raising Jesus from the dead.

Peukert's resurrection theology is vulnerable to such an interpretation, but it is not the only theological option available. Glebe-Möller ultimately opts out of theistic theology entirely on the grounds that the God-concept is unthinkable today and in any case is not needed to give an adequate account of the ideal communicative fellowship. The question then concerns the conditions of possibility for maintaining such a fellowship under the conditions of historical adversity and amnesia. What enables "thoughtfulness," or better, "discursive rationality,"[82] to prevail against the radical perversion of reason that is present in the twisted logic of the death camps and nuclear war games?

History, I have suggested, is a battle not of reason versus unreason but of reason versus reason, of discursive rationality versus systemic distortion. It is precisely reason run amok that gives evil its terrible power. My theological claim is that humanity on its own cannot overcome this self-concealing perversion of reason. Liberation is then, to be sure, experienced as a "deliverance"—but in the form of an empowerment from within, not of a supernatural rescue—an empowerment experienced as something gratuitous, which makes it possible for us to think and act anew, to break through distorted communication, to shape communities of freedom afresh, when all the resources at our disposal have been exhausted. This is the work of God in history, "the rose in the cross of the present."

Shapes of Freedom and Historical Process

What Hegel called "the cross of the present" entails recognizing and enduring the contradiction between communicative freedom and the structures of domination and oppression that threaten to overwhelm it. But there is a "rose" in this cross, which is reason, dialectical reflection, the capacity for grasping every contradiction rationally, struggling toward its resolution rather than fleeing or denying it. Such dialectical reflection demands of us "hard labor" because we must inquire about God's redemptive activity in this unfinished, fragmented, ambiguous process known as history, not in a fairy-tale world where good always triumphs and evil is vanquished. The shape in which God appears is liminal, found at the margins of the dominant world-formations, and hidden within a multiplicity of worldly shapes of freedom. The hard labor required for its discernment is not a theoretical but a practical and self-engaging reason, a taking up of this shape, which is the shape of suffering and liberating love, into one's own emancipatory praxis.[83]

An example of this hard labor is found in the debate among black theologians over the question whether the "definitive event" of black liberation has taken place. If it has not, contends William R. Jones, then blacks have no alternative but to conclude that God—should there be a God—is a "white racist." What Jones demands of black theology, and of James Cone in particular, is a *deus ex machina,* a miracle-working God, who will set blacks free all at once, in one "mighty act" such as the Exodus of the Israelites from Egypt.

> How can blacks know that God disapproves of black suffering except by his elimination of it, except by his bringing it to an immediate halt? . . . Cone must identify what he regards as the definitive event of black liberation. . . . The scandal of the particularity of black suffering can be answered only by an appeal to the particularity of God's liberating activity—an Exodus-type event for blacks.[84]

The painful reality is that such a "definitive event of black liberation" has not taken place and in all likelihood will not take place. God does not intervene supernaturally in human affairs to bring about "definitive" or "immediate" or "total" liberation of any people or condition. The theological alternative demanded by Jones (either God intervenes supernaturally or God is not a liberating God) cannot tolerate the dialectical insight that redemption comes about and shapes of freedom appear in a not-yet-redeemed world, that liberation entails conflict, struggle, suffering, defeat, death and resurrection, that there are setbacks and advances in the history of freedom but never triumphal, unambiguous progress.

Cone refuses the alternative posed by Jones. He and others have shown that freedom has in fact been experienced, affirmed, and sung about in the black community, not only after emancipation but also before it in the days of slavery, not only in the struggle for civil rights or the black power movement but also in the period of Reconstruction and segregation. This is not to diminish the enormous importance of such events as the end of slavery, the dismantling of the legal structure of segregation, or the movement toward full human and civil rights. But it is to say that God's liberating action is not limited to such historical break-throughs as these, and that God can set and hold a people free even in the midst of historical oppression and reversals. Indeed, the black spirituals make it clear that Christ was experienced as present precisely in the slave community, clearing a space of freedom in the midst of bondage and brutality, and the same has continued to be true for the black church as the central institution of a segregated, suffering people.[85] The experience of the presence of the living Christ, rendered concrete by the Gospel stories of Jesus' life and death as well as by the Old Testament accounts of God's acts on behalf of the people Israel, took on the character of a powerfully transformative gestalt. This gestalt—the shape of the crucified and risen Christ, the Messiah of Israel who will set all oppressed peoples free—has been the definitive event of liberation for blacks, but it is a shape that appears in the world liminally, for those who have eyes to see, and it does not work miracles or provide supernatural rescues.

A similar conclusion about the character of God's redemptive presence in history is arrived at, via a somewhat different route, by contemporary feminist theology, notably in the work of Rosemary Radford Ruether. In opposition to the antihistorical, otherworldly eschatology of mainstream Christianity, which has assumed a thoroughly ambiguous attitude toward women (negating the female body in its physical form yet appropriating it in spiritualized form), she intends to reaffirm a "historical escha-tology," but without adopting "a linear view of history as a single universal project leading to a final salvific end point." This is the old salvation history mythos, secularized in modern revolutionary movements. Such a view tends eventually either to become purely eschatological, relying on a suprahistorical divine intervention, or to absolutize a particular social revolution. Moreover, it is increasingly evident that it is anti-ecological, disregarding finite limits and exploiting the nonhuman environment.[86]

Against this linear image, Ruether introduces the image of *metanoia,* "conversion to the center." "Conversion suggests that, while there is no one utopian state of humanity lying back in an original paradise of the 'beginning,' there are basic ingredients of a just and livable society. These ingredients have roots in nature and involve acceptance of finitude, human scale, and balanced relationships between persons and between human and nonhuman beings." A "humane acceptance of our historicity demands that we liberate ourselves from 'once-and-for-all' thinking," and attend rather to the needs and possibilities at hand. Ruether notes that Hebraic thought combined both linear and cyclical patterns, and she suggests that this conversion to the center, a "return to harmony within the covenant of creation," is not a cyclical return to what existed before, but rather involves ever-new achievements of "livable, humane balances" under new and different historical circumstances. "It is a historical project that has to be undertaken again and again in changing circumstances." The most adequate image for such a view of history is one that I shall develop in the next chapter, namely, that of a spiral rather than of a line or a circle. Ruether herself makes no mention of this image, but she does quote an old Shaker hymn:

> 'Tis a gift to be simple; 'Tis a gift to be free;
> 'Tis a gift to come down where you ought to be. . . .
> To turn, turn will be our delight,
> Till by turning, turning, we come round right.[87]

What is this center to which we are turning ever afresh—toward which we are spiraling with new projects under new circumstances? The central biblical images for it, Ruether suggests, are the *shalom* of God and the kingdom of God, but she herself fleshes it out in a feminist vision of an integrative society. This is a society that would affirm the values of democratic participation, the equal value of all persons, and equal access to educational and work opportunities. It would be "a democratic socialist society that dismantles sexist and class hierarchies, that restores ownership and management of work to the base communities of workers themselves, who then create networks of economic and political relationships." It would be an organic community in which activities are shared and integrated, and an ecological community in which human and nonhuman systems have been harmonized. Such an alternative society can be built up, she thinks, either through small utopian experiments or by working on pieces of the vision separately. But she is quite clear that "the alternative nonsexist, nonclassist and nonexploitative world eludes us as a global system" because "the powers and principalities are still very much in control of most of the world."[88] They will, one fears, remain in control of the world. The most we can hope to achieve are fragmentary pieces of the vision, which do, however, when realized have the effect of making this world a tolerable place in which to dwell humanly and of interrupting the sway of the worldly powers, constraining their sphere of influence, perhaps to some modest degree even reforming them.

We must insist, then, that there is no triumphal march of God in history, no special history of salvation, but only a plurality of partial, fragmentary, ambiguous histories of freedom. We have learned from Troeltsch that the "damming and shaping [of] the historical stream of life" goes on all the time and is at the heart of historical process. What is shaped are fragile syntheses of values and praxis, or in Ruether's terms "livable, humane balances," which achieve momentary, relative victories over chaos and tyranny through a process of confrontation and compromise. Such syntheses and harmonies endure for a while, but eventually they break down. Temporal passage involves not only a progressive, continuous evolution of practices but also disruptive, discontinuous revolutions and reversals. History is made up of such continuities and discontinuities, which cannot be patched into an overarching linear teleology. Not only are such teleologies indefensible from the point of view of historical reality as we know it, but also they captivate us by a totalitarian vision—the "once-and-for-all" thinking Ruether warns against—which diverts attention from the partial completions that are possible in the present moment and to which it is our responsibility to attend.

But is this enough? Is it enough simply to be able to say that momentary shapes of freedom do occur, and partial integrations of historical life are attained, again and again despite constant adversity, and that we can rejoice in their occurrence while recognizing their transience and limitation? It is important to be able to say this, but is it enough? Is it enough to speak only of more or less random configurations of freedom and not also in some sense of a *history* of freedom, a history of transfigurative praxis? I think not. There is in fact a telos or purpose of history that can be construed as open-ended and nondeterminative of outcomes. Like the work of art or act of love, such a telos has the character of an "open wholeness." It can be described as follows: our responsibility is to work for the enhancement and expansion of freedom—a building up and integration of the various shapes of freedom into a more inclusive, multifaceted, wholesome matrix of communicative action and cultural practices. Freedom is intrinsically dynamic and never finished; if it becomes static it will stagnate. It requires continual enhancement of its qualities and expansion of its inclusiveness; it entails both a continuing transformation of the privileged and a continuing liberation of the oppressed. There is not a fixed quantity of freedom that will "run out" as a consequence of this enhancement and expansion, this transfigurative praxis. As John Cobb observes, such a telos provides a principle for "measur[ing] the advance and decline of history," for "interpreting the meaning of historical movements, whether the end of history will be failure or consummation."[89] We shall explore the possibilities of such an "open teleology" in the Epilogue.

CHAPTER V

Epilogue:
The Beginning of the History of Freedom?

We asked in the introductory chapter whether the end of salvation history might offer the possibility of the beginning of the history of freedom. The mythos of salvation history, with its logic of triumph and causality, its distinction of planes (profane and sacred), its special sequence of events, its linear teleology, and its supernatural, other-worldly eschatology must be allowed to die out in order to enable the enduring conviction that God acts redemptively in history to be reborn in a theology of the history of freedom, one that is oriented to God's shaping presence in a unitary though complex historical process as well as to an open teleology and a this-worldly communicative praxis.

As we have seen, Hegel claimed that the history of the ancient, medieval, and modern worlds was (at least in the West) a history of the progress of the consciousness of freedom. Even if one were to agree with him (as I do not) that this history of consciousness reached its culmination with the theoretically complete definition of freedom found in Hegel's own philosophy of absolute spirit, one would have to insist that history itself does not come to an end with this philosophical culmination. If the goal of history lies not in the cognition of the concept but in the actualization of freedom, then the post-Hegelian period has a new and distinctive task, namely, the actualization of the concept of freedom in various forms of praxis, which we have described as transfigurative, communicative, emancipatory. In this sense, the turn from the modern to the postmodern is a turn from the primacy of theory to the primacy of praxis, as Hegel's left-wing disciples correctly recognized. The relationship of theory and praxis reverses with this turn: further insight into what freedom is will be gained only from and through historical praxis.[1] Conceptual or logical rationality is supplemented by a discursive or dialogical rationality that is capable of engendering (always fragmentarily but often with transformative power) the telos of reason in history, communicative freedom or communicative fellowship, which can be regarded as a postmodern translation of the symbol "kingdom of God."[2]

It may seem presumptuous if not downright delusory to speak of the "beginning" of the history of freedom. After all, the postmodern period is not the first to concern itself with freedom; rather it is the beneficiary of a great heritage of reflection about freedom. And even if there has been a decisive turn from theory to praxis in the transition from modernity to postmodernity, we cannot claim that the praxis of freedom was initiated only since the Enlightenment. Still, if we consider the entire span of human evolution, and the thousands of years that have elapsed since the ancient civilizations of Mesopotamia, Egypt, and the Indus Valley, beginning around 3500 B.C.E., there is a sense in which the history of freedom is relatively young. Karl Rahner suggests that we are now entering into a second period of "hominized" existence, the realm of history that humanity has "opened up for itself" through the consciousness of self, world, time, and being. Hominized existence began with what Karl Jaspers calls the "axial period," the decisive turn to high civilization that occurred in China, India, Iran, Israel, and Greece between 800 and 200 B.C.E. In this frame of reference, the Christ event took place near the beginning rather than at the middle or the end of the history of human self-actualization in freedom, and in the late twentieth century we are now entering upon a new phase of this history, filled with both unprecedented possibilities and enormous dangers.[3]

Christ may stand near the beginning of this history, but we may very well stand near the end of it, for we have arrived at the point where humanity has attained the power to annihilate itself and terminate history as we know it. Thus if it is not presumptuous to speak of the "beginning" of this history, it surely is delusory. But it is this very threat, in its terror and immediacy, which makes it so urgent to take up the praxis of freedom, with a determination to build a global communication community, to keep the conversation of humanity going, to deploy the power of discursive rationality against the systemic and technological distortions of reason that will, if unchecked, destroy civilization or the environment or both. History hangs in the balance and we do not know what the outcome will be. Hence we are able to speak of "the beginning of the history of freedom," if at all, only with a question mark.

We do, however, know what our responsibility is, and we have some sense of the shape such a history would assume if we are allowed a historical future. I shall refer to this as "the history of freedom within history" and speak of it as "an open teleology." For this history we may work, hope, and pray. We also know, strictly by faith, that God is the Alpha and the Omega, the beginning and the end of all things. Thus we may also speak of "the consummation of freedom in God." Whatever happens in the worldly history of freedom, whether it is itself a failure or a consummation or an ambiguous mixture, will be annulled and transfigured in the "eternal history" of freedom that is God. This consummation, which is itself a continuing process, should not be allowed to distract our attention from worldly praxis, as frequently took place with respect to the salvation history paradigm. It should rather have a releasing, empowering effect, allowing us to turn our attention to the field for which we do have responsibility, giving us the courage to struggle against difficult odds or to start over after reversals and defeats. The absolute "absolves" us to go forth into the world and make of it something good. In a complete reversal from the classical outlook, neglect of our worldly mission rather than of our eternal salvation is what is now seen to have deadly consequences.

1. The History of Freedom Within History: An Open Teleology

The Question of the "End" of History

We may speak generally of two senses of the "end" of history. The English word *end*, like the Greek *eschatos*, means both "aim" or "purpose" (*telos*) and "boundary" or "limit" (*terminus*). Taken in the first sense, it refers to an *innerhistorical* process that is both open and teleological. Taken in the second sense, it refers to a *transhistorical* consummation of all things in God. God and God alone is the ultimate terminus or limit of world history—not a chronologically future terminus but an ever-present one, a terminus that is also a transition, a passing over into a new and unimaginable historicality, the triune figuration of the One who loves in freedom.[4] There are obvious connections between these two senses of "end"; for example, the consummation of freedom in God is also an aim or telos of history, but it is one that lies beyond the boundary distinguishing history from God, and it is not an aim that can be accomplished by historical praxis. I am primarily concerned with the latter as the proper object of theology of history, of God in history; but the transhistorical consummation, which is the proper object of eschatology, of history in God, alters the horizon in which historical praxis is interpreted.

I have argued that world history as a whole, both microhistory and macrohistory, is tragicomic; it is an ambiguous process. The final comedy is the divine comedy, not a human comedy. Comic elements are certainly present in history, but the only unambiguous comedy is the consummation of all things in God. At the same time I have insisted that we must find a way beyond a strictly tragic vision of history, and that it is not enough to remain satisfied with ambiguity, which leaves us with a picture of history as an endless, aimless round of configurations and defigurations, of integrations and disintegrations.

Beyond ambiguity there is hope. Paul Ricoeur identifies it as the third level of interpreting history, the first two being progress and ambiguity.[5] Hope refers to a "unity of meaning," which is "the fundamental source of the courage to live in history," but it is a hidden, mysterious meaning, which we cannot see or say; rather, we must "risk it on signs." For Christians, according to Ricoeur, this hope is based on the faith that God "directs this uncertain, noble, and guilty history toward himself." Great "revelatory" events take on a certain pattern, a global shape that constitutes a meaning in history which is neither rational nor irrational but "surrational"—not less but more than rational, as when we speak of something as "surrealist." I accept Ricoeur's formulation with certain modifications: I prefer to think not of God's "directing" but rather of God's "luring" and "shaping"; the patterns or shapes that are the "signs" on which hope is risked are not merely global but also small and provincial; and the "surrational" is not something suprahistorical or eschatological, as Ricoeur implies, but manifests itself precisely in the dialogical rationality that shapes communicative freedom in this world, demonstrating a transformative, unconcealing, unifying power.

It is important to be able to affirm this hope since, as John Cobb points out, we need some kind of "overview" in order to make sense of history and our place in it.[6] The problem, however, is that all philosophical and theological overviews have fallen into disrepute. The most ambitious of recent theological attempts, that of Wolfhart Pannenberg, overextends itself because it insists on "a pre-apprehension of the fulfilling outcome toward which [the course of events] moves." Cobb observes: "The loss of expectation of a consummatory End of history is no doubt a major reason for the decline both of faith and of reflection about the meaning of history. But from the point of view of process theology, the need now is to renew the Christian interpretation of history without presupposing a fulfilling End."[7]

Material for what he calls an "open-ended theology of history" is provided, in Cobb's view, by Whitehead's *Adventures of Ideas* as well as by political and liberation thought; such a theology would call for a continual transformation of society through the enhancement and expansion of freedom.[8] Yet while Whitehead did speak of the increase of freedom, his controlling metaphors were truth and beauty, adventure and peace. In the concluding words of *Adventures of Ideas:*

> At the heart of the nature of things, there are always the dream of youth and the harvest of tragedy. The adventure of the universe

starts with the dream and reaps tragic beauty. This is the secret of
the union of zest with peace: that the suffering attains its end in a
harmony of harmonies. The immediate experience of this final
fact, with its union of youth and tragedy, is the sense of peace. In
this way the world receives its persuasion towards such
perfections as are possible for its diverse individual occasions.[9]

A profound vision—but one whose telos is not so much the
enhancement and expansion of freedom as it is the harmony of
adventure and peace. What is needed is a conversation partner
with a more natural affinity to a postmodern political-liberation
theology as it attempts to work out an open-ended theology of
history. Such is afforded, in my view, by the complex of materials
from Hegel, Troeltsch, critical social theory, and hermeneutical
and praxis philosophies, which I have attempted to identify in
the preceding pages. But Cobb's contribution from a Whiteheadian perspective is valuable because he provides not only
independent confirmation of the validity of this agenda but also
many original insights.

An Open Wholeness, a Helical Spiral

Our "teleological" responsibility in history is to shape, on both
large and small scales, new cultural syntheses, new communities
of freedom and emancipatory praxis, out of the resources of the
past, attendant to the demands of the present, lured toward new
possibilities by the paradigmatic shape of love in freedom. This
is a responsibility that must be exercised again and again in
each new age and context, recognizing that only partial and
contingent solutions are possible, and that all formulations of
both the paradigm and the telos are culture-specific and relative,
valid only for a time. Through this continuing shaping process,
certain matrices of historical practice may be built up that
provide a basis for further enhancements and expansions of
freedom; and these matrices, if they can be joined together and
sustained, may constitute a trajectory of the history of the praxis
of freedom.

Elements of such a trajectory appropriate to our time might include: the continuing liberation of the oppressed and transformation of the privileged, the protection of individual rights, the enhancement of democratic institutions, the articulation of integrative purposes and values for a people, the fashioning of nonexploitative and just economic systems, the repudiation of nuclear warfare and ecological devastation, the promotion of dialogue and shared concerns among the religions, the creation of a truly global communication community in which national and ethnic differences are both honored and transcended, the bringing of discursive rationality to bear upon situations of distorted communication wherever they are found, whether interpersonal or structural. Any such trajectory remains highly fragile, subject to setbacks and reversals; it does not advance along a steadily progressive line; the struggle against the systems of domination and alienation, to say nothing of personal sin and pathological destruction, is endless.

This teleology scarcely constitutes a total design or a consummatory end of history. As Austin Farrer observes, we can no longer think of the world as a total design but at best only as a loose society of partial harmonizations. What is achieved in history by these momentary syntheses is valuable for its own sake, not for the sake of some unattainable utopian consummation.[10] The teleology that we have in mind is not an enclosed and finished totality but an "open wholeness." It has the character not of a straight line or of a circle but of a spiral, an open-ended, "helical spiral." These metaphors, both of which reflect a Hegelian way of thinking, require closer attention.

1. For Hegel, history could not be an endless succession of random stories; this would be a "bad infinite," a process of becoming that never comes to any genuine realization. Rather, the events of history manifest a "true infinite," a forming or shaping of successive moments into meaningful wholes by acts of recollection and anticipation. But how can this be if the future is the "not yet" and the past the "no more"? William Desmond

suggests that for Hegel the work of art is a model of the kind of wholeness that can be achieved in history. The art work gathers time and space into a meaningful presence, but the perfection it achieves is dialectical rather than univocal. Perfection is found in art not just once but again and again in a plurality of possible actualizations. The true work of art has an "energizing dynamism" or a "compacted fullness" that is analytically inexhaustible; it is not just a "recollective gathering up of the past" but also an "implicit spanning of the future" since it contains the "promise of repeated reinterpretations, repeated resurrections." It is a specific spatio-temporal shape that does not enclose or enframe but rather opens out into infinity. It offers an "open wholeness" rather than a "totalitarian closure." It opens out because "what its wholeness makes manifest is the sense of the presence of infinite inexhaustibility." Thus the perfection of one work of art does not exclude that of another.[11]

The same perfection characterizes works of love or the practice of love in freedom. In such acts, history reaches completion again and again, yet it remains ever incomplete since the wholeness of such acts does not close off but opens out into an infinite inexhaustibility and leaves the future undetermined. Hegel inquired about the possibility of a new wholeness in his own time, after the emergence of both "infinite subjectivity" and "infinite grief." He was deeply aware of the "discord" of modernity and glimpsed the coming traumas of a secularized, privatized, and instrumentalized world. He knew there could be no return to the primitive (as Nietzsche thought and perhaps Heidegger) but only a pressing on to a new telos, a new wholeness "beyond both the passing of the classical and the decomposing forces of modernity."[12] What might this be? Hegel did not attempt to predict it. Is it too much to suggest that it might be a freedom that is communicative, a praxis that is emancipatory, a rationality that is dialogical, and that this new shape of freedom is being called forth precisely in response to traumas and threats more terrible than any Hegel could imagine—total war, total devastation, total meaninglessness, total annihilation of a people?

2. The second metaphor to which I have referred, that of a spiral, is also suggested by Hegel, whose philosophy of history envisioned a "cyclical movement" of spirit (which, it should be remembered, is fundamentally an *inter*subjective concept).[13] This cyclical movement is imbedded in the dialectical process by which spirit becomes spirit, namely, the triadic process of self-immediacy, self-differentiation, and self-reunification. The third moment of this process is not simply a return to the original immediacy but an advance to a new and more complex identity of the self. This new identity or synthesis then discovers that it is not the whole, that it is confronted by a new form of otherness, and thus it becomes a new thesis to a new antithesis, which generates a new synthesis. And so it goes in history, in an open-ended, never finished process of the formation and deformation of syntheses, harmonies, balances, on both microhistorical and macrohistorical scales. Such a process clearly is not linear, an undialectical advance along a straight line. Nor is it circular, although a cyclical movement is involved. At the end of each cycle there is a return to a point that is analogous to the starting point but also different; what has happened between the two points constitutes the difference. Although there may be recurrent patterns in history, history does not repeat itself: the fruit brought to maturity by the life of a nation "does not . . . fall back into the womb from which it emerged."[14]

Probably the best spatial metaphor by which to envision this process is that of the spiral—not an inward or outward spiraling in a single plane, but a coiling through constantly changing planes, which is the shape of a helix.[15] That around which the spiral coils can be imagined as either a cone of decreasing or increasing diameter or a cylinder of constant diameter. I prefer to think of the helix as open-ended and hence as cylindrical; one could, however, think of the diameter as both decreasing and increasing in a wavelike fashion, so that, though there may be significant advances and declines, the question of an innerhistorical consummation of history is left open. Historical process will undoubtedly at some point come to an end like everything finite; but whether that termination will be a consummation of freedom or an apocalyptic failure of the human project is unknown.

Paul Tillich envisions a very similar spatial image of the temporal-historical process. The circle, he observes, is "the spatial analogy to time's coming back to itself in eternal return." It is difficult to introduce genuine change into this model as well as any kind of telos, aim, or purpose; thus the circle imaged well the Greeks' fundamentally tragic world view, and it suited equally well Nietzsche's ironic-satiric emplotment of history. When the circle becomes a labyrinth, as with Derrida and Taylor, a more or less complete deconstruction of history as a meaningful category occurs. Augustine, Tillich argues, made a tremendous advance when he replaced the analogy of the circle with that of a straight line, "beginning with the creation of the temporal and ending with the transformation of everything temporal." Tillich notes, however, that this linear image "does not indicate the character of time as coming from and going to the eternal," and thus it is not surprising that for Augustine the City of God really hovers above the line and never enters into temporal-historical process. This made it possible for modern progressivism, by extending the line indefinitely, to deny a beginning and an end, "thus radically cutting off the temporal process from eternity." Against these two images, Tillich searches for a spatial metaphor that unites the qualities of "coming from," "going ahead," and "rising to."

> I would suggest a curve which comes from above, moves down as well as ahead, reaches the deepest point which is the *nunc existentiale,* the "existential now," and returns in an analogous way to that from which it came, going ahead as well as up. This curve can be drawn in every moment of experienced time, and it can also be seen as the diagram for temporality as whole. . . . Beginning from and ending in the eternal are not matters of a determinable moment in physical time but rather a process going on in every moment, as does the divine creation. There is always creation and consummation, beginning and end.[16]

A helical spiral, when stretched out along a linear plane, approximates the shape of a continuous parabolic curve such as described by Tillich.

Something like this image is in mind when Tillich undertakes a reinterpretation of the idea of a "history of salvation." If justified at all, this term "must point to a sequence of events in which saving power breaks into historical processes, prepared for by these processes so that it can be received, changing them to enable the saving power to be effective in history." To avoid misleading connotations of a separate sacred and suprahistorical history, Tillich thinks it is better to speak of "manifestations of the kingdom of God within history" (that is, of God's spiritual presence), and asks whether there is a "rhythm" in these manifestations. The rhythm is based on the "central manifestation" of the kingdom, Jesus as the Christ; "maturation toward [this] center" is a continual process and constitutes the rhythm of history. A "kairos" is a moment at which history has "matured to the point of being able to receive the breakthrough of the central manifestation of the Kingdom of God." The central kairos is of course the Christ event, but kairoi have come again and again both before and after this event, both within the history of the churches and beyond them; they are ever-new manifestations of the prophetic spirit. With regard to the image of the parabolic curve, kairoi would seem to take place with the transition from one upward swing of the curve to the next downward swing, which are the moments when the eternal is most unambiguously present in history. Kairoi are for Tillich macrohistoric events and represent cultural rather than personal moments of transformative disclosure. Speaking existentially or microhistorically, the curve, as he says, "can be drawn in every moment of experienced time." Tillich reminds us that "history does not move in an equal rhythm but is a dynamic force moving through cataracts and quiet stretches. History has its ups and downs, its periods of speed and of slowness, of extreme creativity and of conservative bondage to tradition."[17]

Instead of speaking of "the kingdom of God within history," I propose to speak of "the history of freedom within history." Much in Tillich's interpretation is helpful to the present argument: history indeed seems to move in irregular rhythms or cycles, which, though not repetitive, do not constitute a progressive advance toward an innerhistorical consummation; rather, the "end" of history comes whenever an authentic kairos takes place. I believe we must hold that the shaping power or gestalt of God is present in every moment of the process—in the building up, the preservation, and the breaking down of shapes of freedom, as well as in the transition to new shapes, new cultural configurations. Tillich's kairoi, then, would mark the times of transition from one significant cultural synthesis to another. In my view, however, the rhythmic, cyclical, or spiraling movement is not an "up and down" movement from the temporal to the eternal to the temporal (as seems to be required by Tillich's ontology), but rather the dialectical movement of identity-difference-reintegration by which spirit advances toward the telos of communicative freedom. The divine gestalt drives, shapes, lures the historical process as a whole, which reaches its telos in many distinct moments of "open wholeness," but it remains a process that is never finished and always subject to demonic distortion.

A Single Goal of History?

We have described a process by which shapes of freedom are engendered in history by a normative shape, which we have dared to call the divine shape, the shape of love in freedom, the shape associated with Jesus' ministry and death. From Habermas, Peukert, and Glebe-Möller we have learned to think of what is engendered as "communicative freedom" or "communicative fellowship," which is a postmodern expression of the symbol "kingdom of God." Is it appropriate to think of these shapes of freedom, this communicative freedom, as a single goal or telos of history? If so, are we then permitted to speak of a *history* of freedom within history?

In 1949, four years after the end of the most devastating war in world history, Karl Jaspers published a remarkable book, *The Origin and Goal of History*. The book is remarkable for its determination not to yield to the temptation of nihilism or retreat into the complacency of which Hegel speaks, a complacency that smugly contemplates the "confusion and wreckage" of history. Jaspers says that his approach is based on an "article of faith," that "humankind has one single origin and one goal," which are unknown to us and can "only be felt in the glimmer of ambiguous symbols." The ultimate goal, which thought can never reach, is simply this: "guided by history to pass beyond all history into the Comprehensive [*das Umgreifende*]." But there is also a proximate goal, which is attainable in the open and incalculable process of history: freedom.[18]

This historical future, while concealed in the past and present, is not inevitable, says Jaspers, but lies in our hands. What humanity may come to is glimpsed in the concentration camps, a peril that goes even deeper than the atom bomb because it "menaces the soul of humanity." "The only hope is for horror to become conscious. Nothing but the most lucid consciousness can help us. Dread of such a future may perhaps prevent it. The terrible forgetting must not be allowed to take place."[19] Rather than projecting images of the future, Jaspers proposes to call to mind three basic tendencies of the present—socialism, world unity, and faith—which "converge in the goal of accomplished human freedom."[20] Socialism is "every outlook, every tendency and every plan that aims at the ordering of the life and work of the community according to the criteria of justice accompanied by the repudiation of privileges," and with the goal of freedom. World unity will be accomplished in the form either of world empire ("the static peace of despotism") or world order ("a peaceful community of all subject to transmutation in perennial democratic unrest and self-rectification"). Faith is our link with the origin and goal of history, the matrix and consummation of our being.[21] A remarkable and prophetic vision, and as relevant today as it was forty years ago.

Is there a unity of history constituted by a single goal? Experience seems to testify against it, often quite strongly, but the essential, underlying fact, claims Jaspers, is that human beings are concerned with one another, recognize themselves in the other, are related to all others—often in a kind of immediacy that transcends political relations and conflicts. Ordinary citizens sense this even if their leaders do not. "The phenomenon of humanity in the dispersal of history," writes Jaspers, "is a movement toward the One—perhaps it is provenance from a single matrix [*Herkunft aus einem Grunde*]."[22] Jaspers recognizes that this movement is not steadily progressive; the "essential fact" about humanity is frequently concealed, distorted, repressed. History moves by "break-throughs," "leaps," "unique creations," which are "like revelations from some other source than the mere course of happening."[23] Unity is not a fact but a goal, a goal that appears in the form of many goals: the civilization and humanization of humanity, freedom and the consciousness of freedom (which includes the recognition that "what freedom is has no end"), cultural creativity, the manifestation of being or divinity in humanity. Such goals are gained and regained in history "in a perennial process of loss and devaluation." But the single, overall goal of history is not attained; "all supposed goals do indeed become factors within history," but they are not the final end of history, which is simply the Comprehensive.

Thus all attempts at constructing the unity of history break down. History is not closed with respect to either its past or its future; it does not reveal its origin and end. The ultimate question, says Jaspers, is this: "Does the unity of humankind consist in unification on the basis of a common faith, . . . in an organization of the one eternal truth by an authority that spans the earth?" Or is it attainable only

through communication of the historically manifold origins, which are mutually concerned with one another, without becoming identical in the manifestation of idea and symbol—a unity which leaves the One concealed in manifoldness, the One that can remain truly one only in the will to boundless communication, as an endless task in the interminable testing of human possibilities?[24]

Jaspers' answer to the question is clearly the second option, and rightly so. As far as our project is concerned, this answer means that we are not permitted to speak of God's presence in history in terms of "the shape of freedom" but only in terms of "shapes of freedom." Even what for us is the normative, paradigmatic shape of love-in-freedom, the shape of God-in-Christ, is finally only one shape among many in the inexhaustible manifold of history.

But notice what Jaspers says: the One concealed in manifoldness "can remain truly one only in the will to boundless communication." "Boundless communication" is at the heart of what Habermas calls "communicative competence" or "communicative action," and what we are calling "communicative freedom." Boundless communication requires a discursive or dialogical rationality in which literally everything is open to question, in which reasons must be given for every claim, in which consent is sought only through agreement rather than by the imposition of authority. Such communication levels all hierarchies, dissolves all privileges, transcends all provincialisms, overcomes all distortions and concealments. Expressed in the central image of Jesus' parables, it is the "kingdom of God." Expressed in a Pauline metaphor, it is the "wisdom of God," which destroys all "cleverness" and "boasting" (I Cor. 1:18-31). Expressed in Hegelian terms, it is the power of reason in history. But it is not simply rationality, not simply discourse or intellectual talk about something: rather, it issues in communities of solidarity and mutuality; it engenders the praxis of its own substance, which is freedom. Communicative freedom is the presence of God, of God's "kingdom," in history; it is the goal of history; but in history it appears only in a manifold of ambiguous and incomplete shapes.

2. The Consummation of Freedom in God

"Guided by history to pass beyond all history into the Comprehensive—that is the ultimate goal," writes Jaspers. Similarly, Cobb reminds us, following Whitehead, that the consummation of the world is in God, not in the creation of an earthly utopia. The future is open and the stakes are very high; we have no assurances whatsoever regarding the final outcome of history. The goal of communicative freedom may or may not be attained, and if it is attained, even partially, it may not endure. "Such a consummating event, if all goes well, could have penultimate significance, but it would not bring an end to the process. Eventually this planet will become uninhabitable. Our resurrection cannot be here or on any other planet revolving around some other sun. It must be in God."[25]

What is this end that is the transhistorical terminus of world-historical process, as distinct from its innerhistorical telos? What is this Comprehensive into which all things ultimately pass? Is it something that in itself is not historical but rather static presence, eternal bliss, unending rest? The tradition has usually thought of it this way, but at the price of dehistoricizing God. When does the "passing" take place? Only at the end of time or in every moment of time? The tradition has usually understood it to be the former, by way of a chronologically future package of "last things." What is the content of eternal life? Is individual identity in any sense preserved, or are all things merged into an undifferentiated whole? The tradition has usually maintained the former, but on the basis of a literal understanding of the resurrection body.

We do not know the answers to these questions. We lack the categories in which to frame the answers; we have only "the glimmer of ambiguous symbols" and intuitions based on faith. For me it seems intuitively right to say that, just as God does not cease to be God in virtue of God's immanence in the world, so also the world does not cease to be the world in virtue of the world's immanence in God (not just a future immanence but a continuous, ever-present immanence). Is it too much to say that the world introduces historicality into the divine life? Of course we do not really know what it means to say this, for historicality would be transfigured in the process. It would be a historicality in which there is both temporality and yet the utter coinherence of the modes of time—a concordance *without* discordance (as Paul Ricoeur might say).[26] The dialectic of identity-difference-mediation would spiral back upon itself in an eternally complete process of becoming. Negativity, destruction, evil, death would remain present only as something conquered, rejected, refined away. Eternal blessedness would not be an immovable perfection but the eternal conquest of the negative and the sublation of the positive in a process of "essentialization." Individual identity would be preserved by being taken up into, embodied by, a whole that is radically communitarian. The problem with these statements is that they are paradoxical to the point of bordering on unintelligibility because they are an attempt to introduce the world into God, the finite into the infinite, the real into the ideal, the temporal-historical into the eternal. The notion of an "eternal divine history" is paradoxical, but it is a necessary thought if we are to take seriously the historicization of God in and through God's self-involvement in world process. The inner, preworldly life of God may be a dynamic, "logical" process, but it is not yet a historical process. God becomes historical in relation to the world, but what this means with respect to the consummation of all worldly things in God we can only faintly imagine.[27]

Perhaps it is enough to say that "in God" communication becomes truly and perfectly boundless. God as the consummation of all things is simply the perfection of "communicative freedom." In God the many shapes of freedom are transfigured into one encompassing shape, which *is* God, the One who loves in freedom.

Notes

CHAPTER I. INTRODUCTION:
THE END OF SALVATION HISTORY

1. H. Richard Niebuhr, *The Meaning of Revelation* (New York: Macmillan, 1941), p. 80.

2. This expression is Edward Farley's. On the concept of salvation history and the logic of sovereignty, see his *Ecclesial Reflection: An Anatomy of Theological Method* (Philadelphia: Fortress Press, 1982), pp. 28-34, 93-94, 155-65.

3. See Langdon Gilkey, "The New Watershed in Theology," in *Society and the Sacred: Toward a Theology of Culture in Decline* (New York: Crossroad, 1981), pp. 7-12.

4. See Gerhard von Rad, *Old Testament Theology*, vol. 1: *The Theology of Israel's Historical Traditions*, trans. D. M. G. Stalker (Edinburgh and London: Oliver and Boyd, 1962), pp. 129-35, 334-36.

5. This is the central thesis of L. G. Patterson's *God and History in Early Christian Thought* (London: Adam & Charles Black, 1967), upon which I rely for the next few paragraphs. See esp. p. vii.

6. Hegel described Roman religion as the religion of "expediency" or "utility" (*Zweckmässigkeit*). See G. W. F. Hegel, *Lectures on the Philosophy of Religion*, ed. and trans. P. C. Hodgson et al., 3 vols. (Berkeley and Los Angeles: University of California Press, 1984–87), vol. 2, esp. pp. 207-11, 508-10, 697-98.

7. Patterson, *God and History in Early Christian Thought*, p. 62.

8. Ibid., pp. 21-26.

9. See Tertullian, *Apology*, 10-11, 25.1-12, 26.1, 40.13, et passim.

10. Patterson, *God and History in Early Christian Thought*, pp. 62-63; cf. pp. 56-67.

11. Ibid., pp. 74-96.

12. Augustine, *The City of God*, 5.pref., 5.1, 21. References (by book and chapter) are to the abridged version of the Fathers of the Church translation prepared by Vernon J. Bourke (New York: Image Books, 1958). Augustine did not use the expression "cunning of providence." It is suggested rather by Hegel's "cunning of reason," which "sets the passions to work in its service, so that the agents by which it gives itself existence must pay the penalty and suffer the loss." G. W. F. Hegel, *Lectures on the Philosophy of World History, Introduction: Reason in History*, trans. H. B. Nisbet with an introduction by Duncan Forbes (Cambridge: Cambridge University Press, 1975), p. 89.

13. Augustine, *City of God*, 5.1, 8-11; 12.6. See Langdon Gilkey, *Reaping the Whirlwind: A Christian Interpretation of History* (New York: Seabury Press, 1976), pp. 165-68.

14. Patterson, *God and History in Early Christian Thought*, pp. 121-23. See *City of God*, 14.28.

15. Augustine, *City of God*, 18.1; cf. 11.1.

16. Ibid., 15.1; 22.24.

17. Ibid., 11.1, 4-10, 16, 21-22; 22.30.

18. Gilkey, *Reaping the Whirlwind*, p. 175; see pp. 169ff. See also Patterson, *God and History in Early Christian Thought*, pp. 124, 126.

19. See the translation of *De veritate* by Robert W. Mulligan published as Thomas

Aquinas, *Providence and Predestination: Truth, Questions 5 & 6* (South Bend, Ind.: Regnery/Gateway, 1961). References are to this edition.

20. Thomas Aquinas, *De veritate*, 5.1-3.

21. Ibid., 5.3-4.

22. Ibid., 5.5, 10.

23. John Calvin, *Institutes of the Christian Religion*, 3.21.5, 7; 3.22.1; 3.23.7. References (by book, chapter, and section) are to the Library of Christian Classics edition, ed. John T. McNeill, trans. Ford Lewis Battles, 2 vols. (Philadelphia: Westminster Press, 1960).

24. Calvin, *Institutes*, 1.16.2-9.

25. Ibid., 1.17.5.

26. Ibid., 1.18.1.

27. Gilkey, *Reaping the Whirlwind*, p. 180. Calvin writes that human beings "cannot by deliberating accomplish anything except what [God] has already decreed with himself and determined by his secret direction" (*Institutes*, 1.18.1).

28. Calvin, *Institutes*, 1.17.11; 3.7.1.

29. Ibid., 3.25.10.

30. Gilkey, *Reaping the Whirlwind*, pp. 176-77, 184-87.

31. Calvin, *Institutes*, 3.23.14.

32. For a brief but illuminating discussion of the treatment of creation and providence in modern philosophy from Descartes to Kant, see Julian Hartt's chapter in *Christian Theology: An Introduction to Its Traditions and Tasks*, ed. P. C. Hodgson and R. H. King, 2nd ed. (Philadelphia: Fortress Press, 1985), pp. 151-58.

33. Gilkey points this out, *Reaping the Whirlwind*, pp. 210-12, but in other respects I do not share his interpretation of Schleiermacher on this question.

34. It is too much to say that Schleiermacher was "a thoroughly unhistorical thinker [*ein ganz unhistorischer Kopf*]," as Wilhelm Dilthey remarked (and also Albert Schweitzer somewhat less sharply), but there is some truth to it. For a discussion of various aspects of this question, see Wilhelm Pauck, "Schleiermacher's Conception of History and Church History," in *Schleiermacher as Contemporary*, ed. Robert W. Funk (New York: Herder and Herder, 1970), pp. 41-56.

35. See Friedrich Schleiermacher, *The Christian Faith*, ed. H. R. Mackintosh and J. S. Stewart (Edinburgh: T. & T. Clark, 1928), §§ 4, 5, 29, 30, 50, 51. On Schleiermacher's underlying determinism, see Albert L. Blackwell, *Schleiermacher's Early Philosophy of Life: Determinism, Freedom, and Phantasy*, Harvard Theological Studies, no. 33 (Chico, Calif.: Scholars Press, 1982). I recognize that these sweeping judgments are rather harsh and not entirely fair to Schleiermacher, but perhaps they are sufficient to indicate why, with respect to theology of history, I do not find myself oriented to his way of thinking.

36. Ernst Troeltsch points this out quite forcefully in "Half a Century of Theology: A Review," in *Writings on Theology and Religion*, trans. and ed. Robert Morgan and Michael Pye (London: Duckworth, 1977), pp. 53-81.

37. Karl Barth, *Church Dogmatics*, vol. 3/3, trans. G. W. Bromiley and R. J. Ehrlich (Edinburgh: T. & T. Clark, 1961), §§ 48-49.

38. Ibid., pp. 3-6.

39. Hegel, *Lectures on the Philosophy of Religion*, 1:308n.

40. Barth, *Church Dogmatics*, vol. 3/3, p. 36; cf. pp. 7-8, 34-43.

41. Ibid., pp. 16-17, 19-25, 44, 157-61, 184-86.

42. Ibid., pp. 164-70, 189.

43. Ibid., pp. 176-84.

44. Ibid., pp. 196-97, 199.

45. Ibid., p. 168.

46. It is true that, according to Barth, God's providential ordering includes not only the "divine ruling" (§ 49.3) but also the "divine preserving" (§ 49.1) and the "divine accompanying" (§ 49.2). While there is promise in these latter concepts, for Barth

they are governed by certain Protestant scholastic distinctions, and they are all construed as means by which "God fulfils his fatherly lordship over his creature." Throughout the entire discussion, the metaphors "lord" and "father" dominate.

47. See Jürgen Habermas, "Modernity—An Incomplete Project," reprinted in *The Anti-Aesthetic: Essays on Postmodern Culture,* ed. Hal Foster (Port Townsend, Wash.: Bay Press, 1983), pp. 3-15. See also Habermas's *The Philosophical Discourse of Modernity* (Cambridge, Mass.: M.I.T. Press, 1987). Stanley Rosen, in *Hermeneutics as Politics* (New York: Oxford University Press, 1987), agrees with Habermas in his insistence that the postmodern turn is a phase within the Enlightenment paradigm.

48. See Langdon Gilkey, "The New Watershed in Theology," pp. 3-14; and Mark C. Taylor, *Erring: A Postmodern A/theology* (Chicago: University of Chicago Press, 1984), pp. 3-18. I have discussed the first four of these crises more fully in the introduction to *Revisioning the Church: Ecclesial Freedom in the New Paradigm* (Philadelphia: Fortress Press, 1988), pp. 13-16.

49. On the concept of postmodernism, see, in addition to the Foster volume cited in n. 47, Frank Lentricchia, *After the New Criticism* (Chicago: University of Chicago Press, 1980); Alan Wilde, *Horizons of Assent: Modernism, Postmodernism, and the Ironic Imagination* (Baltimore: Johns Hopkins University Press, 1981); Jean-François Lyotard, *The Postmodern Condition: A Report on Knowledge,* trans. Geoff Bennington and Brian Massumi (Minneapolis: University of Minnesota Press, 1984); and Ihab Habib Hassan, *The Postmodern Turn: Essays in Postmodern Theory and Culture* (Columbus: Ohio State University Press, 1987). The latter work discusses the "twilight of subjectivity" as an aspect of postmodernism to which I have not attended. I am indebted to David Fisher and Mark Kline Taylor for several of these references.

50. Hal Foster in *The Anti-Aesthetic,* p. xii.

51. Gilkey, "The New Watershed," pp. 11-12.

52. This paragraph and the next are informed by Gilkey's lucid analysis in "Events, Meanings and the Current Tasks of Theology," *Journal of the American Academy of Religion* 53 (December 1985): 718-27.

53. The French biologist Jacques Monod has appropriated the famous words of Democritus for the title of his book, *Chance and Necessity: An Essay on the Natural Philosophy of Modern Biology* (New York: Vintage Books, 1972). A. R. Peacocke provides a very helpful evaluation of and response to the questions raised by Monod in his *Creation and the World of Science* (Oxford: Clarendon Press, 1979). Rather than being apotheosized as metaphysical principles destructive of all meaning, chance and necessity, Peacocke suggests, can be regarded as "creative agents" by means of which the potentialities of universes are being "run through" or "explored" (p. 70).

54. *The Journal of Religion* 66 (July 1986): 261-81.

55. Ibid., 261-62.

56. Ibid., 266-68. The last quotation is from Richard Rorty, *Consequences of Pragmatism: Essays 1972–1980* (Minneapolis: University of Minnesota Press, 1982), p. xxv.

57. Richard Rorty, *Philosophy and the Mirror of Nature* (Princeton, N.J.: Princeton University Press, 1979), pp. 9-10.

58. Ibid., p. 12.

59. Ibid., pp. 373-79, 389, 392-94.

60. See the ironic closing words to Hegel's first lectures on the philosophy of religion: "How things turn out [in the world] is not our concern" (*Lectures on the Philosophy of Religion,* 3:162). Just this is the "partiality" of philosophy, and the words are intended partly, I think, as a self-criticism of the philosopher's vocation, which is to interpret what has happened in the past and preserve the possession of truth for the future. It is religion, according to Hegel, that ought to concern itself with the world but no

longer does so. The question may be implicit for Hegel whether philosophy, given the default of religion, is prepared to relinquish concern for the world to those empirical sciences and secular leaders who have no inkling of the truth.

61. English translation by A. M. Sheridan Smith (New York: Pantheon Books, 1972). On Foucault, see further below, pp. 164-66.

62. Ibid., pp. 3-11.

63. Ibid., pp. 12-17.

64. Ibid., p. 131. Emphasis mine.

65. English translation by Donald F. Bouchard and Sherry Simon in *Language, Counter-Memory, Practice: Selected Essays and Interviews* (Ithaca, N.Y.: Cornell University Press, 1977). I quote from the reprint in *The Foucault Reader,* ed. Paul Rabinow (New York: Pantheon Books, 1984).

66. *The Foucault Reader,* p. 85.

67. Ibid., pp. 88-89. The English translation renders *wirkliche Historie* as "effective history," which in German would probably be *wirkende Historie.* The quotation within the quotation is from Friedrich Nietzsche, *The Dawn of Day* (1881; New York: Gordon Press, 1974), no. 130.

68. See Dean, "The Challenge of the New Historicism," p. 279.

69. Mark C. Taylor, *Erring: A Postmodern A/theology* (Chicago: University of Chicago Press, 1984). In what follows I draw upon some materials from my review of this book, which appeared in *Religious Studies Review* 12 (July-October 1986): 256-59. Published by the Council of Societies for the Study of Religion. See also Thomas Altizer, *History as Apocalypse* (Albany, N.Y.: State University of New York Press, 1985); Carl Raschke, *The Alchemy of the Word: Language and the End of Theology* (Missoula, Mont.: Scholars Press, 1979); and Charles Winquist, *Epiphanies of Darkness: Deconstruction in Theology* (Philadelphia: Fortress Press, 1986). Theodore W. Jennings' *Beyond Theism: A Grammar of God-Language* (New York: Oxford University Press, 1985), and Joseph S. O'Leary's *Questioning Back: The Overcoming of Metaphysics in Christian Tradition* (Minneapolis: Winston Press, 1985), represent rather different theological appropriations of deconstruction. See the reviews by Robert P. Scharlemann and David H. Fisher in *Religious Studies Review* 13 (October 1987): 312-17.

70. Taylor, *Erring,* pp. 36-39, 47-51, 71-72.

71. Ibid., pp. 105-7, 114-17.

72. For the concept of "appresentation," see Edward Farley, *Ecclesial Man: A Social Phenomenology of Faith and Reality* (Philadelphia: Fortress Press, 1975), pp. 194-205, 215-34.

73. Taylor, *Erring,* pp. 70-71; cf. pp. 52-73.

74. Taylor does not note that J. G. Herder long ago employed the image of the labyrinth as a metaphor of history in his *Ideen zur Philosophie der Geschichte der Menschheit* (1784-1791). See the selection contained in Patrick Gardiner, ed., *Theories of History* (Glencoe, Ill.: Free Press, 1959), p. 43. Several other Nietzschean images are found here, such as Ixion's wheel, Sisyphus's stone, the spider's web, the slender thread (pp. 42-44).

75. Taylor, *Erring,* pp. 157-58; cf. pp. 149-69.

76. See further below, pp. 166-67.

77. Gilkey, "Events, Meanings and the Current Tasks of Theology," 720-21, 723-24, 727.

78. Taylor, *Erring,* p. 6.

79. Frank Lentricchia has pointed this out in *After the New Criticism,* pp. 168-88.

80. Gilkey, "Events, Meanings and the Current Tasks of Theology," 728.

81. The similarities of this proposal to Richard J. Bernstein's *Beyond Objectivism and Relativism: Science, Hermeneutics, and Praxis* (Philadelphia: University of Pennsylvania

Press, 1983) are not accidental, and I shall draw upon Bernstein's work and other recent philosophies of praxis in ch. 4.1. I am also indebted here to Gilkey's discussion of "praxis, dialectic and paradox" in "Events, Meanings and the Current Tasks of Theology," 728-34.

82. See Ernst Troeltsch, *Christian Thought: Its History and Application,* ed. Baron F. von Hügel (London: University of London Press, 1923; repr. Westport, Conn.: Hyperion Press, 1979), esp. pp. 69-129.

83. Gertrud von le Fort, *Der Kranz der Engel,* 6th ed. (Munich: Ehrenwirth Verlag, 1953), p. 210. Quoted in Wilhelm Pauck, *Harnack and Troeltsch: Two Historical Theologians* (New York: Oxford University Press, 1968), p. 91n. Emphasis mine.

84. *Aufhebung* is the key to all of Hegel's logical and historical transitions. See Charles Taylor, *Hegel* (Cambridge: Cambridge University Press, 1975), esp. p. 119; and G. R. G. Mure, *A Study of Hegel's Logic* (Oxford: Clarendon Press, 1950), esp. chs. 1, 20. Mure shows that Hegel's sublations (or for that matter anybody's sublations) necessarily remain incomplete.

85. Gilkey, "Events, Meanings and the Current Tasks of Theology," 722-23, 730-34.

86. See n. 39.

87. I have in mind especially Ricoeur's *Time and Narrative,* trans. Kathleen McLaughlin and David Pellauer, 3 vols. (Chicago: University of Chicago Press, 1984–88). White's study of the role of figurative imagination in the work of the historian is highly valuable; see his *Tropics of Discourse: Essays in Cultural Criticism* (Baltimore: Johns Hopkins University Press, 1978); and *Metahistory: The Historical Imagination in Nineteenth-Century Europe* (Baltimore: Johns Hopkins University Press, 1973).

88. Karl Barth, *Church Dogmatics,* vol. 2/1, ed. G. W. Bromiley and T. F. Torrance (Edinburgh: T. & T. Clark, 1957), § 28: "The Being of God as the One Who Loves in Freedom."

89. White, *Metahistory,* ch. 2.

90. Hegel, *Lectures on the Philosophy of World History,* pp. 54, 71.

91. "Radical historicality" is a possible translation of Troeltsch's term *Historismus.* See ch. 3, n. 63.

92. The German word *Gestalt* means "shape," "form," "figure," "structure." I use it as a loan word in English. See below, p. 84.

93. "The philosophers have only *interpreted* the world in various ways; the point is, to *change* it." Karl Marx, "Theses on Feuerbach" (1845), in *Writings of the Young Marx on Philosophy and Society,* trans. and ed. Loyd D. Easton and Kurt H. Guddat (New York: Anchor Books, 1967), p. 402.

94. See Walter Jaeschke, "World History and the History of the Absolute Spirit," in *History and System: Hegel's Philosophy of History,* ed. Robert L. Perkins (Albany, N.Y.: State University of New York Press, 1984), pp. 114-15.

95. This term, suggested by Jürgen Habermas's theory of communicative action, is explained and discussed below, p. 219 ff.

CHAPTER II. GOD: TRIUNE FIGURATION

1. See below, pp. 84-88, 161, 169. I am incorporating at this point a suggestion made by Mark Kline Taylor.

2. Martin Heidegger, *Being and Time,* trans. John Macquarrie and Edward Robinson (New York: Harper & Row, 1962), § 32, pp. 152-53.

3. I am helped by some suggestive remarks by Brian Leftow, "God and the World in Hegel and Whitehead," in *Hegel and Whitehead: Contemporary Perspectives on Systematic Philosophy,* ed. George R. Lucas, Jr. (Albany, N.Y.: State University of New York Press, 1986), pp. 257-59.

4. The term *oikonomia* means the management (*nomos*) of a household (*oikos*); more

generally, it is an arrangement or a plan. The expression "economic trinity" refers to God's arrangement of and involvement in the world's salvation through the creative work of the Father, the redemptive work of the Son, and the sanctifying work of the Spirit. When the word *trinity* was used by the tradition, however, it normally referred to the immanent self-relations of God prior to and apart from the world—the eternal begetting of the Son by the Father and the procession of the Spirit from both. It was believed that God could not have "real" relations outside God.

5. See Karl Rahner, *The Trinity*, trans. Joseph Donceel (New York: Herder and Herder, 1970), pp. 16-22, 39-40, 47-48.

6. Cyril C. Richardson, *The Doctrine of the Trinity* (Nashville/New York: Abingdon Press, 1958), pp. 13-15, 111-12.

7. Ibid., pp. 38, 69, 145-46.

8. Composed over a number of years between 400 and 416 c.e. References are to the translation contained in *Basic Writings of Saint Augustine*, ed. Whitney J. Oates (New York: Random House, 1948), vol. 2, pp. 667-878.

9. Augustine, *On the Trinity*, 8.10; 11.2.

10. Ibid., 9.3; 10.11-12.

11. Ibid., 15.7, 19-27.

12. Ibid., 6.5.

13. Ibid., 15.1, 2, 8.

14. Ibid., 5.5, 8, 9; 7.2, 4, 6.

15. Ibid., 5.11.

16. References to Questions 27-32 are to *Summa theologiae*, vol. 6, *The Trinity*, ed. Ceslaus Velecky (London: Blackfriars, 1965); references to other questions are to *Summa theologica*, part 1, in *Basic Writings of Saint Thomas Aquinas*, ed. Anton C. Pegis (New York: Random House, 1945), vol. 1.

17. *Summa theologica*, Ia.27.1, 3.

18. Ibid., Ia.3.7; 28.1; cf. 14.8; 19.3-4.

19. Ibid., Ia.28.4. These four relations are "characteristics" (*notiones*) of God, who simply is his relations (28.2). There is, however, a fifth characteristic of God that is not a relation of origin, namely, "unbegottenness," since God the Father does not come from another than godself (32.2, 3). Thomas notes the lack of a proper term for the fourth relation, which is the double relation of effect constituting the Spirit, and which is in turn the product of the Spirit's double procession from the Father and the Son as affirmed by the Niceno-Constantinopolitan Creed.

20. Ibid., Ia.29, 30; 32.1; 37.1, 2.

21. Ibid., Ia.43-45.

22. Ibid., Ia.45.3.

23. See M.-D. Chenu, *Toward Understanding Saint Thomas*, trans. A.-M. Landry and D. Hughes (Chicago: Henry Regnery Co., 1964), pp. 301-18.

24. No references to either figure are found in the *Lectures on the Philosophy of Religion* and only a few in the *Lectures on the History of Philosophy*. Whatever Hegel knew about the church fathers and scholastic theologians was gained from secondary sources, with the exception of Clement of Alexandria and Anselm. The latter was of interest to Hegel in connection with the ontological proof, but he made no references whatsoever to Christian theologians in his discussion of the trinity. He was interested, rather, in "anticipations of the triad as the true category" prior to and outside Christianity (in Hinduism, Pythagoreanism, Platonism, Gnosticism, etc.), as well as in Boehme's "rather wild and fanciful speculations." His statement that "Jacob Boehme was the first to recognize . . . the presence of the Trinity in everything and everywhere" indicates that he was unfamiliar with Augustine's discussion of the *vestigia trinitatis* in *De trinitate*. See G. W. F. Hegel, *Lectures on the Philosophy of Religion*, ed. and trans. P. C. Hodgson et al., 3 vols. (Berkeley and Los Angeles: University of

California Press, 1984, 1985, 1987), 1:153n., 154n.; 3:286-89. On Hegel's four philosophy of religion lecture courses (1821, 1824, 1827, and 1831) and the distinctive characteristics of each, see the editorial introductions to volumes 1 and 3 of this edition. I draw upon some of this editorial material for the ensuing discussion.

25. G. R. G. Mure, *A Study of Hegel's Logic* (Oxford: Clarendon Press, 1950), pp. 296-99. This is undoubtedly the finest study of Hegel's logic in English, and I shall rely on it in the next few pages. The present section also draws on materials from my article, "Logic, History, and Alternative Paradigms in Hegel's Interpretation of the Religions," *Journal of Religion* 68 (January 1988): 1-20. © 1988 by The University of Chicago.

26. See Alan White, *Absolute Knowledge: Hegel and the Problem of Metaphysics* (Athens, Ohio: Ohio University Press, 1983), pp. 3-6. On the distinction between "transcendental" and "transcendent" as Hegel understood it, see *Encyclopedia of the Philosophical Sciences*, trans. William Wallace and A. V. Miller, 3 vols. (Oxford: Clarendon Press, 1975, 1970, 1971), § 42 *Zus.* Vol. 1 contains *The Science of Logic* (§§ 1-244 [the "Shorter Logic" or "Encyclopedia Logic"]); vol. 2, *The Philosophy of Nature* (§§ 245-376); and vol. 3, *The Philosophy of Spirit* (§§ 377-577). The *Zusätze* (*Zus.*) or "additions" in the translated edition are not from Hegel's published *Encyclopedia* but from notebooks of lecture courses in which this work was used as a textbook.

27. In this respect I disagree with the interpretation offered by White, who insists that Hegel's dialectic is ideal throughout and does not claim to reconstruct a real process. It ends, he argues, not with any world, experienced or ideal, but merely with the logical principle of determination, the absolute idea. White's view seems to be that the *Logic* is dialectically complete apart from the *Realphilosophie*, the philosophies of nature and spirit. He does not seem to notice that Hegel's absolute, precisely to be absolute, requires worldly self-mediation and self-divestment. See *Absolute Knowledge*, pp. 63, 74, 88, 156-57, et passim.

28. The expression "communicative freedom" (to which I return in ch. 4.3) is suggested by Jürgen Habermas's "communicative action"; see *Communication and the Evolution of Society*, trans. Thomas McCarthy (Boston: Beacon Press, 1979). On the freedom of the concept, see Hegel, *Encyclopedia*, § 160. I have been helped here and elsewhere in this section by conversations with Robert R. Williams.

29. As Mure puts it, God "is Hegel's proximate metaphor for the Absolute" (*A Study of Hegel's Logic*, p. 298).

30. *Lectures on the Philosophy of Religion*, 1:369, 373, 419.

31. "Without the world God is not God" (ibid., 1:308n.). Although this famous statement is probably not Hegel's own formulation but that of one of his auditors and editors, H. G. Hotho, it does, properly interpreted, express one of Hegel's deepest insights.

32. Ibid., 3:292. See below, pp. 69, 172, 178.

33. Martin Heidegger, "The Onto-theo-logical Constitution of Metaphysics," in *Identity and Difference*, trans. Joan Stambaugh (New York: Harper & Row, 1969), pp. 42-74; see also Mark C. Taylor, *Erring: A Postmodern A/theology* (Chicago: University of Chicago Press, 1984), chs. 1-2.

34. Mure, *A Study of Hegel's Logic*, pp. 33-35, 299-302, 350-51. On the dialectic of being, nothing, and becoming, see *Encyclopedia*, §§ 86-88.

35. Hegel, *Encyclopedia*, §§ 181-92; and *Science of Logic*, trans. A. V. Miller (London: George Allen & Unwin, 1969), pp. 664-704.

36. See William Desmond, *Art and the Absolute: A Study of Hegel's Aesthetics* (Albany, N.Y.: State University of New York Press, 1986), pp. 75-76.

37. Mure, *A Study of Hegel's Logic*, pp. 300-301, 332. Mure believes that Hegel himself recognized this by showing that the contradictions expressed in the coupled categories of the doctrine of essence ("his most brilliant achievement in logic") could never be resolved within essence itself (p. 342).

38. Ibid., pp. 315-16, 319-21, 329, 332.

39. See *Lectures on the Philosophy of Religion*, 3:12-13. Hegel resolved the tension he encountered at this point in his original lecture manuscript of 1821 only in the lectures of 1824.

40. Ibid., 3:26-27, 185-89.

41. Ibid., 3:39, 271-75.

42. *Encyclopedia*, §§ 244, 381.

43. *Lectures on the Philosophy of Religion*, 3:284-85.

44. Ibid., 3:77, 186-87, 327-28.

45. See Walter Jaeschke, "World History and the History of the Absolute Spirit," in *History and System: Hegel's Philosophy of History*, ed. Robert L. Perkins (Albany, N.Y.: State University of New York Press, 1984), pp. 106-8, 111-12. On the term *economic trinity*, see above, n. 4.

46. *Lectures on the Philosophy of Religion*, 3:16, 77-78.

47. Ibid., 3:86-87. On the two trinities in Hegel's thought, see Emil L. Fackenheim, *The Religious Dimension in Hegel's Thought* (Bloomington, Ind.: Indiana University Press, 1967), pp. 149-54.

48. Brian Leftow, "God and the World in Hegel and Whitehead," in *Hegel and Whitehead: Contemporary Perspectives on Systematic Philosophy*, pp. 262-63.

49. Hegel drew an important categorial distinction between "being" (*Sein*) and "existence" (*Dasein, Existenz*) as regards God. God is or has being apart from the world, but God exists determinately only in relation to the world. See *Lectures on the Philosophy of Religion*, 1:57-58.

50. Leftow, "God and the World in Hegel and Whitehead," pp. 262, 264. This is especially evident in those passages of the *Lectures on the Philosophy of Religion* where Hegel is rejecting the charges brought against him of "pantheism" and "atheism"; cf. 1:346-47, 370, 374-78, 432; 2:259-62, 572-75.

51. *Lectures on the Philosophy of Religion*, 3:15-16, 28, 39-40, 77-86, 189-98, 275-90.

52. Ibid., 3:16-17, 86-88.

53. Ibid., 3:292; see below, pp. 172, 178. *Ent-lassen* is for Hegel the Germanic equivalent of the Latin *ab-solvere*. Creation might be described in Heideggerian terms as the divine *Gelassenheit* ("releasement").

54. Ibid., 3:39-41, 290-94; cf. 125, 326.

55. Ibid., 3:53, 370; cf. 323n.-324n.

56. Hegel, *Faith and Knowledge* (1802), trans. W. Cerf and H. S. Harris (Albany, N.Y.: State University of New York Press, 1977), p. 191.

57. Hegel, *The Phenomenology of Mind*, trans. J. B. Baillie, rev. 2nd ed. (London: George Allen & Unwin, 1949), p. 808.

58. Mure, *A Study of Hegel's Logic*, pp. 322-28.

59. Ibid., p. 363. This can be demonstrated in detail from the new edition of the *Lectures on the Philosophy of Religion*, which, by separating and reconstructing the four lecture courses, reveals Hegel's continuous struggle with "the empirical and historical factor," as well as his willingness to experiment with new interpretative paradigms. See especially the editorial introduction to vol. 2.

60. Ibid., p. 325.

61. *Lectures on the Philosophy of Religion*, 3:87-89.

62. Ibid., 1:374-78; 2:565-68, 572-75.

63. See Martin Jay, *Marxism and Totality: The Adventures of a Concept from Lukács to Habermas* (Berkeley: University of California Press, 1984), and Emmanuel Levinas, *Totality and Infinity: An Essay on Exteriority*, trans. Alphonso Lingis (Pittsburgh: Duquesne University Press, 1961).

64. Mure, *A Study of Hegel's Logic*, pp. 296, 323-24, 331-32, 363, 367.

65. Wolf-Dieter Marsch, *Gegenwart Christi in der Gesellschaft: Eine Studie zu Hegels Dialektik*

(Munich: Chr. Kaiser Verlag, 1965). For the following see especially pp. 236-45, 260-63, 271-75.

66. Hegel, *Lectures on the Philosophy of Religion*, 2:248: "To recognize the actual existence of what is substantive in the idea . . . involves hard labor: in order to pluck reason, the rose in the cross of the present, one must take up the cross itself." This famous metaphor, which is used also in the preface to the *Philosophy of Right*, trans. T. M. Knox (Oxford: Oxford University Press, 1952), p. 12, was apparently suggested to Hegel by Luther's coat of arms (a black cross in the midst of a heart surrounded by white roses) or by the emblem of the Rosicrucians (a cross with a red rose in the center).

67. Hegel, *Lectures on the Philosophy of World History. Introduction: Reason in History*, trans. H. B. Nisbet from the Hoffmeister ed. (Cambridge: Cambridge University Press, 1975), p. 54.

68. Eberhard Jüngel, *God as the Mystery of the World: On the Foundation of the Theology of the Crucified One in the Dispute Between Theism and Atheism*, trans. Darrell L. Guder (Grand Rapids: Wm. B. Eerdmans Publishing Co., 1983); see pp. 63-104, 224, 346-47.

69. Leftow, "God and the World in Hegel and Whitehead," p. 264. See Alfred North Whitehead, *Process and Reality* (New York: Macmillan, 1929), pp. 527-28.

70. This vision was set forth in its essentials in *Religion in the Making* (New York: Macmillan, 1926), esp. pp. 67-120, but many details were added in *Process and Reality* (see esp. pp. 519-33). A valuable summary of Whitehead's doctrine of God is provided by John B. Cobb, Jr., *A Christian Natural Theology Based on the Thought of Alfred North Whitehead* (Philadelphia: Westminster Press, 1965), pp. 143-68.

71. Cobb, *A Christian Natural Theology*, pp. 176-214. See also John B. Cobb, Jr., and David Ray Griffin, *Process Theology: An Introductory Exposition* (Philadelphia: Westminster Press, 1976), ch. 3.

72. Langdon Gilkey, *Reaping the Whirlwind: A Christian Interpretation of History* (New York: Seabury Press, 1976), pp. 247-50. These modifications take Gilkey in the direction of a more traditional theism, and the argument about the self-limitation of God certainly is not new. Although Gilkey employs Whiteheadian conceptualities, his basic theological outlook is closer to Tillich's.

73. Ibid., pp. 43-44, 251, 301.

74. Ibid., pp. 252, 303-6, 310-17.

75. Lewis S. Ford, *The Lure of God: A Biblical Background for Process Theism* (Philadelphia: Fortress Press, 1978), pp. 102-3, 107.

76. Ibid., pp. 109-10.

77. Charles Hartshorne, *The Divine Relativity: A Social Conception of God* (New Haven: Yale University Press, 1948), pp. ix, 6-9, 67-69, 72-74, 76-77, 83, 86-88.

78. Schubert Ogden, *The Reality of God and Other Essays* (New York: Harper & Row, 1966), pp. 47-48, 59-61, 65, 175-78.

79. See below, pp. 200-203.

80. Grace Jantzen, *God's World, God's Body* (Philadelphia: Westminster Press, 1984).

81. Ibid., pp. 16, 90. Ogden also holds for the immediacy of God's world-embodiment, but in his case this does not lead to an interventionist view; see *The Reality of God*, pp. 175-78.

82. Hegel, *Encyclopedia of the Philosophical Sciences*, §§ 181-89; cf. §§ 567-71, 575-77. See also Emil L. Fackenheim, *The Religious Dimension in Hegel's Thought* (Bloomington, Ind.: Indiana University Press, 1967), pp. 85-112.

83. See Hegel, *Phenomenology of Spirit*, trans. A. V. Miller (Oxford: Clarendon Press, 1977), p. 265; see also below, pp. 205-7.

84. I return to these metaphors in more detail in ch. 4.2.

85. On Troeltsch's use of the category *Gestaltung*, see below, pp. 139-40; on Hegel's use of *Gestalt*, see pp. 206-7.

86. Hayden White, *Tropics of Discourse: Essays in Cultural Criticism* (Baltimore: Johns Hopkins University Press, 1978), p. 2.

87. Hayden White, *Metahistory: The Historical Imagination in Nineteenth-Century Europe* (Baltimore: Johns Hopkins University Press, 1973), pp. 31-38; see also *Tropics of Discourse*, pp. 252-55, 260n.

88. White, *Tropics of Discourse*, pp. 6-7, 12-13, 197-217, 260n.; and *Metahistory*, pp. 31-33n.

89. *Tropics of Discourse*, pp. 5-7, 260n.

90. Hegel, *Encyclopedia of the Philosophical Sciences*, § 187; *Science of Logic*, p. 667. See above, pp. 63-64. In speaking of "the three figures of the syllogism," Hegel was following Aristotelian tradition. The term used by Aristotle for "figure" in *Prior Analytics* 1.4-7 was *schēma*, which in Latin came to mean a rhetorical figure, hence the Latin loan word used by Hegel, *Figur*.

91. The following correlations are not worked out by White, but he hints at them when he shows the connection between Hegel's four phases in the history of any civilization, or the four periods of world history, which are reenactments of logical distinctions, and the four archetypal tropes (*Metahistory*, pp. 123-27). He also observes that "the model of the syllogism itself displays clear evidence of troping." The move from major to minor premise is "a tropological move, a 'swerve' from the universal to the particular which logic cannot preside over, since it is logic itself that is being served by this move" (*Tropics of Discourse*, p. 3). Hegelian logic, however, includes the tropological swerve as an essential moment.

92. Paul Ricoeur, *Time and Narrative*, trans. Kathleen McLaughlin and David Pellauer, 3 vols. (Chicago: University of Chicago Press, 1984, 1985, 1988), 1:52. Ricoeur's third volume has just appeared in English, and I have relied on a summary of it found in his article, "Narrated Time," *Philosophy Today* 29 (Winter 1985): 259-72. My discussion here of Ricoeur's central thesis is foundational for parts of chs. 3 and 4. *Time and Narrative* sums up and builds on all of Ricoeur's recent work, including especially *Interpretation Theory: Discourse and the Surplus of Meaning* (Fort Worth, Tex.: Texas Christian University Press, 1976); *The Rule of Metaphor*, trans. Robert Czerny et al. (Toronto: University of Toronto Press, 1977); and the essays collected in *Hermeneutics and the Human Sciences*, ed. and trans. John B. Thompson (Cambridge: Cambridge University Press, 1981).

93. Ricoeur, *Time and Narrative*, 1:xi. Aristotle, *Poetics*, 50a1. On Aristotle's *Poetics*, see ch. 2 of Ricoeur. The words used by Aristotle for the three key terms *plot*, *imitation*, and *action* are *muthos*, *mimēsis*, and *praxeōs*. These terms link figuration to historiography and praxis.

94. *Time and Narrative*, 1:xi, 53.

95. Ibid., p. 61; cf. pp. 54-64. See Martin Heidegger, *Being and Time*, §§ 78-83.

96. Ricoeur, *Time and Narrative*, 1:64-70.

97. These connections are explored more fruitfully by Hayden White (see *Metahistory*, ch. 2) than by Ricoeur, and I shall return to them in ch. 3.1.

98. Ricoeur, *Time and Narrative*, 1:70-87.

99. Participation in the cultic acts of a religion would be comparable to reading in this respect.

100. See Heidegger's essays "Building Dwelling Thinking" and ". . . Poetically Man Dwells . . ." in *Poetry, Language, Thought*, trans. Albert Hofstadter (New York: Harper & Row, 1971).

101. Ricoeur, *Time and Narrative*, 3:11-96. This volume has been published too recently for me to take adequate account of it in the present work.

102. Another Heideggerian phrase, from *Being and Time*, p. 499.

103. Karl Barth, *Church Dogmatics*, vol. 1/1, trans. G. T. Thomson (Edinburgh: T. & T. Clark, 1936), pp. 407, 413. Barth's excursus on the classical concept of *persona*,

pp. 408-11, is helpful. See also Karl Rahner, *The Trinity,* pp. 73-76.

104. This Barthian formulation will be discussed and evaluated below. See Karl Barth, *Church Dogmatics,* vol. 2/1, ed. G. W. Bromiley and T. F. Torrance (Edinburgh: T. & T. Clark, 1957), § 28: "The Being of God as the One Who Loves in Freedom."

105. This is suggested by Barth in his ingenious treatment of the derivation and distribution of the divine attributes (or "perfections"), *Church Dogmatics,* vol. 2/1, §§ 29-31; see esp. pp. 344-50, 352, 441.

106. Augustine, *De trinitate,* 1.1, 4; 5.11; et passim.

107. See below, p. 172. This is similar to Paul Tillich's view as well. See *Systematic Theology,* vol. 1 (Chicago: University of Chicago Press, 1951), pp. 249-50: "God *is* spirit. This is the most embracing, direct, and unrestricted symbol for the divine life. It does not need to be balanced with another symbol, because it includes all the ontological elements. . . . Spirit is the unity of power and meaning. . . . Spirit is not a 'part,' nor is it a special function. It is the all-embracing function in which all elements of the structure of being participate."

108. Barth, *Church Dogmatics,* vol. 1/1, §§ 4, 8-9.

109. On the reasons for doing so, see *Church Dogmatics,* vol. 2/1, pp. 297-321.

110. Ibid., pp. 348-49.

111. Ibid., §§ 29-31, esp. pp. 321, 324-25, 344-50, 351-58, 640-77.

112. Ibid., p. 263.

113. Ibid., pp. 284-87. See Barth's excursus on the discussion of the personality of God in nineteenth-century and early–twentieth-century theology, pp. 287-97. Barth argues that it was the Hegelian theologians (notably Strauss and Biedermann) who concluded that if God is "absolute spirit," God cannot be personal. But he does not point out that it was precisely Hegel who not only did not abandon the language of personality with reference to God and *Geist,* but who also insisted, in comparing Judaism and Hinduism, that God must be understood as "the personal One" (*der Einer*) as opposed to "the neuter One" (*das Eine*). See *Lectures on the Philosophy of Religion,* 2:128-30, 339-40.

114. Jüngel, *God as the Mystery of the World,* p. 369.

115. Ibid., pp. 369-70; Rahner, *The Trinity,* p. 22.

116. Jüngel, *God as the Mystery of the World,* p. 371.

117. Ibid., pp. 314, 380-81.

118. Joseph A. Bracken, *The Triune Symbol* (Lanham, Md.: University Press of America, 1984); William J. Hill, *The Three-Personed God: The Trinity as a Mystery of Salvation* (Washington, D.C.: Catholic University of America Press, 1982); Robert W. Jensen, *The Triune Identity* (Philadelphia: Fortress Press, 1982); Walter Kasper, *The God of Jesus Christ,* trans. Matthew J. O'Connell (New York: Crossroad, 1984); James P. Mackey, *The Christian Experience of God as Trinity* (London: S.C.M. Press, 1983); Jürgen Moltmann, *The Trinity and the Kingdom,* trans. Margaret Kohl (San Francisco: Harper & Row, 1981). See the review essay on all but the last of these by Catherine Mowry LaCugna, "Current Trends in Trinitarian Theology," *Religious Studies Review* 13 (April 1987): 1-7.

119. Hegel knew it in a twofold sense. On the one hand, he recognized that the relationship expressed by the terms *Father* and *Son* is "a childlike relationship, a childlike form"; it is "merely a figurative relationship," into which Spirit does not properly or clearly enter (*Lectures on the Philosophy of Religion,* 3:194). On the other hand, he recognized that the term *Father* symbolizes an abstract God, a supreme being—a divine abstractness that is "given up in [the death of] the Son" and is reborn in the "unity of Father and Son" as concrete, world-embracing "love, or the Spirit" (ibid., p. 370). Hegel's second sense anticipates Ricoeur's critique, described below.

120. Paul Ricoeur, "Religion, Atheism, and Faith" and "Fatherhood: From Phantasm to Symbol," in *The Conflict of Interpretations: Essays in Hermeneutics,* ed. Don Ihde (Evanston, Ill.: Northwestern University Press, 1974), pp. 440-67, 468-97; see esp. pp. 441, 467, 481-97.

121. See Phyllis Trible, *God and the Rhetoric of Sexuality* (Philadelphia: Fortress Press, 1978); Rosemary Radford Ruether, *Sexism and God-Talk: Toward a Feminist Theology* (Boston: Beacon Press, 1983), ch. 2; Elisabeth Schüssler Fiorenza, *In Memory of Her: A Feminist Theological Reconstruction of Christian Origins* (New York: Crossroad, 1983), pp. 130ff.; Sallie McFague, *Models of God: Theology for an Ecological, Nuclear Age* (Philadelphia: Fortress Press, 1987), esp. ch. 4.

122. Ricoeur, *Conflict of Interpretations,* p. 493.

123. For Hegel, Judaism plays a key role in the history of religions because it was the first to attain the true idea of God as "spiritually subjective unity." See *Lectures on the Philosophy of Religion,* 2:669.

124. See above, n. 62.

125. Hegel, *Lectures on the Philosophy of Religion,* 3:131-41.

126. Jüngel, *God as the Mystery of the World,* pp. 221-22, 317-20, 326-29.

127. Ibid., pp. 185ff., 204, 210-15, 217-19 (the long quotation is from the last page). An analysis similar in many respects is found in Jürgen Moltmann's *The Crucified God: The Cross of Christ as the Foundation and Criticism of Christian Theology,* trans. R. A. Wilson and John Bowden (New York: Harper & Row, 1974), esp. ch. 6.

128. H. Richard Niebuhr recognized this many years ago. See *The Purpose of the Church and Its Ministry: Reflections on the Aims of Theological Education* (New York: Harper, 1956), pp. 44-46: "The most prevalent, the most deceptive and perhaps ultimately the most dangerous inconsistency to which churches and schools are subject in our time (perhaps in all the Christian centuries) arises from the substitution of Christology for theology, of the love of Jesus Christ for the love of God and of life in the community of Jesus Christ for life in the divine commonwealth." This critique by no means entails an abandonment of christology by either Niebuhr or myself. I believe, rather, that the problems of christology must be taken up afresh in light of recent challenges, and possibly along lines suggested later in this book (see ch. 4.2). That, however, is an agenda for another project.

129. Karl Barth has seen this quite clearly in *Church Dogmatics,* ed. G. W. Bromiley and T. F. Torrance, vol. 3/2 (Edinburgh: T. & T. Clark, 1960), p. 211 (cf. the whole of § 45.1); and vol. 4/2 (Edinburgh: T. & T. Clark, 1958), pp. 180-92.

130. For a detailed elaboration, see my *New Birth of Freedom: A Theology of Bondage and Liberation* (Philadelphia: Fortress Press, 1976), esp. ch. 3.

131. Barth, *Church Dogmatics,* vol. 2/1, § 28.3, pp. 297-321.

132. Ibid., pp. 313-14. Emphasis mine; translation slightly modified.

133. Ibid., pp. 317, 320.

134. Hegel, *Encyclopedia of the Philosophical Sciences,* § 381 Zus.

CHAPTER III. HISTORY: DE-CONFIGURATIVE PROCESS

1. For a discussion of figures of speech, see ch. 2.3.

2. Hayden White, *Metahistory: The Historical Imagination in Nineteenth-Century Europe* (Baltimore: Johns Hopkins University Press, 1973), part 2.

3. Ibid., pp. 38-42, 79-80, 138-43, 268-69, 276-80.

4. Ibid., p. 433; cf. pp. 427-34.

5. Among the important works shaping the discussion are the following: Raymond Aron, *Introduction to the Philosophy of History: An Essay on the Limits of Historical Objectivity* (London: Weidenfeld and Nicolson, 1961); Marc Bloch, *The Historian's Craft* (New York: Random House, 1953); Jacob Burckhardt, *Reflections on History* (London: Allen & Unwin, 1943); David Carr, *Phenomenology and the Problem of History* (Evanston, Ill.: Northwestern University Press, 1974); R. G. Collingwood, *The Idea of History* (Oxford:

Clarendon Press, 1946); Benedetto Croce, *History as the Story of Liberty* (London: Allen & Unwin, 1941); Arthur C. Danto, *Narration and Knowledge* (New York: Columbia University Press, 1985); Wilhelm Dilthey, *Der Aufbau der geschichtlichen Welt in den Geisteswissenschaften, Gesammelte Schriften*, vol. 7 (Göttingen: Vandenhoeck & Ruprecht, 1965); William Dray, *Laws and Explanation in History* (Oxford: Oxford University Press, 1957); William Dray, ed., *Philosophical Analysis and History* (New York: Harper & Row, 1966); Emil Fackenheim, *Metaphysics and Historicity* (Milwaukee, Wis.: Marquette University Press, 1961); Michel Foucault, *The Archaeology of Knowledge* (New York: Pantheon Books, 1972); W. B. Gallie, *Philosophy and the Historical Understanding* (New York: Schocken, 1964); Patrick Gardiner, *The Nature of Historical Explanation* (Oxford: Oxford University Press, 1952); Patrick Gardiner, ed., *Theories of History* (Glencoe, Ill.: Free Press, 1959); Pieter Geyl, *Use and Abuse of History* (New Haven: Yale University Press, 1955); Michael A. Gillespie, *Hegel, Heidegger, and the Ground of History* (Chicago: University of Chicago Press, 1984); H. Stuart Hughes, *History as Art and as Science* (New York: Harper & Row, 1964); Karl Jaspers, *The Origin and Goal of History* (London: Routledge & Kegan Paul, 1953); Karl Löwith, *Meaning in History* (Chicago: University of Chicago Press, 1949); Louis O. Mink, *Historical Understanding*, eds. Brian Fay, Eugene Golob, Richard Vann (Ithaca, N.Y.: Cornell University Press, 1987); Paul Ricoeur, *Time and Narrative*, 3 vols. (Chicago: University of Chicago Press, 1984, 1985, 1988); Alfred Schmidt, *History and Structure: An Essay on Hegelian-Marxist and Structuralist Theories of History* (Cambridge, Mass.: M.I.T. Press, 1983); Paul Veyne, *Writing History: Essay on Epistemology* (Middletown, Conn.: Wesleyan University Press, 1984); W. H. Walsh, *Philosophy of History: An Introduction* (New York: Harper & Row, 1960); Hayden White, *Metahistory: The Historical Imagination in Nineteenth-Century Europe* (Baltimore: Johns Hopkins University Press, 1973); Hayden White, *Tropics of Discourse: Essays in Cultural Criticism* (Baltimore: Johns Hopkins University Press, 1978). The issues with which I am engaged in this chapter are discussed in these books from many different points of view, and some of the works relating to current trends in the philosophy of history will be considered in section 3 below.

6. G. W. F. Hegel, *Lectures on the Philosophy of World History. Introduction: Reason in History*, trans. H. B. Nisbet with an introduction by Duncan Forbes (Cambridge: Cambridge University Press, 1975), pp. 11-23. This is a translation of *Vorlesungen über die Philosophie der Weltgeschichte*, vol. 1: *Die Vernunft in der Geschichte*, ed. Johannes Hoffmeister (Hamburg: Felix Meiner Verlag, 1955). Although this is the best edition of the *Introduction* to the philosophy of world history presently available, it is far from satisfactory. Hoffmeister made only minor revisions to the first volume of the 4-volume edition of the text prepared by Georg Lasson in 1917. Passages from student transcripts of the lectures of 1822–23, 1824–25, and 1826–27, as well as from the 2nd German edition of 1840 prepared by Karl Hegel, are collated—without being specifically identified as to their sources—with surviving fragments of two of Hegel's own lecture manuscripts, one used in 1822–23 and 1828–29, the other in 1830–31. An appendix contains additional important materials on "the natural context or the geographical basis of world history" and "the phases of world history," which are unidentified as to their source(s). The effect of all of this is to make it very difficult to discern the significant changes Hegel introduced into his lectures over the course of ten years, changes that bear upon substance as well as structure. The remaining volumes of Lasson's 1917 edition, containing everything following Hegel's *Introduction*, have not been translated into English, and we are forced to rely on John Sibree's 1857 translation of Karl Hegel's 1840 edition; Sibree's translation is available in a reprint (New York: Dover Books, 1956).

7. G. W. F. Hegel, *Aesthetics: Lectures on Fine Art*, trans. T. M. Knox, 2 vols. (Oxford: Clarendon Press, 1975), vol. 2, pp. 986-89, 993-95. See Hayden White, *Metahistory*,

pp. 86-92. White's discussion of Hegel's philosophy of history in ch. 2 of *Metahistory* is the best of those with which I am familiar, and I refer to it several times in this section.

8. Hegel, *Philosophy of World History*, pp. 24-27; White, *Metahistory*, pp. 92, 141, 268.

9. See W. H. Walsh, "Principle and Prejudice in Hegel's Philosophy of History," in Z. A. Pelczynski, ed., *Hegel's Political Philosophy: Problems and Perspectives* (Cambridge: Cambridge University Press, 1971), pp. 181-98.

10. Cf. also the work of the modern philosophical biologist Jacques Monod, *Chance and Necessity: An Essay on the Natural Philosophy of Modern Biology* (New York: Vintage Books, 1972), whose views are influenced by Camus, Sartre, and other French existentialists.

11. Hegel, *Philosophy of World History*, pp. 27-34.

12. Ibid., pp. 35-55.

13. Ibid., pp. 66-67; cf. pp. 35-36, 40-43.

14. These two approaches correspond roughly to the second and third parts of Hegel's treatment of "philosophical world history" in the introduction to the 1830-31 lectures. Hegel's first part, the "general concept" of world history, and the first section of the second part, "the realization of spirit in history" (pp. 27-67 of the Nisbet translation), are included in our discussion of "reason in history"; the remainder of "the realization of spirit in history" (pp. 68-124) comprises the treatment of history as "synchronic structure"; and Hegel's third part, "the course of world history" (pp. 124-51) is its treatment as "diachronic process."

15. White, *Metahistory*, p. 106.

16. Hegel, *Philosophy of World History*, pp. 68-69.

17. Ibid., p. 69.

18. White, *Metahistory*, p. 107.

19. Hegel, *Philosophy of World History*, pp. 69-70. Translation slightly revised.

20. Ibid., p. 71. Translation revised (see German ed., p. 83); the English edition destroys the image by reversing the order of the terms *weft* and *warp*.

21. It is interesting to observe that deconstructionists under the influence of Nietzsche and Derrida have also been attracted to the image of weaving, but for them the dominant theme is the "unraveling" of the fabric, the disintegration of coherence.

22. Hegel, *Philosophy of World History*, p. 208.

23. Ibid., pp. 71-72, 75.

24. Ibid., pp. 73-76, 89.

25. Ibid., pp. 85, 89. Churchill made just this observation when he was unceremoniously cast aside by the English people in the election of 1945.

26. Ibid., p. 90. Translation altered.

27. G. W. F. Hegel, *Lectures on the Philosophy of Religion*, vol. 2: *Determinate Religion*, ed. and trans. P. C. Hodgson et al. (Berkeley and Los Angeles: University of California Press, 1987); see pp. 86-87, 90.

28. Sibree translation of the 2nd German ed. of 1840 (New York: Dover Publications, 1956), p. 73 (see above, n. 6). This passage is not exactly duplicated in the Hoffmeister edition translated by Nisbet, but cf. pp. 32-33, 124-29 of the latter.

29. *Philosophy of World History*, p. 128 (translation altered).

30. White, *Metahistory*, p. 116. I am following White's interpretation closely here; cf. pp. 112-17.

31. *Philosophy of World History*, pp. 58-63, 124-28.

32. See above, pp. 60-61, 63-64.

33. *Philosophy of World History*, p. 130; cf. p. 54.

34. Ibid., pp. 129, 130-31. These passages are from student notebooks of lectures that most likely predated 1827.

35. Ibid., p. 131.

36. Ibid., pp. 196-207. The lectures to which these passages belong cannot be identified with certainty on the basis of the present edition.

37. See above, pp. 87-88, where I discuss Hayden White's contention that Hegel's logic, corresponding to the four principal tropes, exhibits the four stages of thesis, antithesis, synthesis, and dissolution or negation of synthesis (the transition to the beginning of a new triad).

38. See *Philosophy of World History,* pp. 133-34, 138-39, 149-50, 208-9. See also my article, "Logic, History, and Alternative Paradigms in Hegel's Interpretation of the Religions," *Journal of Religion* 68 (1988): 1-20.

39. White, *Metahistory,* p. 117; cf. pp. 117-31, upon which I depend for much of what follows.

40. Hegel, *Philosophy of World History,* p. 32.

41. White, *Metahistory,* p. 120.

42. See Walter Jaeschke, "World History and the History of Absolute Spirit," in *History and System: Hegel's Philosophy of History,* ed. Robert L. Perkins (Albany, N.Y.: State University of New York Press, 1984), pp. 113-15.

43. See William Desmond, *Art and the Absolute: A Study of Hegel's Aesthetics* (Albany, N.Y.: State University of New York Press, 1986), pp. 70-75.

44. Hegel, *Philosophy of World History,* pp. 78-79.

45. The current Troeltsch renaissance in English seems to have begun with the volume edited by John P. Clayton, *Ernst Troeltsch and the Future of Theology* (Cambridge: Cambridge University Press, 1976). Since then a number of important monographs have been published in German and English, including K. A. Apfelbacher, *Frömmigkeit und Wissenschaft: Ernst Troeltsch und sein theologisches Program* (Munich: Paderborn, 1978); Walter Wyman, *The Concept of Glaubenslehre: Ernst Troeltsch and the Theological Heritage of Schleiermacher* (Chico, Calif.: Scholars Press, 1983); Toshimasa Yasukata, *Ernst Troeltsch: Systematic Theologian of Radical Historicality* (Decatur, Ga.: Scholars Press, 1987); and Sarah Coakley, *Christ Without Absolutes: A Study of the Christology of Ernst Troeltsch* (Oxford: Oxford University Press, 1988). (I appreciate Coakley's willingness to make available to me a typescript and proofs of her work, which had not yet been published at the time this book went to press.) I have also been helped by Wilhelm Pauck, *Harnack and Troeltsch: Two Historical Theologians* (New York: Oxford University Press, 1968). See the bibliographical essay contained in the chapter on Troeltsch by Trutz Rendtorff and Friedrich Wilhelm Graf in *Nineteenth Century Religious Thought in the West,* ed. Ninian Smart et al. (Cambridge: Cambridge University Press, 1985), vol. 3, pp. 305-32.

46. Ernst Troeltsch, "Half a Century of Theology: A Review" (1908), in *Writings on Theology and Religion,* trans. and ed. Robert Morgan and Michael Pye (London: Duckworth, 1977), pp. 53-81. For an understanding of the structure of Troeltsch's theological program, I am indebted to Yasukata, *Ernst Troeltsch,* ch. 3.

47. Ernst Troeltsch, "Religion and the Science of Religion" (1906), in *Writings on Theology and Religion,* pp. 82-123; see esp. pp. 111-12, 114-18.

48. Ernst Troeltsch, "The Dogmatics of the 'Religionsgeschichtliche Schule'," in *The American Journal of Theology* 17 (1913): 1-21.

49. Troeltsch, "Religion and the Science of Religion," p. 120.

50. Ibid., pp. 82-84; cf. pp. 102-10. Translation slightly altered.

51. Ibid., pp. 103-5.

52. Ibid., p. 117.

53. See Ernst Troeltsch, "Die Krisis des Historismus," *Die neue Rundschau* 33 (1922): 579-90.

54. Coakley, *Christ Without Absolutes,* ch. 1. The first phase of Troeltsch's thought about these issues culminated with the publication in 1902 of *The Absoluteness of Christianity and the History of Religion,* trans. David Reid (Richmond, Va.: John Knox Press, 1971). The second phase was marked by two editions of the essay "What Does 'Essence of Christianity' Mean?" (1903, 1913), translated in *Writings on Theology and Religion,*

pp. 124-81. The third phase, beginning about 1915 when Troeltsch moved from Heidelberg to Berlin, is represented by the materials collected in the first (and only) volume of *Der Historismus und seine Probleme* (Tübingen: J. C. B. Mohr, 1922; repr. Aalen: Scientia Verlag, 1977), and by the lecture prepared for delivery at Oxford in 1923, "The Place of Christianity Among the World-Religions," published in *Christian Thought: Its History and Application*, ed. Baron F. von Hügel (London: University of London Press, 1923; repr. Westport, Conn.: Hyperion Press, 1979).

55. Troeltsch, "Über historische und dogmatische Methode der Theologie" (1900), in *Gesammelte Schriften*, vol. 2 (Tübingen: J. C. B. Mohr, 1913; repr. Aalen: Scientia Verlag, 1981), pp. 729-53; see esp. pp. 737, 747, 751.

56. Troeltsch, *The Absoluteness of Christianity*, pp. 90, 107, 114.

57. Coakley, *Christ Without Absolutes*, p. 11.

58. Troeltsch, *Christian Thought*, pp. 22-26.

59. Ibid., p. 34.

60. Coakley, *Christ Without Absolutes*, pp. 13-14, 17, 31-40, 42-43. On types of relativism and their significance for religious discourse, see also Joseph Runzo, *Reason, Relativism and God* (New York: St. Martin's Press, 1986).

61. Cf. Troeltsch, *Der Historismus und seine Probleme*, p. 684.

62. Troeltsch, *Christian Thought*, p. 32.

63. This is Yasukata's suggestion of a possible translation of the term *Historismus*. It is an apt suggestion since the word had positive and constructive connotations for Troeltsch, whereas in English we tend to think of "historicism" primarily in negative terms as an obsessive preoccupation with history or a surrender to a value-free relativism—which, as we have seen, was far from Troeltsch's intention.

64. Troeltsch, *Der Historismus und seine Probleme*, p. 772. On Troeltsch's distinction between "the formal logic of history" and "the material philosophy of history," see pp. 27-83.

65. My interpretation of both these matters has been aided by Yasukata, *Ernst Troeltsch*, ch. 4.

66. Troeltsch, *Historismus*, pp. 27-29.

67. Ibid., p. 33.

68. See above, pp. 63-64.

69. Troeltsch, *Historismus*, pp. 33-34.

70. Troeltsch identified a number of other categories under the formal logic of history, all of which serve to elaborate and supplement the notion of individual totality. These include: originality and uniqueness (the distinctive character of a *Gestalt* cannot be derived from its context; it has the character of something given afresh, a breakthrough); narrow selection (the historian must make a "deeply penetrating" selection out of the inexhaustible wealth of material); representation (historical objects are depicted representationally and imaginatively rather than by laws of classification); unity of value or meaning; tension between common and individual spirit (or between society and person, or objective and subjective spirit, in Hegel's terms); the unconscious, creativity, and freedom of choice as historical factors; the role of chance or contingency; the process of development (historical entities are part of an uninterrupted flow of becoming, out of which the historian constructs a narrative presentation of events, which gives the impression of a movement with an inner consistency); and the concept of time. See *Historismus*, pp. 38-57. These and other categories, such as the principles of analogy, criticism, and continuity, which are also discussed in Troeltsch's article on "Historiography" for *Hastings Encyclopedia of Religion and Ethics*, vol. 6 (New York: Scribner's, 1914), pp. 716-23, could be elaborated at some length, but they are not directly germane to our argument.

71. Troeltsch, *Historismus*, pp. 111-12.

72. Ibid., pp. 171-74, 188.

73. ". . . sondern die Teleologie des seine Vergangenheit zur Zukunft aus dem Moment herausformenden und gestaltenden Willens." Ibid., p. 112.

74. Ibid., pp. 113-15. The quotation is from Karl Marx, "Theses on Feuerbach" (1845), in *Writings of the Young Marx on Philosophy and Society,* trans. and ed. Loyd D. Easton and Kurt H. Guddat (New York: Anchor Books, 1967), p. 402. While Hegel's philosophy of history is scarcely "contemplative," one would have to insist against Hegel that the consciousness of freedom is not enough; this consciousness must be put to practice. Hegel was aware of the need for world-transforming praxis but apparently did not regard it as the role of philosophy to engage in it, this being its "partiality" and "isolation." See *Lectures on the Philosophy of Religion,* ed. and trans. P. C. Hodgson et al., vol. 3: *The Consummate Religion* (Berkeley and Los Angeles: University of California Press, 1985), pp. 161-62.

75. Troeltsch, *Historismus,* pp. 116-19. "Es ist doch das immer neue und selbige Problem des Rückgangs der Gegenwart auf ihre historischen Quellen, eine Beurteilung des Historischen, die zur Umgestaltung der Gegenwart zugleich führt, der enge Zusammenhang der Bewertung des Vergangen mit der Gestaltung der Zukunft" (p. 118).

76. Ibid., pp. 164-67.

77. Troeltsch, "Ethics and the Philosophy of History," in *Christian Thought: Its History and Application,* pp. 37-129; quotation from pp. 128-29; cf. pp. 43, 93.

78. Troeltsch, "Politics, Patriotism, and Religion," in *Christian Thought,* pp. 131-67; see pp. 159-67.

79. Troeltsch, "Ethics and the Philosophy of History," pp. 50-68.

80. See Troeltsch, *Historismus,* pp. 78-79, 83, 112, 114, 118, 132, 135, 137, 148, 169, 178, 221, 235, 272, 296, 337, 364, 388, 417, 487, 704, 710. See also Yasukata, *Ernst Troeltsch,* pp. 42, 133, 137-38.

81. Troeltsch, *Historismus,* pp. 173-75. Emphasis mine.

82. Ibid., pp. 166-68.

83. Ibid., pp. 173, 177.

84. Ibid., pp. 176-79.

85. Ibid., p. 200.

86. Ibid., p. 68.

87. Ibid., pp. 209-12; cf. pp. 656ff., esp. pp. 673, 684.

88. Ibid., pp. 184-85; cf. pp. 183-86.

89. See my "Logic, History, and Alternative Paradigms in Hegel's Interpretation of the Religions," p. 8.

90. Ernst Troeltsch, *Glaubenslehre* (Munich and Leipzig: Verlag von Duncker & Humblot, 1925). The text is based on Troeltsch's own dictated paragraphs and detailed notes taken by the novelist Gertrud von le Fort. My citations below are from the dictated paragraphs.

91. Ibid., §§ 11-14. He did speak of a "growth" (*Wachstum*) of the divine life, a constant "self-augmentation of God" (*Selbstvermehrung Gottes*) through newly emerging spiritual life, a "co-working" (*Mitarbeit*) of divine and human spirits in the spiritualization and ethicization of the world (pp. 218-19); and he did once use the term "panentheism" of his own position (p. 176).

92. Ibid., § 17.2 (pp. 253-55).

93. Ibid., § 18.1 (pp. 266-68).

94. Ibid., § 18.2 (pp. 268-69).

95. Troeltsch's discovery that Buddhism and Hinduism are "really humane and spiritual religions" came too late to be significantly incorporated into his thought. See *Christian Thought,* p. 23.

96. Troeltsch, *Glaubenslehre,* § 18.3 (pp. 269-70).

97. R. G. Collingwood, *The Idea of History*, ed. T. M. Knox (Oxford: Clarendon Press, 1946).

98. Ibid., pp. 7-10.

99. Ibid., pp. 210-19, 227, 304-5, 308.

100. Ibid., pp. 232-48.

101. Ibid., pp. 282-89, 296-97, 300-301.

102. Carl G. Hempel, "The Function of General Laws in History" (1942), reprinted in Patrick Gardiner, ed., *Theories of History* (Glencoe, Ill.: Free Press, 1959), pp. 344-56. This anthology contains an excellent selection of classical, analytic, and sociological philosophies of history.

103. Paul Ricoeur, *Time and Narrative*, trans. Kathleen McLaughlin and David Pellauer, 3 vols. (Chicago: University of Chicago Press, 1984, 1985, 1988), 1:115; cf. pp. 111-20. On pp. 121-43, Ricoeur chronicles in some detail "the breaking up of the covering law model."

104. See the articles reprinted in Gardiner, ed., *Theories of History*, pp. 356-475, as well as Gardiner's own *The Nature of Historical Explanation* (Oxford: Oxford University Press, 1952), and Dray's *Laws and Explanation in History* (Oxford: Oxford University Press, 1957). In *Theories of History*, pp. 265-74, Gardiner provides a convenient summary of the debate.

105. Alan Donagan, "Explanation in History" (1957), in *Theories of History*, pp. 428-43; see pp. 436, 439, 443. Dray reached similar conclusions in *Laws and Explanations in History;* and it is a position that Ricoeur seems to adopt from the analysts, namely, that historical explanation entails "singular causal attribution" (*Time and Narrative*, 1:181).

106. Michael Scriven, "Truisms as the Grounds for Historical Explanation" (1959), in *Theories of History*, pp. 443-75; see pp. 456-58, 470-71.

107. Arthur C. Danto, *Narration and Knowledge* (New York: Columbia University Press, 1985), pp. x-xii. W. B. Gallie's work, *Philosophy and the Historical Understanding* (New York: Schocken Books, 1968), published three years after *Analytical Philosophy of History*, further contributed to an analysis of history in terms of the structural principles of narrative, especially the concept of the "followability" of a story. Paul Ricoeur's summary of "narrativist arguments" in *Time and Narrative*, 1:143-74, is quite helpful. Danto and Gallie are analyzed in this section as well as Louis O. Mink, Hayden White, and Paul Veyne.

108. Danto, *Narration and Knowledge*, pp. 356-57. Vico and Hegel are the targets of the criticism.

109. See Louis O. Mink, "The Autonomy of Historical Understanding," *History and Theory* 5 (1966): 24-47; "Philosophical Analysis and Historical Understanding," *Review of Metaphysics* 11 (1968): 667-98 (a helpful analysis and critique of the work of Danto, Gallie, and Morton White); "History and Fiction as Modes of Comprehension," *New Literary History* 1 (1970): 541-58; and "Narrative Form as a Cognitive Instrument," in *The Writing of History: Literary Form and Historical Understanding*, ed. R. H. Canary and H. Kozicki (Madison, Wis.: University of Wisconsin Press, 1978), pp. 129-49. These and other articles are now collected and available in Louis O. Mink, *Historical Understanding*, eds. Brian Fay, Eugene O. Golob, and Richard T. Vann (Ithaca, N.Y.: Cornell University Press, 1987); see esp. pp. 48-53, 85-88, 136-37, 195-203 of this edition. See also Ricoeur's discussion of Mink in *Time and Narrative*, 1:155-61. Ricoeur is critical of Mink's claim (pp. 50-51) that the ideal aim of all comprehension is that of totality, the grasping of the world, *sub specie divinitatis*, as a *totum simul*. Mink's configurational comprehension tends, he says, to reduce the discordance present in every narrative.

110. Hayden White, *Metahistory: The Historical Imagination in Nineteenth-Century Europe* (Baltimore: Johns Hopkins University Press, 1973). White's central thesis is set forth most fully in ch. 1 of this book, "The Historical Imagination Between Metaphor and Irony"; but aspects of it are also elaborated in *Tropics of Discourse: Essays in Cultural*

Criticism (Baltimore: Johns Hopkins University Press, 1978).

111. White, *Metahistory*, p. 2.

112. Ibid., pp. 5-7.

113. Ibid., pp. 7-11. Ricoeur, rightly I think, questions White's sharp distinction between story and emplotment, which has the effect of limiting emplotment to a categorization of types. See *Time and Narrative*, 1:164-66.

114. White, *Metahistory*, pp. 11-21.

115. Ibid., p. 21; see for the following, pp. 22-29.

116. Ibid., p. 27.

117. Ibid., pp. 29-38. White gives the table, but without the first column, on p. 29. On the figures of speech, see above, pp. 84-87.

118. Ibid., pp. 29-31. Hegel, for example, offered a tragic emplotment of history on the microcosmic scale and a comic on the macrocosmic; both emplotments appealed to an organicist argument employing synecdochic tropes (while recognizing the force of irony), from which either radical or conservative ideological implications could be derived.

119. Ibid., pp. 433-34.

120. Ibid., p. 432; cf. p. 26.

121. See ch. 2.3.

122. I shall advance a similar claim with respect to "historical shapes" or *Gestalten* in ch. 4 (see ch. 4, n. 44).

123. Ricoeur, *Time and Narrative*, 1:91-92, 175-225.

124. This is the topic of part 4, "Narrated Time," of *Time and Narrative*, comprising volume 3, which has just appeared in English. The following synopsis is based on Ricoeur's article, "Narrated Time," *Philosophy Today* 29 (Winter 1985): 259-72. See esp. pp. 260-61, 267-71. Ricoeur also provides an anticipatory summary of "mimesis$_3$" in *Time and Narrative*, 1:70-87.

125. Ricoeur, "Narrated Time," p. 260.

126. Ibid., p. 269.

127. Ibid., p. 270; *Time and Narrative*, 1:82. See above, p. 123, also p. 120.

128. This is suggested by Ricoeur's discussion, "The Metamorphoses of the Plot," in *Time and Narrative*, 2:7-28. He argues that the simple rules of emplotment set forth in Aristotle's *Poetics* are rendered much more complex by the modern novel with its "infinitely ramified praxis," its complex character development, and its "exploration of the abysses of consciousness" (pp. 8-10). Yet Ricoeur contends that the basic structure of emplotment is not broken by these metamorphoses. The classic salvation history mythos (or "plot") of Christian theology might be compared to the Aristotelian rules of emplotment with regard to its simplicity or even naiveté; it too must undergo a metamorphosis in light of modern and postmodern challenges.

129. My familiarity with Derrida is limited. The following is guided by the very helpful discussion of his work provided by Frank Lentricchia, *After the New Criticism* (Chicago: University of Chicago Press, 1980), pp. 157-88.

130. Jacques Derrida, "Structure, Sign, and Play in the Discourse of the Human Sciences" (1966), in *Writing and Difference*, trans. Alan Bass (Chicago: University of Chicago Press, 1978), pp. 278-93.

131. Lentricchia, *After the New Criticism*, pp. 160-61.

132. Ibid., p. 164; see Jacques Derrida, *Of Grammatology*, trans. G. C. Spivak (Baltimore: Johns Hopkins University Press, 1976), pp. 249-51.

133. Northrop Frye, *Anatomy of Criticism: Four Essays* (New York: Atheneum, 1967), p. 118 (quoted in Lentricchia, p. 166).

134. Derrida employs these two images in his 1967 essay "Ellipsis." Alluding to the work of Edmond Jabès, he writes: "The dwelling is inhospitable because it seduces us, as does the book, into a labyrinth. The labyrinth here is an abyss: we plunge into the

horizontality of a pure surface, which itself represents itself from detour to detour" (*Writing and Difference*, p. 298). A pointed hint in the same direction is found a year later in the essay "Différance," where we are told that "*différance* is not. It is not a present being, however excellent, unique, principal, or transcendent. . . . Not only is there no kingdom of *différance*, but *différance* instigates the subversion of every kingdom. Which makes it obviously threatening and infallibly dreaded by everything within us that desires a kingdom, the past or future presence of a kingdom" (*Margins of Philosophy*, trans. Alan Bass [Chicago: University of Chicago Press, 1972], pp. 21-22). Further on the same page, Derrida says that there is no depth to "this bottomless chessboard" on which the "play of the trace" of *différance* takes place. This employment of the image of the kingdom is reminiscent of Foucault, while the images of the abyss and the labyrinth are found in Nietzsche, and the latter at least can be traced back to J. G. Herder (see above, ch. 1, nn. 67, 74). That these images coalesce for Derrida into an attack on the category of history is noted almost incidentally by the remark that the word *history* conveys "the motif of a final repression of difference" (*Margins*, p. 11; cf. p. 122).

135. *After the New Criticism*, pp. 168-69.

136. These include, according to Lentricchia, Geoffrey Hartman, J. Hillis Miller, Paul de Man, and to some degree Harold Bloom (see ibid., pp. 169-73, 185-87). Among theologians, Mark C. Taylor has clearly been influenced by this line of Derrida interpretation.

137. Ibid., pp. 175-76.

138. See above, pp. 34-35.

139. Michel Foucault, *The Archaeology of Knowledge and the Discourse on Language*, trans. A. M. Sheridan Smith (New York: Pantheon Books, 1972), pp. 138-40.

140. Michel Foucault, "Nietzsche, Genealogy, History" (1971), reprinted in *The Foucault Reader*, ed. Paul Rabinow (New York: Pantheon Books, 1984), pp. 76-100; quotation from pp. 76-77.

141. Ibid., pp. 77-86; quotations from pp. 83, 85.

142. See Lentricchia's concluding remarks on Derrida and Foucault, *After the New Criticism*, pp. 209-10.

143. Foucault, *The Archaeology of Knowledge*, p. 25.

144. Ibid., pp. 26-27.

145. See above, pp. 36-38. Mark C. Taylor, *Erring: A Postmodern A/theology* (Chicago: University of Chicago Press, 1984), chs. 3, 7 (quotation from p. 157).

146. It is ironic that the deconstructionist critics of *logocentrism* (a Derridean term, see *Of Grammatology*, p. 18) are themselves very much word oriented, so much so that they might be described as "logomonists." For them, as Richard Rorty observes, it is a matter of "words all the way down" (*Consequences of Pragmatism* [Minneapolis: University of Minnesota Press, 1982], p. xxv).

147. Taylor, *Erring*, pp. 69-71.

148. Ibid., p. 67.

149. Ibid., p. 71.

150. See ibid., ch. 7.

151. Michael Allen Gillespie, *Hegel, Heidegger, and the Ground of History* (Chicago: University of Chicago Press, 1984).

152. Ibid., p. 114; cf. pp. 96-103, 113-14.

153. Ibid., pp. 114-15.

154. Ibid., pp. 164-75.

155. To be sure, it has been impossible entirely to avoid introducing these matters insofar as they are already present in the work of Hegel, Troeltsch, and Ricoeur that we have analyzed in the preceding sections. These analyses are applicable to ch. 4 as well.

156. Collingwood, *The Idea of History*, pp. 232-48.

157. Troeltsch, *Der Historismus und seine Probleme*, p. 772.

158. See R. M. Hare in *New Essays in Philosophical Theology*, ed. Antony Flew and Alasdair MacIntyre (London: S.C.M. Press, 1955), pp. 100-101.

159. Troeltsch, *Christian Thought: Its History and Application*, p. 34.

160. Troeltsch, *Historismus*, p. 212.

161. I have argued above, pp. 62, 69, that Hegel used the term *absolute* in the active sense of "absolving." This interpretation is also suggested by William Desmond; see below, p. 178.

162. Troeltsch, *Historismus*, p. 68.

163. Hegel, *Lectures on the Philosophy of World History*, p. 32.

164. William Desmond, *Art and the Absolute: A Study of Hegel's Aesthetics* (Albany, N.Y.: State University of New York Press, 1986), pp. 91-92. This book contains excellent studies of the relation of Hegel's aesthetics to philosophy, religion, history, dialectic, and deconstruction.

165. These terms are partly indebted to process philosophy, which in many respects offers a remarkably similar vision. I am not, however, attempting in this project to synthesize Hegelian and Whiteheadian approaches for reasons indicated earlier.

166. Hegel, *Philosophy of World History*, p. 56. If *Vergestaltung* is substituted for *Verbildung*, then we have the German equivalent of our term *deconfiguration*.

167. Troeltsch, *Historismus*, pp. 38-57.

168. Desmond, *Art and the Absolute*, pp. 92-93.

169. Ibid., p. 94.

170. Ibid., pp. 95-96.

171. Ibid., p. 99.

172. Foucault, *The Foucault Reader*, p. 83.

173. Paul Tillich, *Systematic Theology* (Chicago: University of Chicago Press, 1963), vol. 3, part 4, ch. 1.

174. Ibid., part 5, ch. 1.

175. Paul Ricoeur, "Christianity and the Meaning of History," in *History and Truth*, trans. Charles A. Kelbley (Evanston, Ill.: Northwestern University Press, 1965); see esp. pp. 82-92.

176. Ruth Page, *Ambiguity and the Presence of God* (London: S.C.M. Press, 1985); see ch. 2, "The Ambiguous World."

177. David Tracy, *Plurality and Ambiguity: Hermeneutics, Religion, Hope* (San Francisco: Harper & Row, 1987); see esp. ch. 4, pp. 66-73.

178. Rebecca S. Chopp, *The Praxis of Suffering: An Interpretation of Liberation and Political Theologies* (Maryknoll, N.Y.: Orbis Books, 1986). Four major figures are studied: Gustavo Gutiérrez, Johann Baptist Metz, José Míguez Bonino, and Jürgen Moltmann.

179. Ibid., pp. 1-4, 23-24, 41-44, 119, 122.

180. See Arthur Cohen, *The Tremendum: A Theological Interpretation of the Holocaust* (New York: Crossroad, 1981); and Emil Fackenheim, *To Mend the World: Foundations of Future Jewish Thought* (New York: Schocken Books, 1982).

181. Tracy, *Plurality and Ambiguity*, p. 74.

182. Paul Tillich points this out in *Systematic Theology* (Chicago: University of Chicago Press, 1951), 1:81-83.

183. This is one of the most powerful insights of Jürgen Habermas; see below, ch. 4.3.

184. Paul Ricoeur's study of Hegel in part 4 of *Time and Narrative* (3:193-206) has come into my hands too recently to permit doing justice to his interpretation. It is evident that he does not concur in the "open" reading of Hegel that I have been advocating, concluding instead that it is the "very project of totalization that indicates the break between Hegel's philosophy of history and every model of understanding, however distantly akin, to the idea of narration and emplotment. Despite the seduction of the

idea, the cunning of reason is not the peripeteia that can encompass all the reversals of history, because the realization of freedom cannot be taken as the plot behind every plot" (pp. 205-6). Putting·aside the question of which interpretation of Hegel is more persuasive, the "open teleology" of historical process that I am advocating appears to be quite similar to the direction in which Ricoeur himself is moving in the concluding two chapters of his magnum opus (pp. 207-74). In place of the discredited idea of a "total mediation," he writes, "another way remains, that of an open-ended, incomplete, imperfect mediation, namely, the network of interweaving perspectives of the expectation of the future, the reception of the past, and the experience of the present, with no *Aufhebung* into a totality where reason in history and its reality would coincide" (p. 207). I arrive at a similar view by extending a trajectory I find already present in Hegel's thinking, whereas Ricoeur believes it is necessary to leave Hegel behind, since "we no longer think in the same way Hegel did, but after Hegel" (p. 206). The basic question is indeed how one thinks about history "after Hegel."

185. Troeltsch, *Christian Thought*, p. 129. Relative victories do, however, point to an innerhistorical as well as a transhistorical dimension of the symbol of the kingdom, as I shall contend in chapter 5.

CHAPTER IV. FREEDOM: TRANSFIGURATIVE PRAXIS

1. Richard J. Bernstein, *Beyond Objectivism and Relativism: Science, Hermeneutics, and Praxis* (Philadelphia: University of Pennsylvania Press, 1983).

2. See above, pp. 62, 69, 172, 178.

3. See the summary of the argument contained in part 1 of *Beyond Objectivism and Relativism*, pp. 1-49. The critique of scientific rationality is found in part 2, while parts 3 and 4 execute the constructive moves of the book.

4. Ibid., p. 174. Gadamer is discussed in detail on pp. 118-69, and the analysis summarized on pp. 174-75.

5. Hans-Georg Gadamer, *Truth and Method* (New York: Seabury Press, 1975), pp. 274-89.

6. Bernstein, *Beyond Objectivism and Relativism*, p. 175.

7. Ibid., pp. 178, 180-81, 185-87, 190-92, 195.

8. Ibid., pp. 201-5. See Richard Rorty, *Philosophy and the Mirror of Nature* (Princeton: Princeton University Press, 1979), pp. 372, 377-78, 389-94.

9. Bernstein, *Beyond Objectivism and Relativism*, pp. 207-8, 212, 219-20. See Hannah Arendt, *The Human Condition* (Chicago: University of Chicago Press, 1958), esp. chs. 5, 6.

10. Bernstein, *Beyond Objectivism and Relativism*, p. 223. Emphasis added.

11. Ibid., pp. 229-31.

12. Johann Baptist Metz, *Faith in History and Society: Toward a Practical Fundamental Theology*, trans. David Smith (New York: Seabury Press, 1980), p. 50.

13. Gustavo Gutiérrez, *A Theology of Liberation: History, Politics and Salvation*, trans. Caridad Inda and John Eagleson (Maryknoll, N.Y.: Orbis Books, 1973), pp. 11-12; cf. pp. 6-15. Like the owl of Minerva, philosophy, whose task it is to preserve and interpret the truth that has already been shaped by the historical struggles of consciousness, spreads its wings only at dusk: thus Hegel in the famous preface to the *Philosophy of Right*, trans. T. M. Knox (London: Oxford University Press, 1952), p. 13.

14. Ibid., pp. 307-8. The allusion is to Blaise Pascal, *Pensées*, no. 792 (London: J. M. Dent, 1908), p. 235.

15. For this idea I am indebted to Anselm Min, who is completing a Ph.D. dissertation at Vanderbilt University on the topic of a theology of praxis.

16. Bernstein, *Beyond Objectivism and Relativism*, p. 226 (emphasis mine); cf. pp. 225-29.

17. Ibid., p. 228; cf. p. 191.

18. Ibid.

19. For this phrase I am indebted to Charlotte Joy Martin.

20. See above, pp. 119-22, 161.

21. See above, pp. 139-40, 175.

22. Gutiérrez, *A Theology of Liberation*, p. 153; cf. pp. x, 67-72.

23. Ibid., p. 177 (translation slightly altered); see also p. 153.

24. Ibid., p. 238 (translation slightly altered).

25. See below, ch. 5.2.

26. Owen C. Thomas, ed., *God's Activity in the World: The Contemporary Problem* (Chico, Calif.: Scholars Press, 1983). Thomas has written an introduction and summary analysis to accompany selections from G. Ernest Wright, Langdon Gilkey, Frank Dilley, Rudolf Bultmann, Schubert Ogden, John Cobb, David Griffin, Gordon Kaufman, Frank Kirkpatrick, Maurice Wiles, Austin Farrer, and Etienne Gilson.

27. These five positions are summarized and evaluated by Thomas on pp. 231-39, in a different order than the one presented here.

28. Rudolf Bultmann, *Jesus Christ and Mythology* (New York: Scribner's, 1958), p. 65.

29. The selection in Thomas's anthology is a 1971 article, "Religious Authority and Divine Action," *Religious Studies* 7 (1971): 1-12. Since then Wiles has published two books relating to the subject: *Faith and the Mystery of God* (Philadelphia: Fortress Press, 1982), and *God's Action in the World* (London: S.C.M. Press, 1986).

30. Wiles, *God's Action in the World*, pp. 56-64, 96-98, 103-5; and *Faith and the Mystery of God*, pp. 29, 122, 124.

31. In *The Reality of God and Other Essays* (New York: Harper & Row, 1966), pp. 164-87; see especially the last ten pages.

32. John B. Cobb, Jr., "Natural Causality and Divine Action," *Idealistic Studies* 3 (1973): 207-22; reprinted by Thomas in *God's Activity in the World*, pp. 101-16.

33. Cobb in Thomas, *God's Activity in the World*, pp. 112-13.

34. John B. Cobb, Jr., *God and the World* (Philadelphia: Westminster Press, 1969), pp. 57-66.

35. John B. Cobb, Jr., *Process Theology as Political Theology* (Philadelphia: Westminster Press, 1982), pp. 102-7.

36. Ruth Page, *Ambiguity and the Presence of God* (London: S.C.M. Press, 1985), pp. 129-34. The quoted examples are from Daniel Day Williams, Charles Hartshorne, and Norman Pittenger.

37. Ibid., pp. 127-32. Cf. G. W. H. Lampe, *God as Spirit* (Oxford: Clarendon Press, 1977), p. 17.

38. Ibid., pp. 135-42.

39. Ibid., p. 142 and the whole of ch. 7. See the essentially similar proposal of Sallie McFague that God be thought of in the role of "friend" (*Models of God: Theology for an Ecological, Nuclear Age* [Philadelphia: Fortress Press, 1987], ch. 6).

40. See above, pp. 83-84.

41. See G. W. F. Hegel, *Gesammelte Werke*, vol. 7: *Jenaer Systementwürfe II*, ed. Rolf-Peter Horstmann and Johann Heinrich Trede (Hamburg: Felix Meiner Verlag, 1971), pp. 252-53; cf. pp. 228ff., 260ff. For the references and interpretation in this and the following paragraph I am indebted to conversations with Robert R. Williams.

42. Hegel, *Phenomenology of Spirit*, trans. A. V. Miller (Oxford: Clarendon Press, 1977), pp. 104-7, 264-65, 410-16 (quotation from p. 265).

43. See above, pp. 138-40.

44. The category of gestalt as I am using it is similar to what Ricoeur identifies as the distinctive "entities" of historical investigation, which are not personal agents or characters but rather are social entities, which in the strict sense are anonymous, yet

function in historical narrative as "quasi-characters" (nations, societies, civilizations, social classes, *mentalités*). These are "first-order entities . . . that bear the indelible mark of concrete agents' participatory belonging to the sphere of praxis and narrative." A gestalt would be such a historical entity in Ricoeur's sense. See *Time and Narrative*, trans. Kathleen McLaughlin and David Pellauer (Chicago: University of Chicago Press, 1984), 1:177, 181, 193-206.

45. On "liminality," see Mark Kline Taylor, "In Praise of Shaky Ground: The Liminal Christ in a Culturally Plural World," *Theology Today* 43 (1986): 36-51. On "hard labor" and "taking up the cross," see above, ch. 2, n. 66, and below, n. 83. Taylor has pointed out to me that the terms *liminal* and *marginal* while related are distinct, whereas I have from time to time used them interchangeably. One experiences liminality when, for a variety of reasons, one is plunged into the interstices of a social system, whereas those who are marginalized exist on the periphery of a system, away from the center of power and most likely exploited by those at the center. When I use the two terms more or less synonymously, I am thinking about the kind of liminality that is pulled toward solidarity with the marginalized—and precisely that is characteristic of the divine shape as it appears in history.

46. G. W. F. Hegel, *Lectures on the Philosophy of Religion*, ed. and trans. P. C. Hodgson et al., 3 vols. (Berkeley and Los Angeles: University of California Press, 1984, 1985, 1987), 2:54n., 85, 475-77 (esp. 476n.), 660n., 756.

47. Ibid., 2:476, 660n.

48. "Sensible nature, immediate singularity is nailed to the cross. Spirit as universal, the community, is the soil for God's appearance" (ibid., 2:476n.).

49. For the detailed discussions on which the following summary is based, see my *New Birth of Freedom: A Theology of Bondage and Liberation* (Philadelphia: Fortress Press, 1976), pp. 227-45; and *Jesus—Word and Presence: An Essay in Christology* (Philadelphia: Fortress Press, 1971), pp. 155-202. In the background of my interpretation is the exegetical work of Ernst Käsemann, Gerhard Ebeling, Eberhard Jüngel, Norman Perrin, Robert W. Funk, Dan O. Via, John Dominic Crossan, Elisabeth Schüssler Fiorenza, and others, as well as the political hermeneutic of Dorothee Soelle, Jürgen Moltmann, Gustavo Gutiérrez, and others. The expression "realm of freedom" (*Reich der Freiheit*) is attributable to Hegel, who used it in the *Philosophy of Right*, trans. T. M. Knox (Oxford: Oxford University Press, 1952), § 4. It was adopted and modified by Karl Marx and has been employed by a number of modern theologians (Karl Barth, Jürgen Moltmann, Hans-Joachim Kraus). See *New Birth of Freedom*, p. 228.

50. See Taylor, "In Praise of Shaky Ground," pp. 44-45; and Paul Ricoeur, "Biblical Hermeneutics," *Semeia* 4 (1975): 115-26.

51. See Edward Farley, *Ecclesial Man: A Social Phenomenology of Faith and Reality* (Philadelphia: Fortress Press, 1975), pp. 150-85.

52. See *New Birth of Freedom*, pp. 245-53; and *Jesus—Word and Presence*, pp. 202-17. My interpretation here has been influenced by Jürgen Moltmann (*The Crucified God: The Cross of Christ as the Foundation and Criticism of Christian Theology*, trans. R. A. Wilson and John Bowden [New York: Harper & Row, 1974], pp. 126-59), and Eberhard Jüngel (*God as the Mystery of the World: On the Foundation of the Theology of the Crucified One in the Dispute Between Theism and Atheism*, trans. Darrell L. Guder [Grand Rapids: William B. Eerdmans Publishing Co., 1983], pp. 210-22, 317-20, 326-29), as well as by Hegel (*Lectures on the Philosophy of Religion*, 3:122-31).

53. See above, pp. 103-4.

54. Hegel, *Lectures on the Philosophy of World History*, trans. H. B. Nisbet (Cambridge: Cambridge University Press, 1975), p. 32; *Lectures on the Philosophy of Religion*, 3:131-41.

55. I am playing on the root sense of the Greek word for "resurrection," *anastasis* (*ana*, in the midst of, throughout + *stasis*, standing), and am suggesting that Jesus takes on a new

kind of communal embodiment in virtue of death and resurrection from the dead. These elusive remarks require, I recognize, considerable elaboration, possibly along lines suggested in this work. I am not yet prepared to undertake this elaboration. My earlier attempts at a theology of resurrection are found in *Jesus—Word and Presence*, ch. 5 (on *anastasis*, see pp. 243-50); and *New Birth of Freedom*, pp. 300-321.

56. See Emil Fackenheim, *God's Presence in History: Jewish Affirmations and Philosophical Reflections* (New York: New York University Press, 1970).

57. See my book, *Revisioning the Church: Ecclesial Freedom in the New Paradigm* (Philadelphia: Fortress Press, 1988), esp. pp. 103-7.

58. See esp. Paul F. Knitter, *No Other Name? A Critical Survey of Christian Attitudes Toward the World Religions* (Maryknoll, N.Y.: Orbis Books, 1985); and John Hick and Paul F. Knitter, eds., *The Myth of Christian Uniqueness: Toward a Pluralistic Theology of Religions* (Maryknoll, N.Y.: Orbis Books, 1987).

59. Further development of the christological implications of this way of thinking about God's presence in history will have to await another project. I am indebted at this point to the critical comments and suggestions of Paul Lakeland.

60. This discussion is based on and in some respects modifies the much more detailed analysis found in *New Birth of Freedom*, pp. 8-10, 131-65, where I rely on Paul Ricoeur, Martin Heidegger, Hannah Arendt, Alfred Schutz, Max Scheler, Karl Rahner, Wolfhart Pannenberg, and other sources in addition to Hegel. In that book I identify a fourth structure of freedom, which I call openness to transcendence or transsubjective freedom. Since it is not directly germane to the argument being pursued in the present work, I omit it here, although I consider it foundational to any theological anthropology.

61. Hegel, *Lectures on the Philosophy of World History*, pp. 47-48 (translation altered slightly). See also Hegel, *Encyclopedia of the Philosophical Sciences*, part 3, *Hegel's Philosophy of Mind*, trans. William Wallace and A. V. Miller (Oxford: Clarendon Press, 1971), § 385. Hegel also established a number of important *connections* between matter and spirit on the basis of this comparison: in nature, spirit "slumbers" and freedom is "implicit"—precisely in the gravitational pull of all material things toward an external center.

62. From *libra*, balance, scales. Although the roots of the terms are different, there is the possibility of a word play in Latin: one becomes free (*liber*) by balancing or weighing (*librare*). The same word play can be extended to English: liberation takes place through deliberation.

63. See Paul Tillich, *Systematic Theology* (Chicago: University of Chicago Press, 1951), 1:182-86. This matter is analyzed at length by Paul Ricoeur, *Freedom and Nature: The Voluntary and the Involuntary*, trans. E. Kohák (Evanston, Ill.: Northwestern University Press, 1966), part 1.

64. Hegel, *Encyclopedia*, § 436.

65. Hegel, *Philosophy of Right*, § 4 (translation altered slightly); cf. *Encyclopedia*, §§ 385-86, 482, 484; *Philosophy of World History*, p. 208. See above, n. 48.

66. "Die Freiheit, zur Wirklichkeit einer Welt gestaltet, erhält die Form von Notwendigkeit, deren substantieller Zusammenhang das System der Freiheits-Bestimmungen . . . ist." Hegel, *Encyclopedia*, § 484.

67. Jürgen Habermas, "Dialectics of Rationalization: An Interview," *Telos* 49 (1981): 7.

68. Bernstein, *Beyond Objectivism and Relativism*, p. 181. This project was first enunciated in Habermas's *Knowledge and Human Interests*, trans. Jeremy J. Shapiro (Boston: Beacon Press, 1971).

69. Jürgen Habermas, *Communication and the Evolution of Society*, trans. Thomas McCarthy (Boston: Beacon Press, 1979), p. 97; and "A Reply to My Critics," in *Habermas: Critical Debates*, trans. John B. Thompson and David Held (Cambridge, Mass.: M.I.T. Press, 1982), p. 221. See Bernstein, *Beyond Objectivism and Relativism*, pp. 185-87, 190-92. On communicative action and its validity claims, see esp. *Communication and the Evolution of Society*, chs. 1, 3.

70. Bernstein, *Beyond Objectivism and Relativism*, pp. 194-95.

71. This is an allusion to a mistaken reading (and mistranslation) of a passage in Hegel's *Philosophy of Right*, § 258 Addition (p. 279). See Shlomo Avineri, *Hegel's Theory of the Modern State* (Cambridge: Cambridge University Press, 1972), p. 176.

72. Martin Jay, *Marxism and Totality: The Adventures of a Concept from Lukács to Habermas* (Berkeley and Los Angeles: University of California Press, 1984), ch. 15, esp. pp. 478-508.

73. These elements are set forth most systematically and fully in Habermas's magnum opus, *The Theory of Communicative Action*, trans. Thomas McCarthy, 2 vols. (Boston: Beacon Press, 1984, 1987). At the end of this work, Habermas claims that the theory of communicative action is intended to replace the Marxist philosophy of history that served as a basis of earlier critical social theory, and he defends it against charges of foundationalism, while admitting that it "aims at the moment of unconditionality that . . . is built into the conditions of processes of consensus formation" (2:378-403).

74. Jay, *Marxism and Totality*, pp. 536-37. Jay quotes Theodor Adorno to this effect: "No universal history leads from savagery to humanitarianism, but there is one leading from the slingshot to the megaton bomb. It ends in the total menace which organized mankind poses to organized man, in the epitome of discontinuity. It is the horror that verifies Hegel and stands him on his head." *Negative Dialectics*, trans. E. B. Ashton (New York: Seabury Press, 1973), p. 320.

75. Helmut Peukert, *Science, Action, and Fundamental Theology: Toward a Theology of Communicative Action*, trans. James Bohman (Cambridge, Mass.: M.I.T. Press, 1984). Michael Theunissen has drawn out some of the theological implications of Habermas's work in the concluding part of his *Hegels Lehre vom absoluten Geist als theologisch-politischer Traktat* (Berlin: Walter de Gruyter, 1970). See also Jens Glebe-Möller, *A Political Dogmatic*, cited below, n. 80.

76. Peukert, *Science, Action, and Fundamental Theology*, pp. 202-14, 217-27, 229, 234-35. Translations altered slightly. The expression "anamnestic solidarity," or solidarity in remembrance, is from Christian Lenhardt (p. 310, n. 107).

77. Max Horkheimer, *Kritische Theorie*, 2 vols. (Frankfurt: S. Fischer, 1968), 1:374. Quoted in Peukert, *Science, Action, and Fundamental Theology*, pp. 209-10 (translation corrected; see Peukert, *Wissenschaftstheorie—Handlungstheorie—Fundamentale Theologie: Analysen zu Ansatz und Status theologischer Theoriebildung* [Düsseldorf: Patmos-Verlag, 1976], p. 282).

78. Walter Benjamin, "Theses on the Philosophy of History," in *Illuminations*, ed. Hannah Arendt, trans. Harry Zohn (New York: Schocken Books, 1969), pp. 256-62; and *The Origin of German Tragic Drama*, trans. John Osborne (London: NLB, 1977), p. 166; quoted in Peukert, *Science, Action, and Fundamental Theology*, pp. 206-8.

79. I hope to return to this question in a future work. See above, n. 55. Mark Kline Taylor has called my attention to a poem by the Guatemalan poet Julia Esquivel, which describes in dramatic terms the effect of the dead upon the living:

They have threatened us with Resurrection,
because they are more alive than ever before,
because they transform our agonies,
and fertilize our struggle.

Threatened with Resurrection, trans. Maria Elena Acevedo et al. (Elgin, Ill.: Brethren Press, 1982), pp. 59-63.

80. Jens Glebe-Möller, *A Political Dogmatic*, trans. Thor Hall (Philadelphia: Fortress Press, 1987). See chs. 3, 6, 7, 8, and esp. pp. 109-12.

81. Ibid., p. 112.

82. For this helpful expression I am indebted to Glebe-Möller.

83. Hegel, *Lectures on the Philosophy of Religion*, 2:248: "To recognize the actual existence of what is substantive in the idea . . . involves hard labor (*harte Arbeit*): in order to pluck

reason, the rose in the cross of the present, one must take up the cross itself." The same metaphor is found in Hegel's *Philosophy of Right,* p. 12. See above, ch. 2, n. 66.

84. William R. Jones, *Is God a White Racist? A Preamble to Black Theology* (New York: Anchor Books, 1973), pp. 115-17.

85. James Cone argues to this effect in *The Spirituals and the Blues* (New York: Seabury Press, 1972), esp. ch. 4; and in *God of the Oppressed* (New York: Seabury Press, 1975), esp. ch. 8, where he deals with questions raised by Jones (see pp. 187-92). Cone's most direct response to Jones, found in a note to this chapter on pp. 267-68, is in terms of a firm insistence that Jesus Christ is the "decisive historical event beyond which no one needs to appeal." But in the text of the chapter, as well as in *The Spirituals and the Blues,* he develops a more nuanced approach, showing how this event has been actually experienced as redemptively efficacious in the black community. See also my *Children of Freedom: Black Liberation in Christian Perspective* (Philadelphia: Fortress Press, 1974), ch. 3; and *New Birth of Freedom,* pp. 295-300.

86. Rosemary Radford Ruether, *Sexism and God-Talk: Toward a Feminist Theology* (Boston: Beacon Press, 1983), pp. 252-53.

87. Ibid., pp. 254-56.

88. Ibid., pp. 232-34.

89. Cobb, *Process Theology as Political Theology,* p. 145; cf. pp. 144-51.

CHAPTER V. EPILOGUE: THE BEGINNING OF THE HISTORY OF FREEDOM?

1. This interpretation is suggested by Walter Jaeschke, "World History and the History of the Absolute Spirit," in *History and System: Hegel's Philosophy of History,* ed. Robert L. Perkins (Albany, N.Y.: State University of New York Press, 1984), esp. pp. 113-15.

2. See Jens Glebe-Möller, *A Political Dogmatic,* trans. Thor Hall (Philadelphia: Fortress Press, 1987), chs. 3, 8. My discussion in this chapter of discursive or dialogical rationality is indebted to conversations with Glebe-Möller.

3. Karl Rahner, *Foundations of Christian Faith: An Introduction to the Idea of Christianity,* trans. William V. Dych (New York: Seabury Press, 1978), p. 169; Karl Jaspers, *The Origin and Goal of History,* trans. Michael Bullock (London: Routledge & Kegan Paul, 1953), pp. 1-27.

4. I have been helped considerably by Tillich's discussion of the kingdom of God "within history" and "as the end of history" in part 5 of his system, but I have identified and applied the two senses of "end" in a different way than he does. Tillich wants to use the term *end* only in a "qualitative-valuing" sense, referring to the "transition" from the temporal to the eternal, not in a "spatio-temporal" sense, referring to "the last in the chain of days." According to Tillich, the "aim" or telos of history is not something innerhistorical but rather "eternal life." See Paul Tillich, *Systematic Theology* (Chicago: University of Chicago Press, 1963), 3:356-61, 394-96.

5. Paul Ricoeur, "Christianity and the Meaning of History," in *History and Truth,* trans. Charles A. Kelbley (Evanston, Ill.: Northwestern University Press, 1965), pp. 93-96. See also above, p. 180.

6. John B. Cobb, Jr., *Process Theology as Political Theology* (Philadelphia: Westminster Press, 1982), pp. 136-42.

7. Ibid., pp. 142-44.

8. Ibid., pp. 144-56.

9. Alfred North Whitehead, *Adventures of Ideas* (New York: Macmillan, 1933), p. 296. I have avoided Whitehead's frequent capitalization of nouns. See chs. 4, 16-20.

10. Austin Farrer, *Faith and Speculation* (London: Adam & Charles Black, 1967), pp. 149-53.

11. William Desmond, *Art and the Absolute: A Study of Hegel's Aesthetics* (Albany, N.Y.: State University of New York Press, 1986), pp. 67-71, 75.

12. Ibid., pp. 160-65.

13. G. W. F. Hegel, *Lectures on the Philosophy of World History*, trans. H. B. Nisbet (Cambridge: Cambridge University Press, 1975), pp. 58-63, 149.

14. Ibid., p. 62.

15. I am indebted at this point to Ray L. Hart's discussion of the "hermeneutical spiral" in *Unfinished Man and the Imagination* (New York: Herder & Herder, 1968), pp. 60-68.

16. Tillich, *Systematic Theology*, 3:419-20.

17. Ibid., 3:362-72. *Kairos* is the Greek word for time in the sense of a qualitatively significant moment, as distinct from *chronos*, time in the sense of duration.

18. Jaspers, *The Origin and Goal of History*, pp. v, xv, 152 (*Vom Ursprung und Ziel der Geschichte* [Zürich: Artemis-Verlag, 1949], pp. 6, 17-18, 197). The English edition translates *Freiheit* "liberty."

19. Ibid., pp. 148-49.

20. Ibid., p. 152 (German ed., 195).

21. Ibid., pp. 172, 196, 215-18.

22. Ibid., pp. 247-48 (German ed., 310-11).

23. Ibid., pp. 186, 242, 251.

24. Ibid., pp. 256-65; concluding quotation from p. 264, to which might be added Ernst Troeltsch's statement: "To apprehend the One in the many constitutes the special character of love" (*Christian Thought: Its History and Application*, ed. Baron F. von Hügel [London: University of London Press, 1923], p. 35).

25. Cobb, *Process Theology as Political Theology*, pp. 77-81.

26. See above, p. 90.

27. I have been helped in thinking about this by Tillich's discussion of "the kingdom of God as the end of history," *Systematic Theology*, 3:394-423. On Hegel's idea of an "eternal divine history," see above, p. 66.

Index